advancing learning, changing lives

BTEC National Health and Social Care

Book 3

Specialist units

Mary Crittenden
Penelope Garnham
Janet Harvell
Heather Higgins

A PEARSON COMPANY

Contents

Unit 10	Caring for Children and Young People	10
	So, you want to be a...Family Court Adviser	11
	Grading criteria	12
10.1	Understand why children and young people may need to be looked after	13
10.2	Understand how care is provided for children and young people	17
10.3	Understand the risks to children and young people of abusive and exploitative behaviour	26
10.4	Know strategies to minimise the risk to children and young people of abusive and exploitative behaviour	33

Unit 14	Physiological Disorders	40
	So you want to be a...Diagnostic Radiographer	41
	Grading criteria	42
14.1	Understand the nature of two physiological disorders	43
14.2	Understand the processes involved in diagnosis of disorders	50
14.3	Understand the care strategies used to support individuals through the course of a disorder	55
14.4	Understand how individuals adapt to the presence of a disorder	62

Unit 19	Applied Sociological Perspectives for Health and Social Care	68
	So, you want to be a...Community Service Volunteer	69
	Grading criteria	70
19.1	Understand the concept of an unequal society	71
19.2	Understand the nature of demographic change within the unequal society	78
19.3	Understand potential links between social inequalities and the health and wellbeing of the population	88

How to use this book

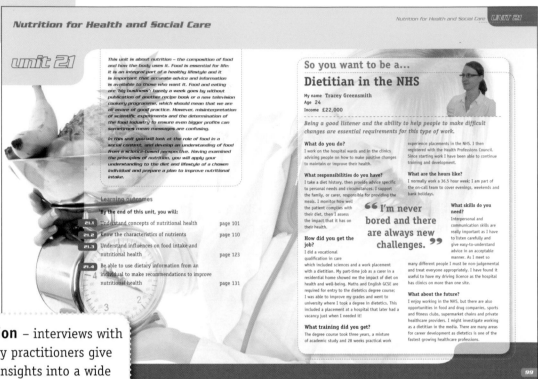

Introduction – interviews with real industry practitioners give invaluable insights into a wide variety of career paths

Key words – easy to understand definitions of key industry terms

Case studies – in-depth focus on industry-specific scenarios show you how the theory works in real-life situations

Grading criteria – learning outcomes and grading criteria are located at the beginning of every unit, so you know right from the start what you need to do to achieve a pass, merit or distinction

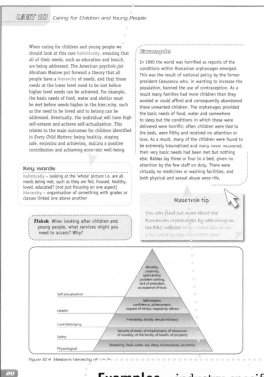

Evidence activities – short activities are spread throughout the unit giving you the opportunity to practice your achievement of the grading criteria in small steps

Think – questions help you reflect on your learning and to think about how it could be applied to real-life working practice

Research tips – direct you to useful websites and key organisations to help you take your study further

Examples – industry-specific examples show you what the theory looks like in practice

Track your progress

This master grid can be used as a study aid. You can track your progress by ticking the level you achieve. The relevant grading criteria can also be found at the start of each unit.

To achieve a pass grade the evidence must show that the learner is able to...	To achieve a merit grade the evidence must show that, in addition to the pass criteria, the learner is able to...	To achieve a distinction grade the evidence must show that, in addition to the pass and merit criteria, the learner is able to...
Unit 10		
P1 Describe the main reasons why children and young people may need to be looked after away from their families	**M1** Analyse how policies and procedures help children/young people and their families whilst the child is being looked after	**D1** Evaluate the legislative rights of the child/young person and the rights of their families, bearing in mind that the needs of the child/young person are paramount
P2 Identify the current relevant legislation affecting the care of children and young people	**M2** Compare the care provided by at least two different organisations offering care to children and young people	**D2** Evaluate a range of strategies and methods to support children/young people and their families where abuse is suspected or confirmed.
P3 Describe health and social care service provision for looked-after children and young people	**M3** Explain strategies and methods to minimise the risk to children and young people where abuse is suspected or confirmed.	
P4 Describe signs and symptoms of child abuse		
P5 Describe appropriate responses where child abuse is suspected or confirmed, making reference to current legislation and policies		
P6 Identify the strategies and methods of supporting children, young people and their families where abuse is suspected or confirmed.		
Unit 14		
P1 Describe the course of two different physiological disorders as experienced by two different individuals	**M1** Explain how the course of the disorder in each individual relates to the physiology of the disorder	**D1** Evaluate the contributions made by different people in supporting the individuals with the disorders
P2 Describe the physiology of each disorder and factors that may have influenced its development	**M2** Explain possible difficulties involved in making a diagnosis from the signs and symptoms displayed by the individuals and the results of their investigations	**D2** Evaluate alternative care strategies that might have been adopted for each individual.
P3 Describe the clinical investigations carried out and measurements made to diagnose and monitor the disorder in each individual	**M3** Explain how the care strategies experienced by each individual have influenced the course of the disorder.	
P4 Describe the care processes experienced by each individual case and the roles of different people in supporting the care strategy		

To achieve a pass grade the evidence must show that the learner is able to...	To achieve a merit grade the evidence must show that, in addition to the pass criteria, the learner is able to...	To achieve a distinction grade the evidence must show that, in addition to the pass and merit criteria, the learner is able to...
P5 Explain difficulties experienced by each individual in adjusting to the presence of the disorder and the care strategy		
P6 Compare the possible future development of the disorders in the individuals concerned.		
Unit 19		
P1 Describe the concept of the unequal society	**M1** Explain the concept of the unequal society	**D1** Evaluate potential links between social inequalities and the health of the population.
P2 Describe recent demographic changes in home country	**M2** Explain recent demographic changes in home country	
P3 Use examples to describe the application of demography to health and social care provision	**M3** Explain the value of the application of demography to health and social care service provision	
P4 Describe two examples of social inequalities in home country	**M4** Use six examples to explain potentials links between social inequalities and the health of the population.	
P5 Use six examples to describe potential links between social inequalities and the health of the population.		
Unit 21		
P1 Explain concepts of nutritional health	**M1** Explain the potential risks to health of inappropriate nutrition	**D1** Evaluate the relative importance of different factors affecting the nutritional health and well-being of two different groups of individuals
P2 Describe the characteristics of nutrients and their benefits to the body	**M2** Explain the factors affecting the nutritional health and well-being of different groups of individuals	**D2** Evaluate how the nutritional plan will improve the health of the chosen individual.
P3 Identify the different factors that influence dietary intake for different population groups	**M3** Explain how the nutritional plan will meet the needs of the chosen individual.	
P4 Carry out a quantitative nutrient analysis of the diet of one individual		
P5 Prepare a nutritional plan for the chosen individual.		

To achieve a pass grade the evidence must show that the learner is able to...	To achieve a merit grade the evidence must show that, in addition to the pass criteria, the learner is able to...	To achieve a distinction grade the evidence must show that, in addition to the pass and merit criteria, the learner is able to...
Unit 22		
P1 Explain the purpose and role of research for the health and social care sectors	**M1** Justify the choice of topic and hypothesis	**D1** Discuss how the methodology of the research project could be altered to reduce bias and error
P2 Describe the key elements of research methodologies	**M2** Review the research methods chosen in relation to the results obtained, any sources of bias or error and ethical considerations	**D2** Analyse the purpose and role of research in the sectors, drawing on the piece of research undertaken.
P3 Identify a research topic and carry out a literature search	**M3** Analyse the finding of the research in relations to the original hypothesis	
P4 Carry out the primary research and collect and record appropriate data	**M4** Discuss the possible implications that the research results may have on current practice.	
P5 Present and report findings in a relevant format, identifying sources of bias or error		
P6 Discuss the findings of the research in relation to the original hypothesis		
P7 Outline any possible improvements to the research, referring to any relevant implications and ethical issues.		
Unit 44		
P1 Describe the structure and function of one health or social care organisation	**M1** Explain how development of knowledge and understanding can be linked to improve practice	**D1** Evaluate own development as a result of workplace experiences.
P2 Present and review a portfolio of evidence demonstrating knowledge and understanding of workplace practice	**M2** Explain how improving own personal effectiveness can enhance the experience of the patient/service user.	
P3 Maintain a reflective practice journal to monitor development of own knowledge, understanding and skills		
P4 Identify links between knowledge and understanding and effective practice		
P5 Describe own effectiveness in work in health and social care.		

Research Skills

Before you start your research project you need to know where to find information and the guidelines you must follow.

Types of information

Primary Sources

Information you have gathered yourself, through surveys, interviews, photos or observation. Ensure that you ask the appropriate questions and people. You must get permission before including someone's photo or interview in your work.

Secondary Sources

Information produced by somebody else, including information from the internet, books, magazines, databases and television. You need to be sure that your secondary source is reliable if you are going to use the information.

Information Sources

The Internet

The internet is a useful research tool, but, not all the information you find will be. When using the internet ask yourself if you can trust the information you find.

> Acknowledge your source! When quoting from the internet always include author name (if known)/document title/URL web address/date site was accessed.

Books, Magazines and Newspapers

Information in newspapers and magazines is up to date and usually researched thoroughly. Books have a longer shelf life than newspapers so make sure you use the most recent edition.

> Acknowledge your source! When quoting from books, magazines, journal or papers, always include author name/title of publication/publisher/year of publication.

Broadcast Media

Television and radio broadcast current news stories and the information should be accurate. Be aware that some programmes offer personal opinions as well as facts.

Plagiarism

Plagiarism is including in your own work extracts or ideas from another source without acknowledging its origins. If you use any material from other sources you must acknowledge it. This includes the work of fellow students.

Storing Information

Keep a record of all the information you gather. Record details of book titles, author names, page references, web addresses (URLs) and contact details of interviewees. Accurate, accessible records will help you acknowledge sources and find information quickly.

Internet Dos and Don'ts

Do

- check information against other sources
- keep a record of where you found information and acknowledge the source
- be aware that not all sites are genuine or trustworthy

Don't

- assume all the information on the internet is accurate and up to date
- copy material from websites without checking whether permission from the copyright holder is required
- give personal information to people you meet on the internet

Caring for Children and Young People

unit 10

This unit is all about caring for vulnerable children and young people from birth to 18 years old. By the end of the unit you will be familiar with the most significant legislation and the impact of this on the care provided. You will also begin to understand some of the reasons that may lead to children and young people being looked after, as well as becoming aware of the different organisations that might be involved in this care.

This unit includes an introduction to the difficult topic of child protection, providing you with guidelines on the signs and symptoms of child abuse. At the same time you will be encouraged to consider some of the reasons why such abuse might occur and identify a range of strategies that could be used by adults working with children and young people that could help to minimise these risks.

Learning outcomes

By the end of this unit, you will:

10.1 Understand why children and young people may need to be looked after   page 13

10.2 Understand how care is provided for children and young people   page 17

10.3 Understand the risks to children and young people of abusive and exploitative behaviour   page 26

10.4 Know strategies to minimise the risk to children and young people of abusive and exploitative behaviour   page 33

So you want to be a...

Family Court Adviser

My name Sanjukta Mandy
Age 29
Income £28,137 - £33,765 basic scale

If you enjoy working with a variety of people and are confident that you can represent their views, then you will enjoy this job.

Qualifications and work experience:

Diploma in Social Work, General Social Care Council (GSCC) registration and at least three years' post-qualifying experience in child-focused social work.

What does your job involve?

I am employed by the Children and Family Court Advisory and Support Service (CAFCASS), working with children who are involved in public and family law proceedings. My main work is to get to know these children and gain their trust, so that I can make appropriate recommendations for their care that promote and safeguard their well-being and interests.

What responsibilities do you have?

My main responsibility is to CAFCASS and the children I work with. I need to make sure that I have had sufficient time and opportunity to get to know the children, to ensure that I can represent their views fairly and at the same time ensure that my recommendations will result in the best possible outcomes for the child or young person.

How did you get into the job?

I completed a vocational course in Health and Social Care at my local college before going on to gain my Diploma. After this I started working with Social Services, within the Child Protection team, before deciding that I wanted to become more

proactive in supporting children and their families. As a result I took a job in a Children's Centre as a Family Worker where I worked with families who were experiencing a range of problems. During my work at the centre I sometimes came into contact with Family Court Advisers and became interested in this area of work.

> **" I love my job and being able to make a difference. "**

What training did you get?

Since starting this job, I have attended a range of specialist training such as Child Protection and understanding of court proceedings.

What is a typical day like?

I love the variety of my job as no day is the same. I will check my email/post box, then I might have an appointment with a child or a court appearance. I may have to write a report outlining my recommendations.

What skills do you need

I need to be able get on well with a variety of people, as well as being able to talk confidently with professionals from other departments. I also have to remain objective at all times.

What about the future

I am happy doing what I am at the moment but I might eventually become a Service Manager, who line manages a team of Family Court Advisers.

Grading criteria

The table below shows what you need to do to gain a pass, merit or distinction in this part of the qualification. Make sure you refer back to it when you are completing work so that you can judge whether you are meeting the criteria and what you need to do to fill in gaps in your knowledge or experience.

In this unit there are 4 evidence activities to give you an opportunity to demonstrate your achievement of the grading criteria:

page 16   P1   page 32   P4

page 25   P2, P3, M1, M2, D1   page 39   P5, P6, M3, D2

To achieve a pass grade the evidence must show that the learner is able to...	To achieve a merit grade the evidence must show that, in addition to the pass criteria, the learner is able to...	To achieve a distinction grade the evidence must show that, in addition to the pass and merit criteria, the learner is able to...
P1 Describe the main reasons why children and young people may need to be looked after away from their families	**M1** Analyse how policies and procedures help children/young people and their families whilst the child is being looked after	**D1** Evaluate the legislative rights of the child/young person and the rights of their families, bearing in mind that the needs of the child/young person are paramount
P2 Identify the current relevant legislation affecting the care of children and young people	**M2** Compare the care provided by at least two different organisations offering care to children and young people	**D2** Evaluate a range of strategies and methods to support children/young people and their families where abuse is suspected or confirmed.
P3 Describe health and social care service provision for looked-after children and young people	**M3** Explain strategies and methods to minimise the risk to children and young people where abuse is suspected or confirmed.	
P4 Describe signs and symptoms of child abuse		
P5 Describe appropriate responses where child abuse is suspected or confirmed, making reference to current legislation and policies		
P6 Identify the strategies and methods of supporting children, young people and their families where abuse is suspected or confirmed.		

10.1 Understand why children and young people may need to be looked after

This section will help you to understand the various reasons that children and young people may need to be looked after away from their families.

LOOKED-AFTER CHILDREN

Children who are in the care of local authorities are described as 'looked-after children'. They are one of the most vulnerable groups in society.

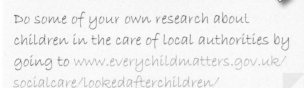

Research tip

Do some of your own research about children in the care of local authorities by going to www.everychildmatters.gov.uk/socialcare/lookedafterchildren/

'Looked after children' refers to children who are **accommodated** by their local authority (LA). The term 'looked after' was first introduced in the **Children Act 1989**. The most recently available figures identify that there are approximately 53,000 children in England who are currently 'looked after'.

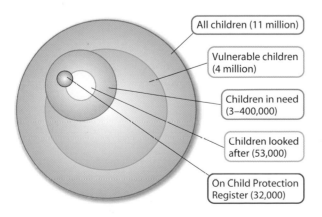

Figure 10.1 Looked-after children in England
Source: DoH Publications Library

What this means in practice is that up until the age of 18 years, a child or young person can be taken into LA care as a result of a court order or parental request. Despite the involvement of the LA, it is important to note that throughout the time that a child remains in care their parents will continue to have joint responsibility with the LA, in making decisions about what will happen to their child. In the majority of cases, a child becomes looked after through no fault of their own and the care will be temporary. The majority of children who remain in care are there as a result of abuse or neglect.

There are two specific sections within the Children Act 1989 which relate specifically to children who are looked after:

- Section 20 refers to parents who have asked for help because for some reason they are unable to stay at home; in this example the parent retains full parental responsibility

- Section 31 allow the court to issue a **care order** if a child is in danger of **significant harm**; in this instance the local authority, together with the parents, have joint responsibility

Consequently, the two main reasons for children being in care are:

- as the result of care orders made by the courts under Section 31 of the Children Act 1989 – approximately two-thirds of all cases

- as the result of a voluntary request under Section 20 of the Children Act 1989 - approximately one-third of all cases

According to the Children Act 1989 S17(1): It shall be the general duty of every local authority:

- to safeguard and promote the welfare of children within their area who are in need, and

- so far as is consistent within that duty, to promote the upbringing of such children by their families, by providing a range and level of services appropriate to those children's needs

Key words

accommodated – this is where a child is provided with accommodation by a LA or voluntary organisation in agreement with parents (and child), e.g. residential children's home, foster parent etc.

Children Act 1989 – this Act came into force in England and Wales in 1991 and defined parental responsibility; it is based upon the belief that children are generally best looked after within the family and where the welfare of the children is the paramount consideration

care order – this is a court order that places a child under the care of the local authority

significant harm – this term was defined by the Children Act 1989 as the point at which compulsory intervention by the local authority is justified in the interests of keeping children and young people safe

> *Think* What reasons can you think of that might result in a child or young person needing to be looked after?

Following imposition of a care order

Care orders are only implemented when a child or young person is suffering, or likely to suffer, significant harm:

'Where a local authority

a [is] informed that a child who lives, or is found in their area –

  i) is the subject of an emergency protection order; or

  ii) is in police protection; or

b [has] reasonable cause to suspect that a child who lives, or is found in their area is suffering, or is likely to suffer, significant harm,

[then] the authority shall make, or cause to be made, such enquiries as they consider necessary to enable them to decide whether they should take any action to safeguard or promote the child's welfare.'

Source: Children Act 1989 S47(1)

The more recent White Paper, Every Child Matters, goes further in stating that all children have a right to certain key expectations, including the right to:

- be healthy

- stay safe

- attain, achieve and enjoy

- make a positive contribution and

- enjoy social and economic well-being.

A child or young person could be seen to be at risk of suffering significant harm should they not have the opportunity to achieve these outcomes. Reasons for this could include poor parenting skills, economic deprivation or regular exposure to domestic abuse. Care orders can only be made for children who are under 17 years of age and will automatically stop if the child marries, is adopted or reaches their 18th birthday.

> *Think* Within this context, can you think of some examples that might lead a local authority to decide that a child or young person is at risk of 'significant harm'?

With the agreement of the parents

Sometimes a family will approach the local authority to look after their child or children because they may feel that they are unable to cope and care for their children, either permanently or on a temporary basis. The local authority will then share parental responsibility for the child with the parents, but the parents will be involved in all decisions that are made.

> *Think* What reasons do you think there might be for parents asking the local authority to take their children into care?

POTENTIAL REASONS

Children and young people may be taken into care for either family- or child-related reasons.

Family related

There are several possible family-related reasons that might lead to children and young people being taken into care. For example, this could include family bereavement – where both parents have been killed and there are no close relatives/ next of kin who can take care of them.

Example

Achmed (5 years) and his sister Nabula (18 months) were travelling in the car with their parents when they were hit by an articulated lorry travelling on the wrong side of the road. Both of their parents were killed immediately but Achmed and his sister were cut out of the wreckage unharmed, having been protected by the car seats that they were strapped into. An emergency care order was issued to place them into temporary care until their grandparents, who lived abroad, were able to make the journey to take over responsibility for their care.

It might also be necessary because of parental illness/incapacity, such as a parent being treated for severe depression which results in them being sectioned under the Mental Health Act; or as a result of substance abuse – with the consequence that a parent is unable to care for their children.

Example

Jessica is 2 years old and lives with her mother who is a registered drug addict; as a result of this she has been identified by the local authority as being 'at risk'. Jessica is underweight for her age and often appears neglected, being unwashed and wearing dirty, inappropriate clothing. On the occasions that the Health Visitor has visited the home, she was very conscious of the unhygienic conditions that the family were living in. Matters came to a head after Jessica was admitted to hospital having swallowed one of her mother's ecstasy pills which she had found. The local authority applied to the court for an emergency care order as they felt that Jessica's mother was no longer able to care for her and that, as a consequence, she was in danger of significant harm.

Child/young person related

A care order might be issued as a result of the particular needs or specific behaviour problems that the child or young person might have. For example, some children may have a disability which requires significant care that their parents or carers are unable to provide and this means that they will need to be placed into care.

> **Think** For what reasons might a young person with a specific learning difficulty or disability be taken into care?

Some children and young people exhibit extreme behaviour problems that their parents or carers are unable to deal with. Because of extreme anti-social behaviour and/or lack of parental control, the court may place the child under local authority care. It could also be the case that the young person has been involved in repeated illegal activities, such as prostitution, and it is felt that a care order is needed for their own protection.

CASE STUDY: SEEKING A CARE ORDER

Jo, who is 13 years old, weighs 15 stone and as a result suffers from a number of health problems. She lives at home with her mother and father and the local authority has applied to the court for a care order to remove her from the family home, as they believe that her obesity is putting her in danger of significant harm, and as such they feel that she is a victim of neglect. Her parents are very angry and intent on getting the order overturned, insisting that her weight is the result of medical problems and not her diet. Obesity is a growing problem among children in the UK and a number of experts feel that this should be treated in the same way as physical or sexual assault.

QUESTIONS

1. Do you support the decision of the local authority in seeking a care order in this instance?

2. What other information would you need to make a valid decision?

3. Do you consider this to be a valid example of a child who is in danger of significant harm as a result of 'family-related' or 'child-related' issues?

Figure 10.2 Every member of the family is affected by a care order

EVIDENCE ACTIVITY

P1

For **P1** you are expected to describe the main reasons that children and young people are looked after away from their families. You work in the Child Protection team of the local authority and have been asked to design a poster that can be used to support staff induction sessions which clearly illustrates why children may be looked after away from their families. Your poster will include a minimum of four examples, and will make reference to both family-related and child/young person-related reasons.

10.2 *Understand how care is provided for children and young people*

LEGISLATION/LEGAL FRAMEWORK

When caring for children and young people it is important to be familiar with the legislation that underlines this care. There are many significant pieces of legislation that need to be followed and some of the most important ones are outlined below.

Children Act 1989

The Children Act 1989 provided a new framework for the care and protection of children and young people. It was the first piece of legislation to recognise that the needs of children are paramount. It also placed a general duty on the local authorities to work in partnership with parents and carers, ensuring that they remain involved and responsible for their child, even if they are in temporary or long-term care.

United Nations Convention on the Rights of the Child 1989

This reinforces the basic rights of all children and identifies the minimum expectations to which every child, wherever they live, has a right.

Human Rights Act 1998

The Human Rights Act 1998, which came into force in England and Wales in October 2000, is a significant piece of legislation that aims to protect the rights of all people. It consists of 12 Articles, with Article Numbers 2, 3 and 5 being particularly significant when looking at issues of child protection. The focus of these articles is:

- Article 2 – The right to life
- Article 3 – The prohibition of torture
- Article 5 – The right to liberty and security.

Data Protection Act 1998

This identifies the type of information that can be held and retained, by different agencies, and the timescales involved. It sets criteria on who should have access to this information, where it will be stored and acknowledges the rights of people to see the information that is held about them.

Framework for the Assessment of Children in Need and their Families 2000

This recognises three specific criteria that need to be taken into account when promoting the safety and welfare of children with special needs and their families. These criteria include the child's developmental needs, family and environmental factors and parenting capacity.

Figure 10.3 The Assessment Framework

This Framework led to the introduction of the Common Assessment Framework (CAF) which is a tool used by professionals involved in assessing the needs of children. This information can then be shared among the different professionals with whom the family will come into contact and stop any unnecessary duplication of information. The Framework is underpinned by 10 key principles which professionals need to keep to the fore at all times. These are shown below.

Principles Underpinning the Assessment Framework

Assessments

- are child-centred
- are rooted in child development
- are ecological in their aproach
- ensure equality of opportunity
- involve working with children and families
- build on strengths as well as identifying difficulties
- are inter-agency in their approach to assessment and the provision of services
- are a continuing process, not a single event
- are carried out in parallel with other action and providing services
- are grounded in evidence-based knowledge

Source: www.dh.gov.uk

Every Child Matters 2003

Every Child Matters was originally a Green Paper which is now incorporated into the Children Act 2004. As with much of the more recent legislation, ECM has its roots in the tragic death of Victoria Climbié, who endured months of abuse at the hands of her aunt and her aunt's boyfriend, before being killed. After consultation with children and young people of all ages, five key outcomes were identified that all children have a right to: to be safe, to be healthy, to attain, achieve and enjoy, to make a positive contribution and to enjoy social and economic well-being.

> **Think** What examples can you think of that would demonstrate how the legislation that has been discussed is implemented by those professionals who care for children and young people?

CASE STUDY: JOSHUA'S ARTHRITIS

Joshua, who is 14 years old, has Juvenile Rheumatoid Arthritis which severely limits his participation in school activities and can lead to long periods of time off school. He and his family work with a number of different professionals, including a physiotherapist who provides an exercise programme that needs to be followed rigorously. Regular meetings are held between Joshua's parents, his doctor, the physiotherapist and his support assistant at school to ensure that the care and support he receives is consistent and meets his needs. Together they work to ensure that his developmental and environmental needs are being met, as well as providing his family with the support and guidance that they need.

QUESTIONS

1 How does the Common Assessment Framework support Joshua and his family?

2 Explain how Joshua's rights, identified by ECM, are being addressed.

3 Who should have access to Joshua's records?

CARE

When children are looked after, there are different options available to meet their individual needs, depending upon their circumstances. At all times it is very important, not least a statutory requirement, that this planning is completed in partnership with the child or young person, their parents or carers and any other organisations that are involved.

Temporary or permanent

When children are cared for by the local authority, it can be on either a temporary or a permanent basis, i.e. to provide temporary respite care or to remove a child permanently from an abusive environment. In the majority of cases children go into care on a temporary basis.

> **Think** What are the different circumstances that might lead that a child or young person being taken into a) permanent or b) temporary care?

Foster care

Foster care is the temporary care of a child or young person in a home environment. Foster care can be either on a long-term or short-term basis, but the child or young person is not a legal member of the family. While the child or young person is fostered they remain the responsibility of the local authority and the foster carers will receive financial support towards their care. Very often fostering is used most effectively to provide respite or emergency care.

Respite care

In some cases, for example when children have serious disabilities, they may go into care for a short period of time in order to provide their parents or carers with a break from the full-time care and the related stresses. This could be a one-off arrangement or a more planned, regular event.

Adoption

Adoption is a legal procedure where the child or young person becomes a permanent member of the family; this is legally binding, the child will take on the name of the adoptive family and the birth parents will have no further legal rights over the child. This is not a step that is taken lightly and it is irreversible.

Adoption is a way of providing a new family for a child when living with their own family is not possible. It is the means of giving a child an opportunity to start again; for many children, adoption may be their only chance of experiencing family life.

> **Research tip**
>
> You can find out more about the process of adoption by going to www.direct.gov. uk/en/Parents/AdoptionAndFostering/ DG_4019657/

Residential care

It is always better for a child or young person to be cared for within a home environment, but for those children or young people with more challenging needs, or those who are particularly vulnerable, residential care may be the only option as it can offer more specialist care.

Planning for care in partnership

Planning for care in partnership with the child or young person, their parents and other agencies (as relevant) is an important principle. At the heart of the Children Act 1989, and the policies that have followed on from this, is the need to involve children and young people in the decisions that are being made about them. This came about as the result of several high profile cases where children were forcibly removed from their homes after allegations of child abuse. The children were not consulted and their views were ignored. The Act recognises that the welfare of the child is of **paramount** consideration and any organisation involved in caring for children and young people must have this principle at the core of their provision.

> **Key words**
>
> **paramount** – of great importance or significance

When caring for children and young people we should look at this care **holistically**, ensuring that all of their needs, such as education and health, are being addressed. The American psychologist Abraham Maslow put forward a theory that all people have a **hierarchy** of needs, and that those needs at the lower level need to be met before higher level needs can be achieved. For example, the basic needs of food, water and shelter must be met before needs higher in the hierarchy, such as the need to be loved and to belong can be addressed. Eventually, the individual will have high self-esteem and achieve self-actualisation. This relates to the main outcomes for children identified in *Every Child Matters*: being healthy, staying safe, enjoying and achieving, making a positive contribution and achieving economic well-being.

Key words

holistically – looking at the 'whole' picture i.e. are all needs being met, such as they are fed, housed, healthy, loved, educated? (not just focusing on one aspect)
hierarchy – organisation of something with grades or classes linked one above another

Think When looking after children and young people, what services might you need to access? Why?

Example

In 1990 the world was horrified as reports of the conditions within Romanian orphanages emerged. This was the result of national policy by the former president Ceausescu who, in wanting to increase the population, banned the use of contraception. As a result many families had more children than they wanted or could afford and consequently abandoned these unwanted children. The orphanages provided the basic needs of food, water and somewhere to sleep but the conditions in which these were delivered were horrific; often children were tied to the beds, were filthy and received no attention or love. As a result, many of the children were found to be extremely traumatised and many never recovered; their very basic needs had been met but nothing else. Babies lay three or four to a bed, given no attention by the few staff on duty. There were virtually no medicines or washing facilities, and both physical and sexual abuse were rife.

Research tip

You can find out more about the Romanian orphanages by searching on the BBC website: http://news.bbc.co.uk/1/hi/world/europe/4630855.stm/

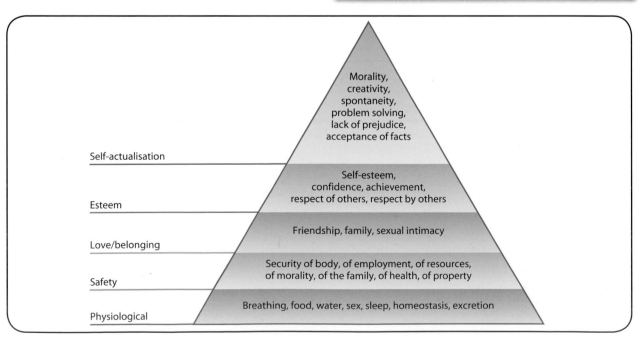

Figure 10.4 Maslow's hierarchy of needs

ORGANISATION OF CARE PROVISION

It is not always the case that children and young people need to be looked after away from their home environment. A range of services can be accessed, which will be overseen at either a central or local government level.

> **Think** What do you think is the difference between central and local government?

Central government

Key departments within central government that have a particular responsibility for the delivery of services related to the care of children and young people include:

- Department of Health – the aim of the DoH is to improve the health and well-being of people in England and it is responsible for setting health and social care policy in England and for the NHS. The Secretary of State for Health is a member of the Cabinet and reports directly to the Prime Minister

- National Health Service - the NHS is the publicly-funded healthcare system in Britain. It provides the majority of healthcare, from local doctors (general practitioners or GPs) to Accident and Emergency departments, long-term healthcare and dentistry

- National Service Framework for Children, Young People and Maternity Services – this was introduced in 2004 as a result of a number of high profile cases that highlighted how the services that were in place with the intention of protecting children and young people were found to be failing.

One of the main catalysts for the framework was the death of Victoria Climbié in February 2000 (see page xx) as a result of sustained abuse at the hands of her aunt and her aunt's boyfriend. The abuse took place over several months during which time Victoria was seen by a range of service providers who failed to recognise and prevent the abuse that led to her tragic death. The framework identifies 11 standards that children's health and social services will be inspected on, and is intended to encourage a co-ordinated approach to services amongst a multi-disciplinary team.

> **Research tip**
>
> Find out more about the Department of Health by going to www.dh.gov.uk/en/Aboutus/index.htm

Local government

Local government is responsible for all local authority services and functions, including those to do with education, health and welfare. It is bound by legislation and government policy but is able to decide on how to deliver this locally.

Integrated services

As a result of previous high-profile cases there is an emphasis on joined-up thinking, and the importance of different services working together to meet the needs of children and young people. The aim is to make the process easier for all parties that are involved.

Children's services

There is a range of services available at local level with the intention of making sure that all children and young people are protected from harm and have the opportunity to fulfil their potential. Each local authority will have a Director for Children's Services whose main objective is to promote the educational achievement of looked-after children and work co-operatively with other services to improve outcomes for all children.

Example

Rashid has diabetes which is controlled by injections. He attends a local nursery where the staff have received training on how to support him. The completion of the Common Assessment Framework allows information to be shared, as appropriate, between the nursery, parents and the primary care teams to prevent unneccesary duplication of notes and discussions and ensure that all services involved are kept up to date with information as necessary.

Children's trusts

These were developed in response to the Children Act 2004, which requires local government to bring all of their children's services under one umbrella in order to facilitate the sharing of information at the same time as providing more responsive services. It is hoped that eventually all children's services will be located on the same premises, whether these are extended schools or children's centres, with the aim of providing parents with a 'one-stop shop' where they can access all health and welfare services in one place.

Children's Centres

These are for families with children under five years old and provide a central location where a range of integrated services can be accessed, including education, care, family support and health services that are delivered by a **multi-disciplinary** professional team. These centres have developed as a result of the government's Sure Start initiative which began in 1999 with the aim of developing services aimed at helping parents in areas of disadvantage. This has since expanded and now there is a wider remit to support all families in achieving better outcomes through a range of Sure Start programmes. These might include providing affordable childcare for families, parenting classes or advice and support for parents wishing to return to work.

Key words

multi-disciplinary – in this context staff working at the Children's Centre will be from different professional backgrounds, such as education and health, and will use their different skills to work together for the best outcomes for the families that use their facilities

Research tip

Sure Start is the government programme that aims to deliver the best start in life for every child. It links together early education, childcare, health and family support. Find out more by going to www.surestart.gov.uk/

Nursery provision

One of the main hurdles that parents face when trying to return to work is the availability of accessible and affordable childcare, the lack of which has often prevented a return to employment. There has been a huge push to provide sustainable, quality childcare provision. Since the launch of the National Childcare Strategy in 1998, more than 500,000 new childcare places have been created – the majority of these places being nursery provision. Nurseries are registered through OfSTED to care for babies and young children from birth to five years; their hours are flexible and will generally support those families who need to drop their children off earlier, or collect them later, in order to fit in with work hours.

Key words

OfSTED – the Office for Standards in Education inspects all registered provision against a set of national standards for care and education

All registered pre-school provision is expected to demonstrate how it plans to meet the care and developmental needs of all children within their setting. In recognition of the important part

Figure 10.5 Pre-school organisations are important for children to socialise and to develop other skills

played by early years care in enabling children to achieve their full potential, the government has funded free nursery provision for all 4 year olds since 1997, and this has since been extended. All 3 and 4 year old children are now eligible for 12 _ hours of funded nursery provision for 38 weeks per year, with the expectation that this will extend to 15 hours in the near future.

To support practitioners in meeting the diverse needs of children in their care, the Curriculum Guidance for the Foundation Stage (CGFS), for children between 3 and 5 years of age, was published in 2000. This identifies children's development in six areas of learning, with each area having a number of early learning goals that most children will be expected to achieve by the time they are five. All settings providing funded nursery provision are expected to implement this guidance and are inspected on this when visited by OfSTED. The *Birth to Three Matters* framework followed in 2002 and, although not compulsory, identifies recognised good practice for practitioners who work with the younger age group and their families. In 2007 the Early Years Foundation Stage (EYFS) was published and from September 2008 it will become mandatory for all early years providers.

The EYFS is a single quality framework from birth to the age of five. It brings together and replaces *Birth to Three Matters*, the Curriculum Guidance for the Foundation Stage and the National Standards for Under 8s Day Care and Childminding.

Research tip

Find out more about the Early Years Foundation Stage, by going to www.teachers.gov.uk/_ doc/11324/00109-2007FLY-EN.pdf

Extended schools

Another government initiative is the development of extended schools provision, whereby all schools must have in place, by 2009, both pre- and after-school provision. This means that all families will have access to affordable, registered care for school children between 8.00 a.m. and 6 p.m. This may be delivered on site at the school, or in partnership with another school or registered provider.

Connexions service

Young people who are coming to the end of their formal education will have access to information from their local Connexions partnerships. Connexions is a government service, for young people between 13 and 19 years, that provides advice and guidance about personal development opportunities and further education, as well as preparing them for employment. They can be found in schools and colleges, community centres or dedicated Connexions offices.

Day care

The most common form of care for babies and young children is that of day care, which is where children are looked after, for set periods of time, during working hours. This care is provided by a range of settings within the voluntary, private and maintained sectors.

Voluntary sector

The voluntary sector consists of those organisations that are non-profit-making and run by a volunteer committee. Examples of organisations in the voluntary sector include playgroups.

> **Think** What types of organisations can you think of in the voluntary sector?

Private providers

In contrast private providers are owned and managed independently. They not controlled by the state but are privately owned or run by a company; they are run for profit. Examples of private providers include private day nurseries.

Young offenders

There are also particular providers for young offenders, for example local authority secure children's homes (LASCHs) and young offenders' institutions, where young people have committed crimes for which they have been found guilty and sentenced to custodial care away from the home. LASCHs are the responsibility of both the Department of Health and the Department for Children, Schools and Families and focus on addressing the physical, emotional and behavioural needs of the young people who have been sent there. They are generally used to accommodate young offenders between the ages of 12 and 14 years, or up to 16 years if the young person is identified as being particularly vulnerable. They are often seen as a last resort before being sent to a young offenders' institution whose focus is on imprisonment and the loss of liberty rather than the ethos of rehabilitation and care put forward by the LASCHs.

Young Offender Institutions (YOIs) are prisons for 15 to 21 year olds. They are run by the Prison Service as part of the prison estate as a whole. YOIs are distinct from Secure Training Centres and Local Authority Secure Children's Homes, which focus on different types of youth offenders and therefore have different staffing and accommodation specifications.

The core distinction is that Young Offender Institutions have a lower staff to offender ratio, reflecting the focus of these institutions on incarceration as opposed to rehabilitation and care. YOIs are also generally larger. Perhaps the best-known YOI in England is Feltham in west London. Young offender wings also exist within adult prisons.

> *Research tip*
>
> You can find out more about Young Offender Institutions by going to www.politics.co.uk/issuebrief/public-services/prisons/young-offenders-institutions/young-offender-institutions-$366692.htm/

JOB ROLES

As would be expected, the range and diversity of care available for children and young people is reflected in the variety of job opportunities for people wishing to work in this area. A selection of these jobs would include: Director of Children's Services, social worker, foster parents, support workers, residential care staff, tutors, lecturers, nurses, health visitors, educational psychologists, counsellors, nursing/health care/social care assistants, education welfare officers, learning mentors, play therapists, play workers, Connexions advisers, early years workers, youth workers, youth justice workers and prison officers.

> **Think** What sort of job would you like to do that involved the care of children or young people? What qualifications would you need to this job?

EVIDENCE ACTIVITY

P2 – P3 – M1 – M2 – D1

For **P2** you must identify the current relevant legislation affecting the care of children and young people.

This should be an overview of the legislation that you have looked at during this unit and could be achieved by writing a report based on the following information. You are an early years worker in a Children's Centre and you have been asked to support a family new to the area who are currently living in bed and breakfast accommodation. The mother is 7 months pregnant and has recently left an abusive partner after fears that his physical attacks could transfer to her two other children, who are aged 2 and 4 years. Making reference to a minimum of three different pieces of legislation that you have researched during the study of this section, what services could you provide for this family and which other professionals would you consider involving?

For **P3** you are asked to describe the health and social care provision available for looked-after children and young people.

You could do this by providing a detailed description of the circumstances in which a child or young person may be put into care; you should then describe in detail a minimum of four different types of care provision (both permanent and temporary) that could be accessed. You should also make reference to provision which is particularly appropriate to the specific needs of a) children and b) young people.

For **M1** you must analyse how these policies and procedures help children, young people and their families whilst they are being looked after.

You could do this by looking in much greater detail at a minimum of three different policies and procedures that you have researched. You will be expected to break these down into key aspects before identifying and then describing the key features of these policies, and how they have impacted on the care and provision for children and young people.

For **M2** you are asked to compare the care provided by at least two different organisations offering care to children and young people.

You could do this by developing your answer to P3 and comparing at least two of the different types of care provision that you have described. What are the similarities, and what are the differences?

For **D1** you will need to evaluate the legislative rights of the child/young person and the rights of their families, bearing in mind that the needs of the child/young person are paramount.

You could do this by presenting an appraisal of the issues, including the pros, cons, advantages and limitations of the Human Rights Act 1998 and the United Nations Convention on the Rights of the Child 1989.

10.3 Understand the risks to children and young people of abusive and exploitative behaviour

It is crucially important that everyone who works with children and young people has a thorough knowledge and understanding of child protection issues; they should be aware of those factors that could indicate a greater potential for children and young people being abused. You will also need to be familiar with the signs and symptoms that might indicate abuse.

It is important to realise that this subject may affect people differently and there is a need to be sensitive to the issues that discussions on this topic might raise.

All children have a right to be protected from harm and have their welfare promoted – whoever they are, and wherever they are. Anyone who works for an organisation that comes into contact with children has a responsibility to keep them safe and promote their welfare.

As has been discussed in previous sections, every child has a legal right to be free from fear and safe from abuse. The Human Rights Act 1998, the United Nations Convention on the Rights of the Child 1989, the Children Act 1989 and *Every Child Matters* all make specific reference to the protection of children. Key recommendations from *Every Child Matters* became statutory with the introduction of the Children Act 2004, which now places a statutory duty on key people and organisations to put in place policies and procedures to ensure the safety and promote the welfare of children in their care.

Initially, it would be useful to identify what child abuse is. The World Health Organization defines child abuse as:

> '... all forms of physical and/or emotional ill treatment, sexual abuse, neglect or negligent treatment or commercial or other exploitation, resulting in actual or potential harm to the child's health, survival, development or dignity in the context of a relationship of responsibility, trust or power.'

Research tip

The National Society for the Prevention of Cruelty to Children has much useful information on its website. Go to www.nspcc.org.uk

RISK OF ABUSE

Abuse can happen as a result of either direct action, such as sexual abuse, or indirect action, such as neglect; it can occur anywhere, any place, and at any time – within the family, outside the family, in a care setting - and unfortunately we always have to be alert to this fact.

- At least 150,000 children annually suffer severe physical punishment.

- Up to 100,000 children each year have a potentially harmful sexual experience.

- There are 350-400,000 children who live in an environment low in warmth and high in criticism.

- There are 450,000 children who are bullied at school at least once a week.

Source: National Commission of Inquiry Into the Prevention of Child Abuse 1996

Sadly, in the majority of cases children are abused by someone they know, such as a family member, a close family friend or an adult in a position of trust. The tragic murders of Hollie Wells and Jessica Chapman in 2002 by the school caretaker Ian Huntley provide a sombre example of this abuse of trust. The Protection of Children Act 1999, which came into effect in October 2000, puts a statutory obligation on registered providers to check the criminal records of all potential employees and volunteers. This should make it more difficult for unsuitable people to work with vulnerable children and young people for their own sinister purposes, although there are still serious gaps in the system.

Think Why do you think that most cases of abuse are committed by people that children and young people know?

RISK OF EXPLOITATION

Apart from the more obvious forms of abuse it is also important to be aware of other ways that children and young people may be exploited, for example through visual, written and electronic forms of communication and media. We need to ensure that they do not have access to pornographic literature or films. There is also a significant concern that the huge growth in internet access has placed children at greater risk of contact with paedophiles or other unsuitable individuals who will misrepresent themselves, particularly with the current popularity of teenage chatrooms and social networking websites such as Facebook, Bebo and MySpace. The Child Exploitation and Online Protection Centre (CEOP) wants such sites to install its 'report abuse' button that connects people to the police; in 2006 Microsoft agreed to put the distinctive red icon on MSN Messenger, much used by children and young people. In 2007 around one million children under 16 used Bebo, while 600,000 minors were on MySpace. CEOP research has shown that some sex offenders are starting to use these sites to seek out victims.

Research tip

The website www.chatdanger.com/ has specific examples of how children can be misled and what to do to keep safe on the Internet.

Think Jonathan, 12 years old, has a 'sleep-over' at his friend Jack's house. After tea they go upstairs to Jack's room and put on a 'certificate 18' DVD that Jack has taken from his parents' collection downstairs. Do you consider this to be a child abuse issue? Why?

FAMILY FUNCTIONING

It is important to understand that all families are different and may have practices which might be in direct contrast to our own experiences; but we should respect their individual rights as long as these do not impact upon the safety or welfare of children and young people. For example, there are many different family types and the changing face of the family means that the traditional image of the family – mother married to father with 2.4 children – is no longer true for all. Many children and young people are brought up by single or same sex parents and, with the increase in the incidence of family breakdown, there will often be different partnership arrangements to be taken into account, such as visitation rights, where children will live – all of which will have an impact on the lives of each member of the family. It has also been recognised that family breakdowns, and changes in family circumstances, may lead to stressful events such as altered living arrangements, leaving the family home and a decrease in income; all of which may lead to social disadvantage, as well as emotional distress. Many of the recent initiatives which have been introduced attempt to redress some of these issues.

Different family groups will have their own different concepts of discipline, and again it is important to bear this in mind when working with children and their families. Some will be much stricter when it comes to disciplining their children but we need to respect these practices, even if we do not agree with them, unless the practices could be classified as abuse.

Think Many families still use physical punishment to discipline their children. Do you think this is child abuse? Justify your choice.

It is also important to understand the impact that abuse within families can have; the removal of a family member from the home, or access only through supervised visits, could all put severe pressure on the family.

Mali's brother is currently under investigation with regard to accessing and contributing to child pornographic websites. While the investigation is being carried out he is not to have any unsupervised contact with her, and is no longer able to live at the house or Mali will be removed into care for her own protection. Mali is 5 years old and very close to her brother. She is very upset at the changes that have taken place and the distress that is evident within the family home.

Other important aspects to take into account are the cultural variations that can be found when working with families. Different cultures may have practices which would appear more severe than those we are used to. We must feel confident in recognising what is acceptable behaviour and what would be classed as abuse. Remember that the paramount concern is the health and safety of the child and we should not let the issue of culture stand in the way of child protection. This was one of the points raised in the Victoria Climbié case.

Think Consider the following: the Jehovah's Witness religion prevents their members from having blood transfusions, or any treatment developed from the use of blood or blood products, even if withholding this treatment will mean certain death. If such life-saving treatment was withheld from a child or young person, would you consider this to be a child protection issue?

PRE-DISPOSING FACTORS

A key factor in preventing, or stopping, child abuse is a knowledge and understanding of the impact that certain circumstances could have when considering the care and welfare of children. These circumstances may be specific to the potential abuser or in relation to the child or young person, and families under stress are particularly vulnerable. For example, substance abuse within the home could put young children at risk of ingesting tablets that are left lying around, or accidentally piercing themselves with syringes that had not been disposed of correctly.

For some families, particularly those where the parents are very young, their lack of role models and knowledge about children's needs may mean that they put their children's safety at risk unintentionally, for example, through poor diet, not realising the long-term effects this might have on their child's health. Mothers suffering from postnatal depression may demonstrate a lack of attachment to their babies which, if allowed to continue without intervention, could lead to detrimental effects on the child's emotional development.

In families where there are or have been instances of specific social problems, such as a history of violent behaviour, personality disorders, such as schizophrenia, or a history of mental illness, children and young people are more vulnerable to being abused or exploited.

The age of sexual maturation for girls, i.e. the onset of puberty and menstruation and the development of breasts, is lowering, and this pre-maturity can mean that children are more susceptible to sexual abuse.

Children and young people who have a disability are also more at risk of abuse as they are often unable to communicate clearly and are more easily taken advantage of by unscrupulous carers.

TYPES OF ABUSE/NEGLECT

Abuse is generally classified under four different categories: physical, emotional, sexual and neglect; and children may experience one or more types of abuse at any one time.

Physical abuse

Physical abuse is non-accidental and causes physical injury. It is the most obvious form of abuse because, in the majority of cases, the results are visible. Physical abuse includes hitting, biting, punching, burning, severe shaking, extreme methods of corporal punishment or any other action that inflicts pain or physical injury. It must be remembered that many of these injuries can occur as the result of normal childhood rough and tumble, but regular occurrences, with no reasonable explanation, must be cause for concern and investigation.

Emotional abuse

Emotional abuse, or mental abuse, is the consistent disregard of emotional needs. Even though the child or young person may appear to be physically well-cared for, emotional abuse means that they start to see themselves as unworthy of love and this will result in an extremely low self-concept. Instead of receiving messages that they are valued, the child is starved of love and affection. Examples could include constant criticism, ridicule, unreasonable expectations, name calling, threatening behaviour, and offering love but only conditionally.

Sexual abuse

Sexual abuse applies to any way in which a child or young person takes part either willingly, or not, in any form of sexual activity; this could also include the intentional/unintentional exposure to pornographic material.

Neglect

Neglect is the failure to provide for the essential physical needs of the child or young person. This could manifest itself in inadequate or inappropriate clothing, failure to provide adequate shelter or lack of appropriate supervision.

> **Think** Is it abuse when a parent leaves their 9-year-old child at home alone whilst they go the pub for a drink?

INDICATORS OF ABUSE

Children and young people have a statutory right to be protected from child abuse in any form and it is important that those adults who come into contact with children on a regular basis are familiar with some common indicators of abuse. Where physical abuse is suspected this can sometimes be difficult to confirm, but the chart below identifies common sites for accidental and non-accidental injuries.

Figure 10.6 Common sites for accidental and non-accidental injuries

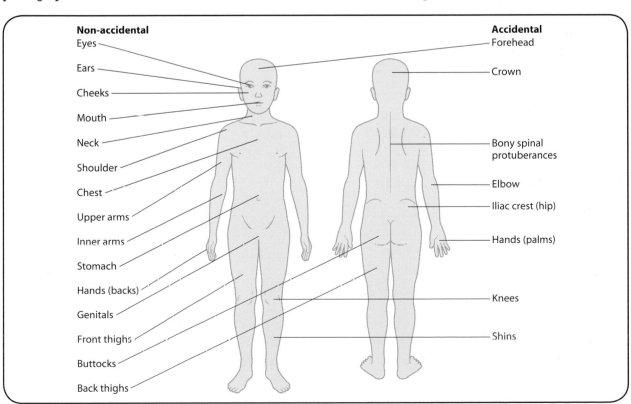

Non-accidental
- Eyes
- Ears
- Cheeks
- Mouth
- Neck
- Shoulder
- Chest
- Upper arms
- Inner arms
- Stomach
- Hands (backs)
- Genitals
- Front thighs
- Buttocks
- Back thighs

Accidental
- Forehead
- Crown
- Bony spinal protuberances
- Elbow
- Iliac crest (hip)
- Hands (palms)
- Knees
- Shins

OTHER SIGNS, SYMPTOMS AND CONSEQUENCES OF ABUSE

Table 10.1 below outlines some of the signs and symptoms of sexual abuse that a carer may observe or that a child or young person may complain about. It is important to remember that these signs do not mean that a child has been abused but may help you to recognise that something is wrong.

Neglect	Physical
Constant hunger	Unexplained injuries, bruises, bites or burns
Poor personal hygiene	Internal injuries, consistent broken bones
Constant tiredness	Improbable excuses given to explain injuries
Poor state of clothing	Untreated injuries
Frequent lateness or non-attendance	Withdrawal from physical contact
Untreated injuries/medical problems	Flinching at sudden movements Low self-esteem
Few social relationships	Arms and legs kept covered up even in hot weather
Compulsive behaviour	Aggressive or destructive behaviour
Weight loss	Fearful of adults or one particular adult
	Difficulty in making relationships
Sexual	**Emotional**
Disclosure of sexual abuse	Changes in behaviour
Genital injuries/soreness or itching of genitalia/bottom	Excessive attention seeking/comfort-seeking behaviour
Sexually transmitted diseases/pregnancy	Self-harming
Vivid details of sexual activity	Self-neglect
Compulsive masturbation	Developmental delay
Torn or stained underwear	Lack of trust in adults
Sexual drawings	Very low self-esteem/self-concept
Sexual play with explicit acts	Difficulty in accepting criticism
Fear or being bathed, changed or put to bed	Withdrawal
Promiscuity	Reluctantance to join in

Table 10.1 Potential signs and symptoms of sexual abuse
Source: Adapted from www.ncma.org.uk

Think These are just some signs and symptoms that might indicate abuse. Can you identify any others?

MODELS OF ABUSE

There are many theories about why child abuse occurs and these theories have been categorised under four different models of abuse: medical, sociological, psychological and feminist.

Medical

The medical model of abuse sees the child or young person as the problem, and the causes of abuse being viewed as a disease to be treated. The module was first defined by the work of Dr Henry Kempe and his colleagues in 1962, with the publication of his paper on 'The Battered Child Syndrome'. It was the first study to provide the medical profession with a clearer understanding of child abuse. Later research became more directly focused on the abuser and the removal of the abuser from the home environment until they had undergone therapy.

Sociological

The sociological model of abuse recognises the effect that poor social conditions have on the quality of children's lives and the impact of poor diet, housing and education on children's outcomes. *Every Child Matters* is based on this model with its commitment to the abolition of child poverty and improved life prospects for children and young people.

Psychological

The psychological model of abuse believes that child abuse is the result of learned behaviour, i.e. the abuser was themselves abused or observed abuse taking part on a regular basis within their home environment. For example, a child who has observed a parent being physically abused is more likely to form an abusive relationship.

Feminist

The feminist model of abuse is based on the difference in strength between men and women and that men will abuse children as a way of exerting their power over them.

RECOGNITION OF ABUSE

It can be a problem to recognise and deal with abuse where children or young people cannot communicate. Suspicions of abuse in babies and very young children, or those children with alternative forms of communication, can be more difficult to confirm. In addition to those signs and symptoms that have already been identified, signs of possible abuse in babies and very young children are outlined in Table 10.2.

Neglect	Physical
Arriving (for example at nursery) with nappies that don't appear to have been changed overnight. **Dehydration** – babies cannot help themselves to a drink. **Not seeking or** expecting attention or comfort. **Untreated nappy rash. Consistent failure** to attend medical appointments, for example, with a health visitor or GP. **Constant hunger** – older children may sometimes steal food from other children.	**Finger bruising** – could indicate that the child has been gripped tightly. Finger bruises to the child's trunk are of particular concern as the child may have been gripped and shaken. This is potentially dangerous and should always be taken seriously. **Injuries to the mouth** – either bruising to both sides of the mouth or cheeks, or injuries inside the mouth. This might be a sign of force-feeding and is of particular concern in bottle-fed babies. **Flinching when** approached or touched.
Sexual	Emotional
Injury, pain or itching in the genital area. **Discomfort when** walking or sitting down. **An indication** that the child has been exposed to, or involved in, pornography, including paedophile activity on the internet.	**Frozen watchfulness** – as the name suggests, this is where children become still and withdrawn but stay 'on guard' from fear of violence, a telling off or punishment. **Indifference to** the parent, passive acceptance of change of carers or being over-affectionate. **Self-stimulation,** such as rocking or head banging.

Table 10.2 *Signs of possible abuse*
Source: *adapted from National Childminding Association*

CASE STUDY: STEPHANIE

Stephanie, who is 12, has been absent from school a number of times without permission. Another parent has mentioned to the teacher that she has seen her looking after her 4-year-old brother on the days she isn't at school, whilst her mother is unsteady on her feet and appears confused. Both children come to school and nursery looking dishevelled and hungry and they are both small for their age. Today Stephanie arrives at school smelling of alcohol.

QUESTIONS

1 Do you consider this to be a child abuse case?

2 If so, what type of abuse, and what are the signs that lead you to this conclusion?

3 What should you do and why?

Example

What is abuse? It is very easy to think that you would recognise child abuse if it occurred, but in real life it is rarely so simple. Consider the following statements and decide which are examples of child abuse:

- while shopping in the supermarket you see a 3-year-old child slapped hard enough to leave a mark
- a father sleeps in the same bed as his daughter
- you overhear your neighbour consistently shouting at and criticising her son for being useless.

How did you decide?

EVIDENCE ACTIVITY

P4

For **P4** you must describe signs and symptoms of child abuse.

You can do this by creating four separate hypothetical case studies which illustrate each category of abuse. You should support these case studies by including a separate chart that you have designed which lists some of the most common signs and symptoms of child abuse.

10.4 Know strategies to minimise the risk to children and young people of abusive and exploitative behaviour

Many of the new government strategies are based on the belief that prevention is better than cure, and so too with issues of child protection. Our practice should be proactive and ensure that we provide children and young people with the skills they need to keep them safe.

It is also of extreme importance that we have policies and procedures to follow in case we have real concerns that abuse is taking place. Anyone who works with children and young people should have access to a written plan of the steps to take when child abuse is suspected. Care providers are required to make sure that all staff are familiar with the policy of the setting.

STRATEGIES WITH CHILDREN AND YOUNG PEOPLE

We will consider here some of the programmes that can be used to empower children and young people if there are problems.

Person-centred approach

This approach was developed in the 1940s and 1950s by the psychologist Carl Rogers and is most well known for the development of 'counselling'. In practice, this means helping children to make sense of what has happened after abuse. The aim is to help them to look towards the future and to realise that they have a choice over what will happen and how they can help themselves. This strategy obviously requires the ability to communicate, which can be more difficult if dealing with younger children.

Provide active support

Active support is where care workers will work at encouraging children and young people who have been abused to participate in everyday activities and not to withdraw; the emphasis is on working with them and not doing it for them.

Promoting empowerment

It is very important to promote empowerment, assertiveness, self-confidence, self-esteem and resilience in all children and young people. Confident children and young people are at less risk of child abuse than those who lack confidence and have low self-concept. It is therefore essential that we provide children with the skills that are necessary to become assertive, whilst developing their confidence and self-esteem; they need the confidence to say 'no' to abuse.

Children should be encouraged to be confident in their relationships with adults so that they will be able to talk to them (family members, teachers etc.) about any concerns they might have. Child abusers are known to target children who they believe will not tell. Strategies that can be used to promote empowerment and assertiveness in children include drama workshops, where the children are encouraged to act out their responses to a range of different scenarios which are appropriate to their stage of development.

Example

Stepping Stones Day Nursery carries out regular role play activities where children take part in dramatic play scenarios acting out their responses to a number of potentially dangerous situations. This culminates in the singing of their song 'Just say NO'.

Sharing information

One of the key factors in preventing abuse is encouraging children not to keep secrets and to have confidence to share their experiances with someone they trust. Often, in cases of child abuse, the abuser will threaten the child with serious consequences if they tell someone about what has happened, such as that they will be taken away from their home into care. It is important that children have someone they are able to trust, who they can confide in and ask for advice. All settings should encourage staff to develop warm and caring relationships with children, so that they know there is someone who will listen to and believe in them. The key worker role supports this effectively.

Key words

key worker – a named carer who is the first point of contact for parents. He or she will record all information regarding your child's daily routine as well as any specific information, such as significant issues or changes in routine or environment which can affect the well-being of children and young people. The key worker will not have sole responsibility for the child/young person but will be the person who has the most rounded overview of their circumstances.

Providing information

It is important to provide information for children to keep them safe, according to their age, needs and abilities – for example, how to respect their bodies and keep themselves safe and, where necessary, about the transmission of disease.

A sound knowledge of child development will support your work with children and young people, in providing developmentally appropriate activities to help children understand how to stay safe. Curriculum guidance, notably the National Curriculum (NC) for children aged 5 to 16 years, and the Early Years Foundation Stage (EYFS) for children aged up to 5 years, gives clear advice on what children are able to understand at different stages. The specific curriculum areas are Personal,

Social and Emotional Development (EYFS) and Personal, Social, Health and Citizenship (NC). Children should learn that they can choose for themselves whom they want to kiss, cuddle or hug, and they need to develop an understanding and awareness of their own personal space and where and when it is appropriate to be touched.

WORKING WITH PARENTS AND FAMILIES

Partnerships

Everyone wants what is best for children, so it is important to work in partnership with parents and families. This means involving parents in the assessment of children's needs, helping parents to recognise the value and significance of their contributions and, where necessary, encouraging the development of parenting skills.

Research continuously recognises that in all but the most extreme cases, where children are at significant risk of harm, it is of crucial importance that children are able to remain living within the home environment. The recognition that parents are their children's first and foremost educators is at the heart of recent policy. Any strategies developed must have this as the cornerstone of their practice so that carers understand the importance of working with parents and families and involving them in their children's learning.

It is not only those who work with children and young people who need to recognise the important role that parents and families play; parents and families also need to understand the significant role they have in developing confident and strong children. They should be encouraged to be involved.

Think How can different care providers encourage families to be involved in the care and education of their children?

When children are first registered at the Children's Centre their family attends a familiarisation meeting where the aims and ethos of the setting are shared, and the importance of the partnership between the family and the setting is stressed. Home visits help to provide continuity and emphasise to the child the importance of this relationship. Each child is allocated a key worker who will share information on their child's day with the parents, and identify any concerns they might have, as well as sharing celebrations and achievements. A home record book encourages parents to share their children's home experiences and individual reports include opportunities for families, and their children, to add comments. A monthly newsletter provides information on the parenting classes being offered, including baby massage and behaviour management.

* not reproduced in this book

Figure 10.7 What To Do If You're Worried a Child is Being Abused Source: www.doh.gov.uk

PROCEDURES WHERE ABUSE IS SUSPECTED OR CONFIRMED

Policies of the setting

It is a statutory requirement that all registered settings must have a policy in place that identifies the procedures to be followed where abuse is suspected and confirmed. All staff must have access to this policy and be familiar with the steps to be taken, relevant to their level of seniority. Policies will identify the named person to be contacted about any child protection issues – the Child Protection Officer – and forms to be completed.

> **Think** What are the key points that you think should be included in a Child Protection Policy?

The government booklet 'What To Do If You're Worried a Child Is Being Abused' provides clear guidelines on the procedures to be followed. The following flow chart identifies the key steps to be followed where there is the suspicion of child abuse.

Safe working practices

When considering issues of child protection it is as important that settings put in place safe working practices that also take into account the safety of their staff, as well as that of the children and young children who they care for. These practices will include criminal checks on all people who come into regular contact with children and young people.

> **Think** What guidance should staff receive about protecting their own safety when working with children and young people?

Whistle blowing

Whistle blowing is the term used when a person reports any form of misconduct. It has connotations of 'telling tales' but it is very important that, where child abuse is suspected, staff understand that it is their duty to report their concerns to the appropriate person, who should be identified within the Child Protection Policy. If this is inappropriate, then the applicable registering body should be contacted, i.e. OfSTED or Social Services. These organisations have confidential helplines which can offer reassurance and advice on the appropriate line of action.

Lines of reporting

In order to safeguard children and staff, there must be clear lines of reporting, accurate reporting and security of records in all settings.

Clear guidelines on the lines of reporting are necessary, i.e. who you go to if you have concerns regarding child protection. This might be the manager of the setting, the designated child protection officer or the head teacher.

In all instances a written record of events will need to be kept and these should be accurate, objective observations that describe the reasons for your concerns. There may be different methods of reporting these concerns. For example, many settings will keep a Register of Concerns where they note down any instances that have worried staff. These may not be definite examples of abuse, for example, bruising on the child; but if several incidences are noted over a period of time without a convincing or valid reason, this could provide appropriate evidence to proceed with the next stage in the child protection procedure. As with all personal information, it is extremely important that any such records are kept in a secure location and that access is restricted to those people on a 'need to know' basis.

Key words

objective observations – an exact record of what has been seen, heard or reported; there should be no interpretation of what this observation might mean

Think What procedures need to be put in place where secure records are electronically stored? What legislation might be involved?

Registration on child protection register

Where concerns about child protection have been verified, and the child/young person has been identified as being at risk of significant harm, there is a sequence of events which lead to registration on the child protection register. The procedures identified in the chart below will be followed.

Where there is a risk to the life of a child, or a likelihood of serious immediate harm, an agency with statutory child protection powers, i.e. social services, police or the NSPCC, should act quickly to secure the immediate safety of the child.

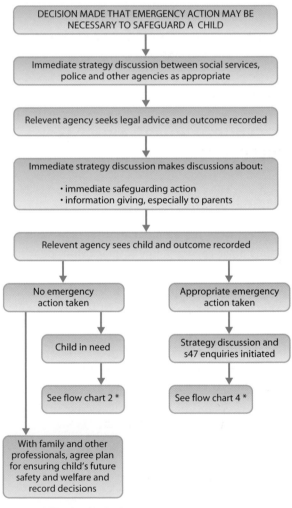

* not reproduced in this book

Figure 10.8 Procedures to be followed if you think a child is at risk Source: www.doh.gov.uk

ROLES AND RESPONSIBILITIES

Policies and procedures of setting

It is important that anyone working with children and young people is not only aware of the policies in place to protect them, but also that they are aware of their role in implementing these policies and procedures.

All staff should receive training on how to recognise the signs and symptoms of abuse and what they should do if a child or young person reveals that they are being, or have been, abused. There should be clear guidelines on what information is recorded and who should have access to this information, as any such information is highly sensitive and confidential, and should only be shared with named members of staff. Immediately abuse has been identified you should follow the procedures that are laid down in the setting's policy documents; these steps should not be delayed.

DISCLOSURE

Disclosure is when a child or young person reveals that they have been, or are experiencing, abuse.

Direct and indirect

Disclosure can be either direct or indirect. Direct disclosure is where a child comes out and talks openly about having been abused; indirect disclosure is where you discover a child is being abused in another way. For example, you might recognise suspicious bruising or burns on a child when they are changing, or you might observe sexually inappropriate behaviour.

Responding to disclosure

An adult's response to disclosure of abuse is crucial. It involves listening carefully and attentively, communicating at the child or young person's own pace and without undue pressure, taking the child or young person seriously and reassuring and supporting them.

When a child admits to being abused it is extremely important that you listen attentively to them, that you allow them to talk freely and that you don't ask leading questions as this could invalidate any evidence in a court. It is very important that you reassure the child who reveals that they have been abused, as frequently they will have been threatened about the consequences of revealing the abuse and will be very concerned and frightened. Also they may be frightened that they will not be believed. It is essential, therefore, to let them know that you believe them, and will help them. However, it is very important that you do not make any promises – for example, that you will not tell anyone else. In order to minimise anxiety, it is recommended that you keep the child or young person informed about what will happen next.

Unconditional acceptance

Those who have been abused will very often feel that they are the guilty person and that the abuse has happened because of something they did. They may also feel guilty about getting the abuser into trouble. It is imperative that you offer unconditional acceptance, and that they know that you do not think worse of them for what they have told you.

Figure 10.9 Listening is important

Boundaries of confidentiality

Very often, when children identify that they have been abused they will begin by asking the adult to keep a secret and not to tell anybody what they are going to reveal. You must never promise not to pass on this information as this will be a promise that cannot be kept and, on discovering this, the child will feel let down once again. Instead it would be appropriate to say that you can't keep a secret, but that you will only reveal the information to somebody who can help; you should also promise to keep the child informed about what is happening.

Dealing with your own feelings and emotions

It is important to be aware of the impact that disclosure of abuse may have on the person who has discovered it. Listening to such disclosures can be extremely distressing and you should consider the offer of counselling if this is offered to you. It is important that you are able to talk to somebody about what you have heard and how this makes you feel.

SUPPORT FOR CHILDREN/YOUNG PEOPLE WHO DISCLOSE

Empowering children and young people

It is important that children and young people who have been abused receive appropriate support and counselling and that they understand that, no matter what someone may do to them, it is not their fault that the abuse has occurred.

ALLEVIATING THE EFFECTS OF ABUSE

Although it is inevitable that abuse will have a devastating effect on children who have suffered it, nevertheless there are certain strategies that can be used to help children cope. These are outlined below.

Encouraging expression of feeling

In order to help them recover from the effects of child abuse, children need to be encouraged to talk through what has happened with a trained counsellor. The counsellor should work with staff who have direct involvement to provide them with information on how they can best support the child or young person that has been abused.

Improving self-image

As identified earlier, children with low self-esteem and poor self-concept are at more risk of abuse than those with high self-esteem. It is therefore very important that those working with children who have been abused look at ways of improving their self-image and help to build up their self-esteem and confidence. Counselling is one way of helping children and young people to feel better about themselves. Play therapy is also a recognised strategy for developing self-esteem and confidence in children and young people who may find communication difficult.

Research tip

Find out more about play therapy by visiting the website of the British Association of Play Therapy: www.bapt.info/

Role of voluntary organisations

There are a number of different voluntary organisations which provide support for children and young people who are in danger or have been abused. These include:

- The National Society for the Prevention of Cruelty to Children (NSPCC) which provides specialist advice and information about child protection

- ChildLine, a free helpline that children can use to contact someone for advice and help

- Kidscape, which provides advice and support on a number of issues, including abuse and bullying

- The National Children's Bureau, which has a database that includes information on child abuse issues.

Research tip

Find out more about some of the different voluntary organisations and the range of support that each one provides. For example, you could visit the website for ChildLine and find out more about its work. Go to www.ChildLine.org.uk

EVIDENCE ACTIVITY

P5 – P6 – M3 – D2

For **P5**, you should write a Child Protection Policy for a child care setting. The policy should include the steps that staff should follow where child abuse is suspected. A separate Appendix will identify the legislation that has been addressed, and how your policy implements this.

For **P6**, you need to identify the strategies and methods of supporting children, young people and their families where abuse is suspected or confirmed. For this you could interview a senior person from your work placement and ask them to identify the procedures that would be followed if they had concerns that one of the children or young people in their care was being abused. What support would they provide for a) the child or young person and b) family members?

For **M3**, you are asked to explain strategies and methods to minimise the risk to children and young people where abuse is suspected or confirmed. You could do this by building upon the answers you were given during your interview for P6. You could explain the procedures that are followed in greater detail, and suggest why the setting has chosen these strategies. How do they help to lessen the risk of abuse?

D2 asks you to evaluate the range of strategies and methods to support children and young people and their families where abuse is suspected or confirmed. This could be done by describing the strengths and weaknesses of the strategies that have been identified in P6 and M3. You could then reflect upon these points and make your own judgement about the effectiveness of these strategies, giving reasons for your decisions. You will provide examples of alternative strategies that you feel would address any weaknesses that you have identified.

Physiological Disorders

If you plan to work in any of the health professions, such as nursing, (adult or paediatric), midwifery, radiography or dietetics, you will need to have an in-depth knowledge of different physiological disorders. These are conditions and illnesses that disturb the way that the body functions – for example, diabetes or asthma. One of the best ways of understanding these disorders is to study real people, if possible, rather than getting your knowledge from textbooks and the internet.

To complete this unit you must produce two case studies of individuals, with very different physiological disorders, who have been referred to professionals for investigation, diagnosis, treatment and care. You may choose to follow the progress of friends or relatives who have been diagnosed with a physiological disorder. However, whoever you choose to study, confidentiality and objectivity are required throughout, including the use in your study of any shared information. These case studies will not be connected with each other until you produce evidence for the final pass criteria (P6), which asks you to compare the future development of the two disorders.

Your work for this unit will be assessed against the unit requirements by your teacher/tutor.

This unit can be linked with several other units in the programme, including Unit 5: Fundamentals of Anatomy and Physiology and Unit 13: Physiology of Fluid Balance.

Learning outcomes

By the end of this unit, you will:

14.1 Understand the nature of two physiological disorders   page 43

14.2 Understand the processes involved in diagnosis of disorders   page 50

14.3 Understand the care strategies used to support individuals through the course of a disorder   page 55

14.4 Understand how individuals adapt to the presence of a disorder   page 62

So you want to be a...

Diagnostic Radiographer

My name Sara Hussein
Age 24
Income £18,240 **Location** Manchester

You will enjoy this job if you like variety and can work closely with the other health care teams in the organisation.

What does your job involve?

I work in the radiology department of a large city hospital, using X-Rays, Magnetic Resonance Imaging and Ultrasound, to investigate and monitor injuries and diseases.

What responsibilities do you have?

We provide a service for most departments, including, accident and emergency, outpatients, the operating theatres and the wards. I work closely with other members of the hospital team. Some patients are apprehensive about the diagnostic procedures and I try to be reassuring and provide a calm, supportive atmosphere. This is particularly important when patients are aware that they may be seriously ill.

How did you get into the job?

I did a BTEC National Diploma in Health and Social Care. This gave me an insight into careers in health and care, and also provided me with an academic foundation for study in higher education. In my second year, I did a short work placement shadowing a radiographer for a week. This really convinced me that this was what I wanted to do. I've always been a 'techie' type of person, but I do love being with people. Radiography combines the two.

How did you find your current job?

I worked here on one of my university clinical practice placements. They happened to have a vacancy just as I graduated, and I was invited to apply. I also looked at the job adverts in specialist magazines, and on websites such as rcnbulletinjobs.co.uk

> ❝ **It sometimes gets a bit hectic, but it is never ever boring!** ❞

What training have you received?

I did a three-year full-time degree, consisting of alternating blocks of academic study and clinical placement. Since joining the City Hospital, I've continued to receive training. For example, I've just done sign language to help me communicate with patients with impaired hearing.

How many hours a week do you work?

I work a five-day, thirty-five-hour week, but I'm also on a rota to provide cover for emergencies at night, weekends and during public holidays.

What skills do you need?

You should be patient, and able to reassure nervous patients. You also need to be competent in performing the techniques used in the job.

What about the future?

I hope to progress to senior radiographer and eventually superintendent radiographer, managing my own department.

Grading criteria

The table below shows what you need to do to gain a pass, merit or distinction in this part of the qualification. Make sure you refer back to it when you are completing work so that you can judge whether you are meeting the criteria and what you need to do to fill in gaps in your knowledge or experience.

In this unit there are four evidence activities to give you an opportunity to demonstrate your achievement of the grading criteria.

page 49	P1, P2, M1	page 62	P4, D1
page 54	P3, M2	page 66	P5, P6, M3, D2

To achieve a pass grade the evidence must show that the learner is able to...	To achieve a merit grade the evidence must show that, in addition to the pass criteria, the learner is able to...	To achieve a distinction grade the evidence must show that, in addition to the pass and merit criteria, the learner is able to...
P1 Describe the course of two different physiological disorders as experienced by two different individuals	**M1** Explain how the course of the disorder in each individual relates to the physiology of the disorder	**D1** Evaluate the contributions made by different people in supporting the individuals with the disorders
P2 Describe the physiology of each disorder and factors that may have influenced its development	**M2** Explain possible difficulties involved in making a diagnosis from the signs and symptoms displayed by the individuals and the results of their investigations	**D2** Evaluate alternative care strategies that might have been adopted for each individual.
P3 Describe the clinical investigations carried out and measurements made to diagnose and monitor the disorder in each individual	**M3** Explain how the care strategies experienced by each individual have influenced the course of the disorder.	
P4 Describe the care processes experienced by each individual case and the roles of different people in supporting the care strategy		
P5 Explain difficulties experienced by each individual in adjusting to the presence of the disorder and the care strategy		
P6 Compare the possible future development of the disorders in the individuals concerned.		

14.1 *Understand the nature of two physiological disorders*

INDIVIDUALS

As you begin, there are some important issues to consider. First, the two individuals whom you will study are real, as are their disorders. A sensitive and tactful approach is essential if you are not to cause them distress. The following points will support you in carrying out your investigations without causing anxiety or embarrassment:

- always check your questions and queries with your teacher/tutor before approaching the individuals

- always check that proposed visits are convenient and will not interfere with any routines or appointments

- remember that the individuals have the right to refuse to provide you with any information

- never offer opinions – you are there to listen, not to suggest

- only ask for the information that will assist your investigations; do not be tempted to feed your curiosity about an individual's personal life

- be prepared to allow the individuals to read what you have written, if they wish to

- maintain confidentiality at all times – it may not be appropriate to include copies of clinical reports, and images such as X-ray films and scans

- remember also that the inclusion of photographs that clearly identify an individual would be considered a breach of trust.

APPROPRIATE DISORDERS

You may wish to study disorders other than those in the following list. However, you must confirm your choices with your teacher/tutor, before beginning your research. Appropriate disorders for study include:

- diabetes (insulin-dependent or non-insulin-dependent)

- coronary heart disease

- stroke (cerebral haemorrhage, cerebral thrombosis or cerebral infarction)

- Parkinson's disease

- Alzheimers's disease

- asthma

- emphysema

- motor neurone disease

- multiple sclerosis

- rheumatoid arthritis

- osteoporosis

- Crohn's disease

- ulcerative colitis

- inflammatory bowel syndrome (IBS)

- cancer – for example, of the lung, bowel, skin, breast, prostate gland.

INVESTIGATE

A case study has many similar issues to a research proposal; first you must decide on the methods you will use to gather information and data. Ethical issues are of paramount importance, and so is the maintenance of confidentiality with regard to the information you have collected.

Remember that you must show your chosen individuals any details that you have written about them. They may have been happy to speak with you, but less happy to read their discussion in print. You must never publish details unless you have the person's full permission. Don't forget to change names, dates of birth and addresses to fictional ones; this will demonstrate that you are adhering to the Care Value Base requirement for privacy. (You can discover more about the Care Value Base in Unit 2: Equality, Diversity and Rights in Health and Social Care, Unit 6: Personal and Professional Development in Health and Social Care and Unit 9: Values and Planning for Social Care.)

Primary research

Primary research is information that you have gathered during the course of your case study. The following points may be useful in helping you focus on the important details:

- evidence of changes in lifestyle in order to cope more easily with the disorder

- changes in employment (including from full-time to part-time)

- visible signs and symptoms such as complaints of pain or signs of discomfort

- changes in daily living, such as having regular visits from a community care assistant to help with domestic chores.

It would be helpful if you noted down your observations directly after a visit with the individual; never write whilst you are visiting as it can appear intimidating to the person.

You may also wish to interview the individuals, and a structured or semi-structured interview will enable the session to remain focused. Do be aware that the individual may just wish to 'chat' with you, and you should allow time for this, in order not to appear unfriendly.

Try to be flexible in arranging visits and remember that the person may not always be feeling well enough to be interviewed; after all, their disorder is the reason you are visiting.

Secondary research

This is information gathered by other people, which you will use in addition to your primary research. The following list contains some suggestions for places where you can start your research, but your teacher/tutor will be able to provide you with further guidance:

- health journals

- *Community Care* magazine/website

- health and social care textbooks

- Department of Health website

- BBC website

- newspaper articles

Remember that you must acknowledge all your sources in the form of a bibliography, and reference any direct quotations within your final piece of work.

Ethical issues

As you begin your investigations, there are several issues that must be considered, in order to ensure that your research is conducted in an ethical manner, which is not offensive to the individuals involved.

- You must obtain informed consent before recording any information provided by the individuals. This means that they fully understand what they are consenting to. It is never acceptable to deceive people in order to obtain the results or information you want.

- The individuals involved should be allowed to withdraw from your study at any time; you must never put pressure on someone who is ill in order to gain information.

- The privacy and dignity of the individual must always be your main concern. Remember that as a future health or social care professional, the Care Value Base must be incorporated into all of your work.

- Never be tempted to ask 'just one more question'; be sensitive to the person's body language, tone of voice and facial expression, which may be signalling distress or fatigue.

- Never be tempted to gossip about your visits to friends and relatives, or to reveal confidential documents. The Care Value Base dictates that you follow its code and respect the privacy of the service user.

- You will need to consider how to incorporate ethical practices when doing your case studies.

HUMAN PHYSIOLOGY

Human physiology is the science that deals with the functions and activities of the body. You will be investigating two conditions that affect those functions and activities, together with the care and treatment involved to control those effects.

Body systems

You will be writing about the body systems that are affected by your chosen disorders. Although several systems may be involved you are only required to describe and explain the major systems affected.

In motor neurone disease, for example, the nervous and musculo-skeletal systems are involved. You may need to describe the basic effects on the skin from the accompanying immobility. Table 14.1 is a summary of the major systems involved in the physiological disorders listed on page 43.

Disorder	Major body systems involved
Diabetes	Endocrine and digestive systems
Coronary heart disease	Cardiovascular and respiratory systems
Stroke	Cardiovascular and nervous systems
Parkinson's disease	Nervous and musculo-skeletal systems
Alzheimer's disease	Nervous system
Asthma	Respiratory system
Emphysema	Cardiovascular and respiratory systems
Motor neurone disease	Nervous and musculo-skeletal systems
Multiple sclerosis	Nervous and musculo-skeletal systems
Rheumatoid Arthritis	Musculo-skeletal system
Osteoporosis	Musculo-skeletal system
Crohn's disease	Digestive system
Inflammatory bowel disease	Digestive system
Breast cancer	Reproductive system
Bowel cancer	Digestive system
Lung cancer	Respiratory system
Prostate cancer	Reproductive system
Skin cancer	Skin

Table 14.1 Major body systems involved in different physiological disorders

As you progress through this unit, you will study the case of Sophia, who has motor neurone disease. This will assist you in setting out your research for your own case studies. The questions in each 'episode' of Sophia's story are designed to test your learning and to provide guidance with regard to your own investigations.

CASE STUDY: SOPHIA

Sophia has motor neurone disease. The major body systems affected by this condition are the nervous and musculo-skeletal systems. There are three types of motor neurone disease, which are:

- amyotrophic lateral sclerosis (ALS)

- progressive muscular atrophy (PMA)

- progressive bulbar palsy.

QUESTION

What are the main characteristics of each type of motor neurone disease?

Research tip

You may find it helpful to consult the BUPA website. Go to http://www.bupa.co.uk/health_information/

Structural and physiological changes caused by the disorder or its treatment

Following your overview of the body system, you will explain how the disorder has affected the anatomy of the system, either macroscopically or microscopically – or both if appropriate. For example, motor neurone disease might show muscle wasting macroscopically and degeneration of nerve fibres and muscle fibres microscopically.

Key words

macroscopic – changes that can be seen without using a microscope

microscopic – changes that cannot be seen without using a microscope

muscle wasting – observable diminishing muscle mass

CASE STUDY: PRELIMINARY INVESTIGATIONS

In order to confirm the diagnosis of motor neurone disease for Sophia, the neurologist ordered the following three tests:

- an electromyogram (EMG)
- a muscle biopsy
- a Magnetic Resonance Imaging Scan (MRI).

QUESTION

Why might the specialist request these tests?

In addition to the structural changes that occur, there are likely to be physiological changes resulting from the disorder. For example, in some cases of non-insulin-dependent diabetes, the individual may experience a reduction in vision, due to the formation of new blood vessels at the back of the eye.

Treatment can also cause structural and physiological changes. For example, invasive procedures involve piercing or cutting the skin and/or deeper tissues, which can leading to scarring and even deformity if large areas of skin or muscle are involved. Biopsies, surgery, injections and blood tests are examples of invasive procedures.

Some individuals may experience discomfort or major side effects from treatment; for example, certain prescribed drugs may cause gastric symptoms. In addition, physiotherapy, designed to reduce stiffness in the joints, may cause the person some discomfort to begin with.

There is a wide-ranging variety of treatments for disorders and you will explain how both the treatment and the disorder affect the anatomy and physiology of the body.

CASE STUDY: THE DIAGNOSIS

Sophia's neurologist confirmed that the tests demonstrated a diagnosis of amyotrophic lateral sclerosis, which is a form of motor neurone disease.

QUESTIONS

1. What are the signs and symptoms that would suggest this particular form of the disease?

2. Who is the famous scientist who has this form of motor neurone disease? (If you don't know, try searching the internet.)

PSYCHOLOGICAL EFFECTS

The majority of the disorders that you will choose to study are long-term, chronic disorders. They are manageable, but incurable. Some of these will be progressive, resulting in a diminished lifestyle for the individual. Examples of this include Parkinson's disease and Crohn's disease. Such conditions can induce bouts of depression and anxiety in the individual, due to the feelings of powerlessness that may be experienced. Furthermore, pain either from the disorder, as in rheumatoid arthritis, or from the treatment, as may be the case in breast cancer, can cause considerable distress.

> ***Think*** What is meant by a 'diminished lifestyle'?

When conducting your research, you should observe and record the mood changes in your subject. However, a sensitive approach is necessary.

> ***Think*** Have you ever felt unhappy for a short time, perhaps when recovering from illness? Find out what you can about the signs of clinical depression and compare them with how you felt.

INFLUENCES ON THE DEVELOPMENT OF THE DISORDER

As you begin your research, you will discover that there are underlying factors that have contributed to the disorder. Some of these are discussed below.

Inherited traits

Research has revealed that many disorders, such as sickle cell anaemia and Tourette's syndrome, are inherited from one or both parents. Alternatively, the mutation of a chromosome has occurred at conception, as with Down's syndrome. In conditions such as autism, there appears to be an inherited tendency.

Lifestyle choices

The government and the medical profession have tried to make us aware of the importance of lifestyle choices in helping to prevent the onset of various disorders. For example, the consumption of excessive alcohol can lead to cirrhosis of the liver, and too much sunbathing, which involves long-term exposure to ultraviolet rays, can lead to skin cancer. The link between obesity and the development of different cancers, stroke and heart disease has also been emphasised.

Therefore, people are encouraged to take exercise and maintain a healthy weight. Other government campaigns have advocated the practice of 'safe sex' in order to reduce the incidence of HIV/AIDS and other sexually transmitted diseases such as chlamydia.

> ***Think*** What do you know about the link between cigarettes and diseases such as lung cancer and emphysema? What would a healthy lifestyle choice be?

You may discover that lifestyle choices have contributed to at least one of your chosen disorders. However, remember not to leap to conclusions as there may be other explanations. Also, be sensitive that you do not give the impression that you are blaming the individual or making them feel responsible for causing their disorder.

Employment

A person's work may also contribute towards the development of a disorder. For example, there are many incidences of coal miners developing a variety of respiratory conditions, including bronchitis and emphysema. Agricultural workers and gardeners have been shown to be more vulnerable to skin cancer than other members of the population, and some scientists have suggested that there may be a link between exposure to some pesticides and chemical solvents and motor neurone disease.

Diet

You will be aware that dietary choices can influence the development of some disorders. For example, a lack of fibre is now known to contribute to the development of bowel cancer. In addition, a diet high in saturated fats and refined sugar is known to contribute to diabetes and coronary disorders.

Environment

Various environmental factors have been linked with either the onset of disorders, or having contributed to the worsening of them. For example, overcrowded and damp housing can encourage the spread of tuberculosis and other infections. Air pollution can add to the discomfort of sufferers of asthma and chronic bronchitis.

Figure 14.1 Poor housing is linked to a variety of illnesses

SIGNS AND SYMPTOMS

Physiological disorders will be diagnosed by the appearance of **signs** and **symptoms** experienced by the individual.

Key words

sign – an objective indication of a disorder observed by a health professional
symptoms – signs noticed by the service user or patient; for example, tiredness and diminished mobility in motor neurone disease, or rectal bleeding in the case of bowel cancer

The following table describes a selection of some common signs and the symptoms they may cause.

Common signs	Common symptoms
Changes in heart rate	Palpitations, chest pain
Changes in mobility	Painful joints
Rash	Itching
Changes in breathing rate	Shortness of breath, chest pain

Table 14.2 Common signs and symptoms of physiological disorders

> ***Think*** Can you add to this list?

In both of your case studies, you are required to describe and explain the signs and symptoms of the disorder.

CASE STUDY: SOPHIA'S SUNBATHING

Sophia had always been fond of sunbathing, declaring that the sun cheered her up. One day, while taking a shower, she noticed that the mole on her back appeared to be enlarged. Sophia had recently read a poster at her local health centre about the need to examine moles regularly and decided to make an appointment with her GP (General Practitioner). When the doctor saw Sophia, she referred her to a dermatologist to gain a second opinion.

QUESTIONS

1. Why would the doctor refer Sophia to a dermatologist?

2. What investigations might the dermatologist arrange for Sophia?

3. How might a diagnosis of skin cancer from the dermatologist affect Sophia psychologically, given that she is already displaying worrying signs of another illness?

EVIDENCE ACTIVITY

P1 – P2 – M1

For **P1**, you are required to describe the course of two different physiological disorders as experienced by two different individuals. The following activities will help to frame your evidence.

1. Create a diary or journal for each individual that charts the progress of their condition. First you will need to select the individuals you choose to study. You can start this by making notes when you have contact with people with physiological disorders, for example about:

- the current stage of their disorder

- the physiological nature of their disorder.

You can use this information to produce a spider diagram for each of the individuals with disorders. Check your diagrams against the unit requirements and discard any that will not provide you with the information you need – for example, anyone whose condition has been recently diagnosed, or anyone with whom you are unable to spend sufficient time to gain the information you will require in a sensitive way.

Discuss the remaining diagrams with your teacher/tutor and decide which two will be the most suitable to study, and also which one you will start with.

2. Remember that you cannot use information about individuals in your diaries without their informed consent. Draft a consent form to be signed by the chosen individual and a witness. Check the form with your teacher/tutor. If the individual is cared for in a residential setting, you must also produce a permission form for the care home manager.

3. Produce a plan of action, including:

- A brief profile of your chosen person that includes first signs and symptoms.

- An explanation of any clinical investigations and measurements undertaken at the first visit to the GP. (These could might include blood pressure readings, urine testing, blood tests and listening to the patient's breathing with a stethoscope.)

- The initial diagnosis at this stage.

- Any physiological changes that had already occurred.

In order to help you understand the progression of the disorder, it would be helpful to gather information in time order. You can do this by organising your questions so that the individual provides you with a timeline. The following are some suggestions for questions to help you with this:

- What made the person visit their GP in the first place?

- What did their GP conclude or advise at the first visit?

- Did their GP order any investigations?

- When was the individual referred for more specialist investigations?

- Is the specialist care still ongoing?

For **P2**, you need to describe the physiology of each disorder and factors that may have influenced its development.

1. Continue your diaries by answering these questions:

- Explain the structure and physiology of the main body systems involved.

- Explain the signs and symptoms of the disorder.

- Identify and explain the factors that have influenced the development of the disorder.

In order to add depth and breadth to your work, and to extend your understanding of the physiology involved, research websites for the disorder on the internet, but be sure to check them for accuracy and reliability. If you are not certain about a piece of secondary information, check with your subject teacher/tutor.

For **M1**, you must explain how the course of the disorder in each individual relates to the physiology of the disorder.

1. Produce a table, or write a report in your diaries, that shows how you can relate the developing disorder to the way in which normal functions of the body are becoming disturbed.

14.2 *Understand the processes involved in diagnosis of disorders*

There may be several stages between the first visit to the GP and a final diagnosis of a disorder.

REFERRAL

If the doctor can make a definite clinical diagnosis of disorder at the first visit, they will make an immediate referral to a hospital consultant. They will do this by contacting the appropriate department and requesting an urgent appointment.

More often, however, the doctor will arrange blood tests and other tests as preliminary measures. The results of these will be sent to the hospital before the patient's appointment, so that the specialist has a more detailed picture of the individual's physiological state before the initial consultation. The GP may also refer a patient directly to other services, such as physiotherapy, and arrange further appointments to discuss the results.

INVESTIGATIONS

An individual will always undergo general investigations such as height, weight, pulse rate, blood pressure and breathing rate to establish a baseline when they first visit their doctor or a specialist clinic. They will also have investigations that are specific to their disorder. For example, a patient who might have motor neurone disease will have the strength of their muscle assessed with an electromyogram (EMG). A medical history will always be taken as well as standard blood tests, such as haemoglobin levels (see blood tests below).

Medical history

The doctor listens to the patient as they describe their symptoms, when they started and how the individual is currently feeling. The doctor will ask appropriate and relevant questions, in order to find out which factors may have influenced the onset of the disorder and the patient's current state of health.

Sometimes the patient will provide information that could point to several conditions, because the symptoms of several disorders may be similar. In this case, the doctor will order tests to make a firm diagnosis (this is known as a differential diagnosis).

Following the medical history, the doctor will usually perform a physical examination, to provide further information and to confirm symptoms. For example, in the case of motor neurone disease, the doctor will test the patient's reflexes as the disorder affects the musculo-skeletal system.

> ### Key words
> diagnosis – the process by which the nature of the disorder is determined
> clinical diagnosis – a diagnosis made on the basis of signs and symptoms
> differential diagnosis – the recognition of one disease from others presenting similar signs and symptoms
> referral – sending the patient to another professional for specialist advice or treatment. For example, if a patient has severe eczema, the GP might refer them to a dermatologist.

Palpation

This is a technique for feeling the shapes, sizes and surfaces of organs with the hands. Doctors are taught this technique and find it particularly useful for examining abdominal organs, such as the liver, spleen and bladder. The doctor will note areas of unusual tenderness or rigidity. They will also note any abnormal masses or lumps.

Blood tests

Blood samples can be obtained in two ways, by venepuncture (inserting a sterile needle into a vein), or by a finger prick using a small, sterile instrument called a lancet. Venepuncture is used when a large sample of blood is required for clinical analysis. The clinical analysis of a blood sample can provide the doctor with vital information that will contribute to diagnosis. For example:

- a low haemoglobin level can indicate anaemia

- a raised level of carbon dioxide in the blood and reduced oxygen (blood gases) can indicate the severity of respiratory disorder

- raised levels of certain female hormones can indicate pregnancy

- raised levels of blood salts (electrolytes) can indicate renal disorders, diabetes and metabolic bone disorders

- raised levels of white blood cells can indicate infection or more serious blood disorders.

The finger prick test is used when small quantities of blood are required. For example, a person with diabetes will check their blood glucose levels in this way before administering their own insulin.

Urine tests

The physical characteristics of urine, such as its colour, odour, clarity, pH (which stands for power of hydrogen, used to indicate whether a solution is acid, alkaline or neutral) and concentration can inform much about the individual's physiological state. The chemical composition of urine such as the glucose, urea, protein, drugs, hormones and any blood content, can reveal an underlying condition such as diabetes. More specific urine tests can provide information on the functioning levels of the placenta in pregnancy. Urine can also be cultured to detect microbial infections.

Key words

urea – a nitrogenous substance resulting from the liver breaking down excess amino acids from the digestion of proteins. Nitrogenous material not required for metabolism cannot be stored in the body. If allowed to accumulate, urea is toxic to body tissues and can result in death.

amino acids – the nitrogenous end-products of protein digestion, normally used to build up new proteins such as enzymes and hormones. However, many western diets contain too much dietary protein and after digestion the unwanted amino acids will be broken down by the liver and eliminated by the kidneys.

Radiological investigations

You will probably have seen plain black and white X-rays that view the skeleton in a non-invasive way. Modern equipment exposes patients to very little radiation; however, clinicians will not request any more X-rays than is necessary.

Some X-rays are taken following the insertion of radio-opaque materials into the patient, in order to highlight areas not visible on regular X-rays. For example, radio-opaque iodine compounds will display the urinary tract as these will be excreted by the kidneys and show the kidney, ureters, bladder and urethra. This will indicate where there are any blockages, such as kidney stones.

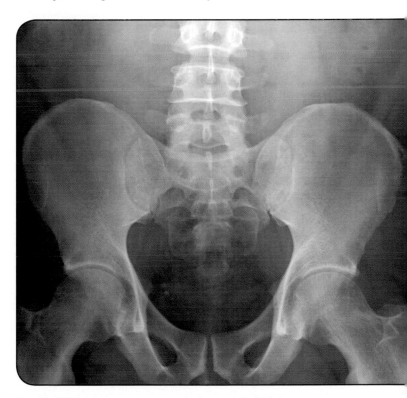

Figure 14.2 An x-ray can reveal much useful information

Scans

The most common form of scan is an ultrasound scan, which is routinely used when monitoring a pregnancy. Women can expect to have at least two scans during the course of their pregnancy and many keep the pictures of the fetus as mementoes – the first baby pictures. Ultrasonic scanning is also used to visualise the gall bladder, liver, pancreas, breast and kidneys. The technique works by bouncing high frequency sound waves off internal organs. The technique does not work well where there is a lot of gas, as in the lungs, or where there is a casing of bone, such as inside the adult skull. Ultrasound scanning is generally considered safe and is used extensively to detect tumours, foreign bodies (such as gall stones and kidney stones), cysts and abnormalities of structure.

Magnetic Resonance Imaging (MRI scan) uses magnetic fields and radio waves to provide high quality three-dimensional images of organs and structures within the body. This technique may be used to assist the diagnosis of, for example, motor neurone disease, by producing images of the brain and spinal column.

Computerised Axial Tomography (CAT or CT scan) uses X-rays passed at different angles through the body, which are then transformed using a computer to produce cross-sectional images, sometimes known as 'slices'. This is useful to produce very detailed images of, for example, brain tissue where a tumour is suspected.

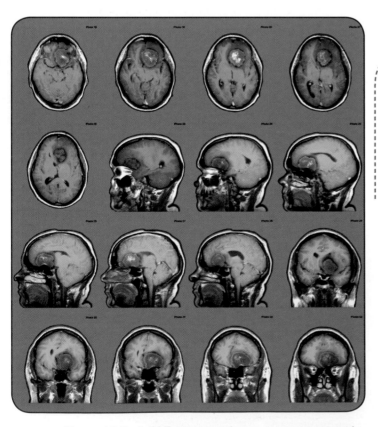

Figure 14.3 A CAT scan produces cross-sectional images

Research tip

You can find out more about MRI and CT scans at www.cancerhelp.org.uk. Click on 'About cancer' and then 'Cancer tests' and select either CT or MRI.

Function tests

These are tests that have been specifically designed to determine the degree of function of particular body parts, to assist diagnosis and also to assess the value of treatment. Function tests for an organ may include various types of scans or X-rays. For example:

- **Liver-function tests**. This is a series of blood tests that look at the way the liver is making new substances and breaking down and getting rid of old ones. It tells the doctors whether the liver is healthy or damaged.

- **Kidney-function tests**. These tests include blood tests and an examination of the urine.

Example

The creatinine clearance test compares the amount of creatinine in an individual's blood with the amount they excrete in their urine over a twenty-four hour period. Creatinine is a waste product excreted by the kidneys. A decreased creatinine clearance rate could indicate a kidney disorder.

MEASUREMENTS

There are certain measurements that are taken routinely during medical investigations, such as breathing rate, pulse rate, blood pressure, body temperature and body weight and height.

Blood pressure is measured using a sphygmomanometer, which measures the force that blood exerts on the walls of blood vessels. The pressure of the blood when the ventricles of the heart are contracting is known as systolic blood pressure. This is the highest reading of the two (usually around 120 mm of mercury for a healthy young adult). The pressure when the ventricles are relaxed and filling is known as diastolic blood pressure. This is the lowest reading of the two (usually 75-80 mm of mercury for a healthy young adult).

Machines for measuring blood pressure can be bought from many high-street pharmacies. However, they do not provide as accurate a reading as those used in health care settings.

Figure 14.5 A peak flow meter provides useful information for adjusting medication

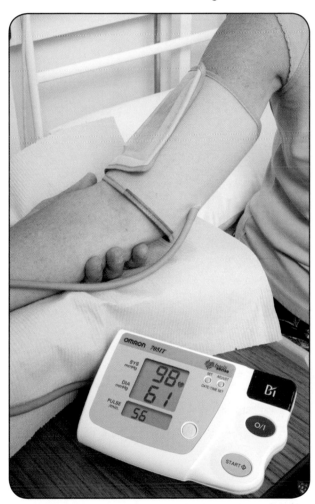

Figure 14.4 A blood pressure reading should be taken by a professional health care worker

Other measurements are specific to particular disorders. For example, individuals with diabetes measure their blood glucose levels before administering insulin. Many adults and children with asthma measure their maximum speed of expiration using a peak flow meter, to monitor their condition and to adjust their therapy.

MONITORING

The timing of repeat consultations with professionals will vary. Some consultations may occur on an annual basis; for example, individuals who have been free from cancer symptoms for some time. Other individuals, such as those with severe asthma, may attend an outpatient clinic at three- or six-monthly intervals. Individuals with high blood pressure monitored by their GP may visit at monthly intervals, reducing their visits to six-monthly as the medication takes effect.

Repeat measurements

Repeat measurements will depend on the nature of the disorder and also on the treatment. Individuals who self-medicate will probably make more frequent measurements than a health care professional would.

CASE STUDY: SOPHIA'S PROGRESS

When Sophia next attended the neurology clinic at her local hospital, she was complaining of the following symptoms, as the disorder progressed:

- muscle spasms

- muscle cramps

- constipation.

QUESTIONS

1. What is likely to have caused Sophia's constipation?

2. How might her constipation be treated?

Repeat investigations

Investigations are likely to be repeated if previous results are inconclusive or if the diagnosis has not yet been made. Investigations will also be repeated to monitor progress. For example, following chemotherapy a scan may be ordered to see whether or not a tumour has shrunk. Ultrasound scans may be repeated in pregnancy to monitor the growth of the fetus, particularly if the professionals are concerned about the progress of the pregnancy.

EVIDENCE ACTIVITY

P3 - M2

1. In journals/diaries that you are keeping for your chosen individuals, record all the investigations that they underwent when their disorder was diagnosed.

You should start by asking your chosen individuals about the diagnosis process they experienced. You will also need to use secondary sources to check current practice and to provide further details about any clinical investigations used to make the diagnosis. (**P3**)

2. Record all the measurements that they had taken both before diagnosis and also during the monitoring of their disorder.

You must also provide examples of measurements that would be used for the particular disorders (for example, blood glucose levels in diabetes). You will not have access to the individuals' records and they may have forgotten readings, if they ever knew them. (**P3**)

3. For each of your chosen individuals, research what difficulties there may have been in reaching a diagnosis of their disorder. Write an account of about 500 to 800 words in your journals/diaries to explain the difficulties that health care personnel may have had in reaching the diagnosis from:

- the signs the individual was showing when they first saw their GP or and when they first saw the consultant

- the symptoms they were experiencing at that time

- the results of any tests that were performed before their diagnosis.

Diagnosis is not always easy; although two people may have the same disorder, the signs and symptoms that each has may not be the same. Everyone is an individual and their body will react in different ways. In addition, if the individual also has another disorder, their intial signs and symptoms may not fit the usual pattern. This will make diagnosis difficult. Multiple sclerosis, for example, can be difficult to diagnose. Sometimes a diagnosis is reached only by eliminating all other possible disorders.

Remember to look at secondary sources to see what difficulties there may be in diagnosing a disorder. Individuals may forget symptoms or even misinterpret them and some disorders, such as strokes, can produce confusion, making the individual an unreliable source or unable to tell you what originally made them seek medical attention.

14.3 *Understand the care strategies used to support individuals through the course of a disorder*

CARE SETTINGS

The individual may be cared for in many different settings, including in their own home, during the course of their disorder.

Primary care

Most individuals will visit their GP at a surgery or health centre when they first experience unusual signs or symptoms. The GP may refer the individual to a specialist, usually based in a hospital clinic, if it is not possible for the GP undertake the specialist tests or treatment required for the disorder. However, the individual may well return to the GP for follow-up care and monitoring of their disorder or treatment. Nursing care, physiotherapy and other specialist care may also be undertaken at the GP's surgery or health centre.

Hospital care

Some patients may spend time in hospital, particularly in the later stages of a progressive disorder, and also during periods of intensive investigation. However, much of the treatment and monitoring can be in the form of visits to outpatient clinics. Chemotherapy for certain forms of cancer, for example, may be given in an outpatient chemotherapy clinic. Other patients may experience 'shared care' in that they visit the hospital clinic at infrequent intervals and their own GP more frequently.

Domiciliary care

This is care delivered in the patient's own home, and it is usually preferred as people like to be in their own homes rather than in hospital. Older people often fear that they will not return home once they have been admitted to either residential care or a hospital ward. Occupational therapists may visit the home to provide advice and assess the home for adaptations and specific aids to mobility and daily life.

Community-based nurses provide vital support to patients, particularly to those in the later stages of a progressive disorder. Patients and their families may also receive support from social services in the form of community care assistance with daily life. Patients with terminal disorders, such as some forms of cancer, may be admitted to a hospice for respite care.

CASE STUDY: SOPHIA'S PROGNOSIS

Using secondary sources, research why Sophia's family may benefit from the use of respite care as her motor neurone disease progresses.

Residential care

Individuals in the later stages of a progressive disease may need 24-hour care. This may not be possible in their own home and they may need to move to residential care. People with Alzheimer's disease or dementia require high levels of care, for example. Admittance to a nursing home may be required. Individuals with reduced mobility - for example, due to the onset of arthritis - may need to be looked after in a care home. Sometimes respite care is offered to give families and other home carers a rest.

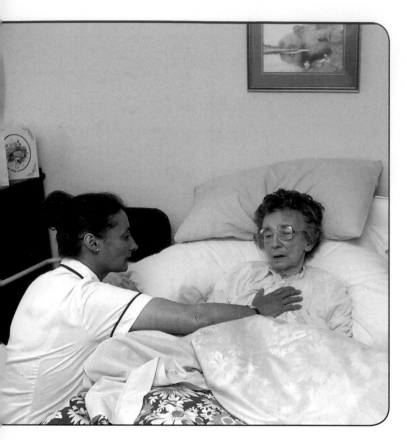

Figure 14.6 A nursing home can provide specialist care

PROFESSIONALS INVOLVED IN DELIVERING SPECIALIST CARE

Many health care professionals may be involved in caring for individuals with acute or chronic disorders.

General Practitioners (GPs)

A GP is a doctor with a medical practice who cares for individuals in the community in which they live. The GP does not usually specialise and is the first point of contact for an individual needing non-emergency medical care.

GPs run their own practices as a business. This may involve working alone or with one or two other GPs in a surgery. GPs may also work with several other GPs in a health centre, employing administrative staff and a team of other health care professionals such as practice nurses or physiotherapists.

Clinical specialists

Clinical specialists are also known as consultants. Medical professionals may become specialists in a particular area of medicine. For example, the specialist who is treating Sophia (see the case studies) is known as a neurologist. A neurologist has developed expertise in all disorders that affect the body's nervous system. The dermatologist mentioned in the case study on Sophia's mole (page xxx) is an expert in skin disorders. These professionals will have gained additional qualifications in their chosen field, and have decided to work solely in that area.

Other specialists are involved in diagnosis work behind the scenes in laboratories. These people include haematologists and pathologists.

> ### Key words
> ------------------------------------
> haematologists – specialists who advise on the diagnosis and treatment of disorders of the blood or bone marrow
> pathologists – specialists who study the causes of disorders and their effects on the body. The pathologist advises on the diagnosis and treatment of a wide range of disorders.

It is not possible for the clinical specialist to always see each individual on their list, so on some visits the individual may be seen by another doctor working in the specialist team, such as a registrar. Many registrars are working towards becoming a specialist in their chosen field.

Nurses

Nurses are specialists in their own field and many nurses have specialist practitioner status – for example, nurses who practice in GP surgeries or health clinics. Other nurses specialise within particular areas of patient care – for example, stoma care nurses. Nurses may also practice in extended roles, such as nurses who are licensed to prescribe medications.

Professionals allied to medicine

The roles of these professionals are vital to the work of the health service. They include:

- chiropodists
- radiographers
- radiotherapists
- speech therapists
- dieticians.

Chiropodists care for feet and treat disorders of the feet. This service is particularly important for elderly diabetic patients who tend to get foot infections.

Radiotherapists administer particular treatments to reduce or remove certain tumours. The treatments are prescribed by the radiologist (a clinical specialist), and performed by the radiotherapist.

Speech therapists work with a variety of patients, including those who have had strokes that have affected their speech.

Dieticians support patients whose disorder requires a particular diet, such as those diagnosed with diabetes or elderly patients with particular nutritional needs. Many people find a new diet regime difficult to follow and will need a lot of support.

Pharmacists

Pharmacists work in hospitals and in the community, usually within a retail setting such as a chemist's shop. Pharmacists dispense medication prescribed by doctors, nurses and dentists, but also provide advice on a variety of issues.

Example

Many pharmacists are now offer advice about programmes for giving up smoking. Pharmacists may also offer other services such as measuring cholesterol and blood pressure levels.

Phlebotomists

Phlebotomists work in hospitals. They are trained to take blood samples by puncturing a vein to withdraw a small quantity of blood through a syringe. Nurses may also be trained to take blood, and nurses employed in community medical practices will usually perform this function. However, within a hospital there will be many more individuals requiring blood tests so this is not usually a nursing task.

Laboratory personnel

Laboratory staff analyse and produce reports on the many types of sample taken as part of investigations for disorders and illnesses. Their work is important both in diagnosing a disorder and in the ongoing monitoring of the treatment for specific disorders.

Example

A specialist may take a biopsy (a small sample of tissue or cells) of an individual's skin if the individual has any signs or symptoms that may be caused by a skin disorder. The biopsy is sent to the laboratory for analysis, through careful preparation of the sample and examination using a microscope. The laboratory will report their findings to the specialist who can then decide whether any further treatment is necessary.

Figure 14.7 The work of laboratory staff is essential for correct diagnosis and treatment

Health care assistants

Health care assistants are skilled in the routine care of hospital patients, such as washing and personal hygiene routines. They work with guidance from a qualified healthcare professional. Their role will vary according to where they work.

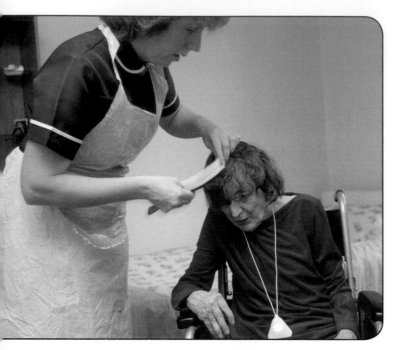

Figure 14.8 Health care assistants are an important part of the team

Care assistants

Care assistants are skilled at caring for patients in their own homes, within a care home or in a day care centre. They provide practical support for people with a range of disorders. Care assistants may work with children, older people, people with physical disorders or people with learning disabilities.

Research tip

Find out about the role of the Health Care Assistant at www.nhscareers.nhs.uk. To find out about the role of Care Assistant visit www.learndirect-advice.co.uk. You will also find more information about working in the Health Sector in Unit 18.

Counsellors

A counsellor may be employed as part of the prescribed care strategy for an individual. For example, for an individual with Auto Immune Deficiency Syndrome (AIDS) counselling is essential to help the individual come to terms with the debilitating effects and terminal nature of the disease. Counselling may also form part of a rehabilitation strategy to enable an individual to manage their disorder.

> **Think** What type of lifestyle changes will an individual newly-diagnosed with insulin-dependent-diabetes have to adjust to?

Figure 14.9 Counselling can help patients to come to terms with managing their condition

INFORMAL CARERS

The care provided by relatives and friends is essential. This care is known as informal care, because it is not provided by health or care professionals, and is not subject to the same regulations. A carer may have to give up their full-time job to look after their relative. This can involve long hours, often with little structure to the day and extending into the night. This can be extremely stressful and exhausting for the carer. A short period of respite care for the sick or disabled relative may allow the carer to recover and carry on looking after their relative.

Care provided by voluntary groups

The involvement of voluntary groups in providing care for vulnerable individuals has been encouraged by government. Voluntary groups are seen as an essential part of the 'care package'. Some groups, such as the Salvation Army, are well-established to receive referrals from social services. Voluntary groups can apply to receive local authority funding to support their work.

There are many voluntary groups who support patients and families affected by particular disorders. They all have websites. The following are a small selection:

- Multiple Sclerosis Society
- Brain and Spine Foundation
- Contact a Family
- Age Concern
- Cancerbackup.

Research tip

To find out more about motor neurone disease, go to www.mndassociation.org or visit http://news.bbc.co.uk/1/hi/health/medical_notes/1500231.stm or http://hcd2.bupa.co.uk/fact_sheets/html/motor_neurone_disease.html

CARE

Medication

Medication may be given as part of the treatment regime for many physiological disorders, or it may be prescribed to relieve and control unpleasant symptoms. Table 14.1 shows some examples of types of medication and the reasons why they are prescribed.

Type of medication	Reason prescribed
anti-inflammatory drugs	reduction of inflammation and swelling, for example following a soft-tissue injury such as a wrench or a strain
laxatives	constipation relief
antihypertensive drugs	reduction of high blood pressure
insulin	correction of hormone deficiency in insulin-dependent-diabetes
antihistamines	to suppress allergic reactions, for example for allergic rhinitis (hayfever)
analgesics	relief of pain, for example headache or joint pain
diuretics	to increase urine flow and remove excess fluid from the body, for example to relieve fluid retention caused by heart failure
antibiotics	to treat infections such as bronchitis and pnuemonia
immunosuppressants	to suppress the body's immune response, for example immunosuppressants will be given following transplant surgery to prevent the body rejecting the new organ
muscle relaxants	to relieve muscle spasm, for example caused by motor neurone disease

Table 14.3 Some common medications and the reasons for prescribing them

Research tip

You will need to do some research to find out about the different types of medication that are usually prescribed for your chosen disorders. If you search the internet using the name of the disorder you are studying, you will usually find a section that tells you what medications the individual is likely to be prescribed.

Aids and adaptations

As the disorder progresses, some patients will benefit from the provision of mobility aids. For example, an individual who has multiple sclerosis may benefit from the use of a walking stick. However, as the disease progresses and their mobility decreases, they may need to use a wheelchair. Other daily living aids include stair lifts, shower seats and bath hoists, and adapted cutlery and plates. This equipment can enhance the quality of life for individuals and help them to remain independent for as long as possible.

Surgery

Surgical intervention (an operation) may be an essential part of the treatment for some disorders. For example, a woman diagnosed as having breast cancer may be advised by her surgeon to have the lump removed. This is known as **lumpectomy**. If the surgeon feels that the lump is in an area where the tumour could spread, or if the lump is quite large, then the surgeon may advise her to have the whole breast removed. This is called a **mastectomy**. There are many other surgical procedures that might also be offered and these include:

- wide local excision – this is removal of an area of normal tissue beyond the diseased tissue to check whether there are any cancer cells in it

- axillary dissection – removal of the lymph nodes in the armpit (axilla) on the affected side to check whether there are any cancer cells in the lymph nodes

- breast reconstruction – this is offered to the individual when the surgeon is confident that there has been no spread of the cancer to surrounding breast tissue. A new breast is created using an implant or muscle from another part of the body.

Key words

lumpectomy –removal of a lump, usually from the breast, which may be benign (not cancer) or malignant (cancer)
mastectomy – removal of one or both breasts to prevent the cancer spreading

Transfusion

Some patients may lose several pints of blood during surgery, which will need to be replaced through a blood transfusion. The surgeon will order the blood before surgery if there is a risk of any serious blood loss. The patient's blood group will be checked by taking a blood sample, so that the correct blood will be administered. Giving blood from the wrong group can be fatal.

Think Where does all the blood come from for transfusions?

Professional advice

Professional advice is varied and may be offered, for example, by health care workers such as doctors, nurses, pharmacists and dieticians. Advice may be verbal, such as that given during a consultation, or written, in the form of leaflets, posters and instructions. For example, when medications are prescribed there is usually a small leaflet in the pack that details how often to take the medicine, along with possible side effects and any other useful information. An individual may require detailed information before an investigation, such as an MRI scan, and health care professionals will often give this in written form to reinforce any verbal instructions.

Other examples include:

- A nurse may offer advice about lifestyle choices, such as the effect of smoking on respiratory and cardiovascular health.

- A dietician may give advice to help an individual manage any changes needed to their diet if they have been diagnosed as having diabetes.

- A physiotherapist can offer advice and support to people about the correct use of aids and adaptations to help them cope with their disorder.

Support for managing the disorder

In addition to professional advice, support may be given by specialist organisations such as the Motor Neurone Disease Association, Arthritis Care, Age Concern and the British Diabetic Association. There are many more. All these organisations have websites that offer information and support to individuals and their families.

Specialist nurses such as health visitors, community nurses and Macmillan or Marie Curie Nurses also offer support to individuals and their families in their own homes.

Support can also be obtained from complementary therapists and rehabilitation services.

Rehabilitation and counselling

Many individuals benefit from rehabilitation programmes. For example, individuals recovering from major surgery can be offered a combination of physiotherapy, relaxation techniques and advice on diet and lifestyle to help them adjust to an altered lifestyle. As already mentioned, many individuals benefit from counselling to help them to come to terms with their disorder and its impact on them and on their families.

Complementary therapies

Some individuals find that their quality of life is enhanced by using a combination of complementary therapy alongside more conventional treatments. Many health care professionals acknowledge the benefits of complementary therapies and will work with complementary therapists to provide an integrated programme of care. For example, for many years acupuncture has been used alongside more conventional treatments to relieve pain. Other complementary therapies include reflexology, hypnosis, massage and naturopathy.

> **Think** Could aromatherapy help a person cope with the symptoms of motor neurone disease?

Key words

acupuncture – a form of traditional Chinese medicine in which very fine, sterile needles are inserted through the skin at key points on the body, depending on what organ or body part is to be treated

Research tip

To find out more about complementary therapies, what they are and how they are used to treat physiological disorders visit www.bcma.co.uk.

EVIDENCE ACTIVITY

P4 – D1

For each of your chosen physiological disorders, you are advised to read the unit requirements and complete the following tasks.

1. In your care journals/diaries, describe the different care strategies that have been provided for your chosen individuals. You should include notes about how each of the different carers is involved in delivering the care strategy, how they use the care plan to do this and how they support the individual in coping with their disorder. (**P4**)

Remember that many care professionals, each of whom may have delivered a variety of care strategies, will have had contact with the individuals you have chosen to study over the progress of their disorders. You could begin this task by producing a timeline of the professionals and the strategies in which they have been involved. Remember that you must include people like the laboratory technicians who analysed samples of blood or urine and the GP who first referred the individuals to the clinical specialist.

You might prefer to include work for Distinction (**D1**) in your work for **P4**, rather than writing additional paragraphs.

2. In your journals/diaries, evaluate the care provided by the different people involved in supporting your chosen individuals. (**D1**)

Remember to examine in detail the strengths and weaknesses of the care provided. You should give your reasons for these; an evaluation must always contain justification.

Note: you are not criticising the carers but examining the value of the care given to the individuals who receive it. For example, did a particular treatment ease the pain; did the physiotherapy increase mobility?

14.4 *Understand how individuals adapt to the presence of a disorder*

DIFFICULTIES

Daily living activities and mobility

Over time, an individual will have to adapt to their illness or disorder, perhaps recognising that the condition is chronic and therefore ever-present. The support of both professionals and informal carers is essential in the transition period when an individual comes to terms with a different future than they had anticipated. For example, the individual's mobility could be decreased through rheumatoid arthritis or multiple sclerosis. This in turn is likely to limit opportunities for travel and holidays. It could also result in the need to change job or even retire earlier than they had planned.

Example

An individual with a kidney (renal) disorder may require regular dialysis, which may mean short periods of hospitalisation. Dialysis involves connecting the patient to a machine for several hours to clear the impurities that have built up in the system as a result of their kidney failure. This usually means huge changes in a individual's lifestyle. Some renal patients may have home units, but it will still mean a restricted lifestyle. They may have to change their job or work part-time, which can lead to financial hardship.

Individuals and their families may also have to adjust to the presence of carers in their home, and interruptions to their daily routine. Carers should take a sensitive approach, remembering that they are guests, who are there by invitation. Although carers are busy people, often with heavy caseloads, they should attempt to fit in with family routines where possible and must always behave in a professional manner. For instance, it would not be seen as acceptable to make personal telephone calls while attending to a service user. Furthermore, cultural and religious differences and conventions should always be respected. For example, during Ramadan (a Muslim period of fasting and prayer), the carer should recognise that an individual or their family may not wish to have times of special prayer interrupted, unless the treatment or care routine is absolutely essential to life and cannot be delayed.

Thalassaemia is an inherited blood disease affecting thousands of children throughout the world. It is a disorder that has an increasing impact on a child's life as they grow up. Individuals with thalassaemia are born without the ability to develop enough healthy red blood cells to carry iron around the body. The treatment for the disorder is for the individual to have regular blood transfusions for the rest of their life. A side effect of the blood transfusions is that iron builds up in the body. Medication has to be given to remove the excess iron, which would otherwise damage the individual's heart and liver. The medication has to be given by a slow injection pump over a period of 8 to 12 hours. How often the injections are needed depends on how much iron has built up. However, this medication may need to be given daily, which will severely limit the individual's ability to go to school, socialise and later on to get a job.

Research tip

Find out more about thalassaemia, and the different types of the disorder, by visiting the website of the UK Thalassaemia Society on www.ukts.org.

For many individuals, as their disorder progresses their normal daily activities have to change. For example, the treatment of diabetes involves following a special diet for life. This can be inconvenient for the rest of the family and make the individual with diabetes feel guilty about being a 'problem' and different to the rest of the family. Alzheimer's disease or multiple sclerosis may cause the individual to need assistance with their daily

personal care, including using the toilet. This can change family relationships, causing stress and strain in the family unit. Admittance to residential care can increase household expenses both in terms of any fees that the individual has to pay and also any travelling expenses for family visits.

Employment

Under the Disability Discrimination Act 2005, disabled people cannot be discriminated against on the grounds of their disability. This includes disabilities caused by a physiological disorder such as multiple sclerosis, HIV/AIDS or cancer. However, long periods of illness may mean that an individual is no longer able to carry out their job, which may lead to retirement on medical grounds.

Research tip

Further information about the Disability Discrimination Act 2005 can be found at http//direct.gov.uk.

Relationships

Some relationships may fall apart as partners find that they cannot with the stresses and strains of a lifestyle altered to cope with a disorder. Other relationships may adapt, and become strengthened. While some people may feel obliged to remain with their partner out of duty, the resentment that builds up may result in added strain for both partners.

There may be problems for the rest of the family; for example, siblings may resent the additional attention paid to a sick or disabled brother or sister, or the lack of family outings that could result from a parent developing a disorder. Constant hospital visits can interrupt family life, even for those who are not ill. The extended family, friends, religious groups and self-help groups can be very supportive and health care professionals should encourage this.

CASE STUDY: NABEELA

Nabeela, a 45-year-old paediatric staff nurse, worked in a large city hospital. Following several viral infections, she woke up one morning to find herself almost completely immobile. Struggling, she managed to find her phone and call a friend. The friend came immediately and contacted Nabeela's GP. The GP was completely puzzled as Nabeela had always been a very active woman; a member of the hospital netball team, and a volunteer at many events at her local mosque. Nabeela was referred to a neurologist who diagnosed Myalgic Encephalitis (ME). ME is a chronic brain disorder that occurs in a vulnerable individual, usually at a time of stress and following one or more viral infections. As ME can last for up to four years, the neurologist recommended that Nabeela take early retirement on medical grounds. Furthermore, depending on the severity of her condition, it was possible that Nabeela might never return to full function.

QUESTIONS

1. What are the common symptoms of this disorder?

2. In addition to her NHS pension, what funding might Nabeela be entitled to?

COPING STRATEGIES

Many people with physiological disorders develop particular coping strategies to enable them to manage their lives. For example, a person with rheumatoid arthritis may shop online, rather than having to ask others to shop for them. Occupational therapists can provide valuable advice on the type of mobility aids that will enhance the quality of life for an individual and assist with coping strategies. For example, additional stair rails or stair lifts can be fitted for those with reduced mobility and raised toilet seats can mean independence for someone who transfers from a wheelchair.

Figure 14.10 An occupational therapist can advise on different aids and adaptations

Some coping strategies are psychological and may be suggested by a counsellor. For example, many individuals use stress management techniques as part of their daily routine, such as meditation or yoga. Some people find strength in their religious beliefs.

Family and friends

Often it is those supporting individuals with chronic illnesses who need to develop the greatest coping strategies. Many families of individuals with physiological disorders receive support from a variety of voluntary groups to help them to cope. The Alzheimer's Society, for example, provides support and advice for families as well as for the individual with Alzheimer's disease. You will find information and contact details for various self-help groups connected with physiological disorders in the telephone directory and also in most health centres and GP surgeries.

Research tip

For each of your chosen physiological disorders, search the internet for the associated voluntary group. Websites will provide you with valuable information and lead you to further sources of information.

Counselling

We have already discussed this as a support service for the individual. However, living with relatives who have a physiological disorder can place a severe strain on the rest of the family. For example, if the individual who is ill or disabled has been the main wage earner there may be a loss of income that will cause worry and stress. Families may find the changes in daily living hard to cope with and may need the services of a counsellor for emotional support.

Example

When he was just 46 years old, Mr South had a stroke that left him partially paralysed and also affected his speech. Mr South became increasingly frustrated with his reduced functioning, and this was expressed through frequent angry outbursts to his family. His daughter Kelly found that she could not invite her friends to the house, and her mother became increasingly depressed. Kelly's college tutor suggested that perhaps they would both benefit from counselling and they agreed to try this strategy. Kelly's GP arranged counselling for her mother and Kelly attended sessions at the college. They both found that the service enabled them to cope more effectively with Mr South, and contributed to their understanding of his frustration.

Lifestyle changes

It is inevitable that coping with a physiological disorder will involve some changes to a person's lifestyle. For example, an individual might need to find alternatives to meet their different dietary needs when going for a business lunch with prospective clients – not always an easy option in some restaurants. Someone who develops rheumatoid arthritis may need to move from their house to a downstairs flat or bungalow. It may be necessary to give up certain hobbies and sports, which can cause the individual to feel angry and depressed. Holidays may require more planning, and some types of holiday will become impossible. However, many travel companies are well aware of the needs of travellers with disabilities and are excellent at finding holidays to suit most needs.

For some people, their disorder may make it necessary for them to sell their homes and move into residential care, which they will inevitably find distressing.

PROGNOSIS

A prognosis is a forecast of the probable course and outcome of a disorder. This is a sensitive subject, and you will need to use secondary research to discover what the prognosis is for each of your chosen individuals. The likely progression of a disorder will depend on:

- the specific disorder

- the stage of the disorder when the diagnosis was made

- how soon afterwards the treatment began

- the individual.

Some individuals diagnosed with cancer or HIV, for example, far outlive the original lifespan predicted for them. Others unfortunately do not survive long, which may be due to genetic tendencies, their general health or other concurrent disorders. Late diagnosis may mean that some individuals will not survive what may have been potentially curable disorders.

Changes to care strategies

Changes will be required to the care and treatment plans to support the individual as their disorder progresses. Care and treatment plans will be reviewed regularly so that the individual receives the maximum benefit of any new care strategies. Cost, both human and financial, must be considered. If a care strategy is no longer benefiting an individual, it will be discontinued. For example, if someone who has rheumatoid arthritis is not being helped by physiotherapy, and the journey to the centre is painful, it is probably not worth continuing the treatment.

CASE STUDY: JUDITH'S STORY

Judith was a biologist living in France. One day after a shower, she noticed a small lump in her right breast. She was aware that breast lumps could mean a serious disease and so she went to see her doctor. The doctor reassured Judith that there was nothing to worry about and that she should just ignore the lump, it would go away in time. Judith did so, but following a move to England she decided to visit her new GP. She showed her the lump that by now had grown.

The GP referred Judith to an oncologist (a cancer specialist) who ordered a biopsy. The lump was found to be malignant and Judith had to undergo a mastectomy followed by radiotherapy. Unfortunately, Judith was found to have a secondary cancer in her brain. The oncologist wrote in her notes that Judith's chances of survival were poor, due to late diagnosis.

QUESTION

How do you think Judith would feel about this prognosis?

CASE STUDY: SOPHIA – A FINAL CONSIDERATION

Sophia's motor neurone disease has progressed and she has developed bulbar paralysis.

QUESTIONS

1. What does the term 'bulbar paralysis' mean?

2. What care strategies might be ordered by the specialist?

3. What care strategies might be ordered by the nurse?

EVIDENCE ACTIVITY

P5 – P6 – M3 – D2

1. Complete the journals/diaries you are keeping for your chosen individuals by explaining the difficulties experienced by each individual in adjusting to their disorder. You will also need to discuss their adjustment to the care strategy prescribed for them and the different types of care that they experience. (**P5**)

You will have to find out what problems have been caused for the patient or service user as a result of their disorder. You will also need to ask them about any problems caused by the different types of care they receive.

To find out about the difficulties caused by the disorder, you might ask questions such as:

• How do you cope with everyday living?

• Has the disorder restricted your movements?

To find out about difficulties caused by the care strategies, you might devise a list of short questions such as:

• What are the differences to daily living that you have noticed since receiving care/treatment?

Confidentiality must always be respected. Remember not to undermine the professional care providers when you discuss these issues with your chosen individuals. You may discover that the individual has adjusted to their disorder and accepts it as part of their life. They may not enjoy repeat investigations but nevertheless appreciate the benefits of their care. Maintain a sensitive approach when questioning people about these issues and never make judgements.

2. In your journals/diaries, choose three or four care strategies that your individual has planned for them. Write a short report explaining whether or not these different types of care have made a difference to the way the individual's disorder has developed. (**M3**)

Depending on the disorder you are studying, questions such as the following may help you to make your report:

- Has the special diet had any effect? Do you feel you have more energy?

- Have the new pain-relieving tablets helped you to sleep more soundly?

Remember that you must design your questions to fit the disorder you are studying and the care that your individual receives. You can use both primary and secondary research to explain the effects of different types of care.

3. Using primary and secondary research, find out what alternative care strategies there might be for your chosen individuals. Record this in your journals/diaries along with the potential benefits and disadvantages of using these alternatives. (**D2**)

For many physiological disorders, there are several care strategies that could have been used. For example, an individual with a hiatus hernia may be treated with surgery or with medication. Not all patients with the same disorder will receive the same treatment. The specialist will first consider all the factors involved. For example, if the individual with the hiatus hernia also has a heart or lung condition, then medication would be a safer option than surgery. Remember that individuals may refuse certain forms of treatment. For example, some people hold religious beliefs that will not allow them to accept blood transfusions.

4. Your final entry in your journals/diaries will compare the possible future developments of the disorders for the individuals concerned. You will need to write about what is the same or similar for the two individuals you have chosen and what is different. (**P6**)

You will first need to research the expected patterns of development for both disorders, using secondary research. You could discuss what future developments your chosen individuals expect to see, and compare these with your research. Remember to include anything that does not follow the usual pattern of development and any reasons for this.

Applied Sociological Perspectives for Health and Social Care

unit 19

This unit builds on the knowledge and understanding that you have already gained through studying Unit 2: Equality, Diversity and Rights in Health and Social care and Unit 7: Sociological Perspectives for Health and Social Care. Some of the concepts you have already met; now you will be able to study them in more depth and apply them to your experiences in health and social care.

Despite a variety of initiatives over the years, there are still many forms of inequality in society in the UK. These are illustrated through studies of differing experiences of health, educational achievement, income and other life chances within the population. The groups which experience poverty and deprivation are some of the most vulnerable in society.

This unit will explore the needs of these groups and how and why they have become marginalised. You will gain an understanding of topics such as discrimination, prejudice and social exclusion. Demographic change will be studied in greater depth, with an exploration of its impact on society – for example, the effect of immigration or the changes in life expectancy. The way in which demographic data is used to assess the needs of the population and to direct policy will be considered.

The links between social inequalities and the health and well-being of the population will be studied. This includes an exploration of the factors that affect the life chances of an individual or group and the implications on their health and well-being.

Learning outcomes

By the end of this unit, you will:

So you want to be a...

Community Service Volunteer

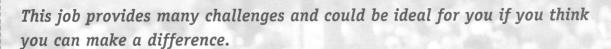

My name **Stephanie Crane**

Age **19**

Income **Weekly allowance and out-of-pocket expenses**

This job provides many challenges and could be ideal for you if you think you can make a difference.

What do you do?

I am supporting a student with disabilities at university. I help her get around in her wheelchair, take notes in lectures, go with her to social and leisure activities and help with cooking and personal care. I live on the university campus.

How did you get into it?

I was not completely sure what aspect of social care I wanted to follow. I heard about Community Service Volunteering (CSV) and made enquiries to see if there might be an opportunity for me. There were lots of options but they were all about enabling people with disabilities and other support needs to remain independent.

So what else could you have done?

I could have worked with other individuals. One person who has needed support is Jackie. She was paralysed following a road accident in which her husband was killed. With the help of CSV volunteers she was able to return to her own home, bring up her children and study for a degree. Another is Ron. He has learning difficulties but lives independently, goes to college and takes part in leisure activities – all with the support of a volunteer who lives with him in his home. Alternatively, I could have worked in an organization, such as a special needs or mainstream school or college, a social services day centre or a homeless shelter.

> **"Despite being hard work, it's a lot of fun too"**

What qualifications do you need?

CSV believes everyone can make a difference! In order to do full-time volunteering you need to be prepared to live away from home for between four and twelve months. The main thing is to be committed, enthusiastic and get on well with others.

What have you gained from your volunteering experienc?

I have gained new skills and it has really changed my life. I have become more flexible, adult, independent and responsible. I have had a great time with lots of fun as well as hard work. It has given me a much clearer focus for the future. I know what I want to do and it has provided me with fantastic experience.

What training have you had?

I have undergone training in skills for life and some occupational qualifications such as first aid, health and safety etc. Everything I have done has improved my chances of getting a job or entering higher education.

What about the future?

I want to be a social worker. My application to university was strengthened by the fact that I had been a volunteer for 9 months. I intend to continue to volunteer on a part-time basis while I am at college.

Grading criteria

The table below shows what you need to do to gain a pass, merit or distinction in this part of the qualification. Make sure you refer back to it when you are completing work so that you can judge whether you are meeting the criteria and what you need to do to fill in gaps in your knowledge or experience.

In this unit there are three evidence activities to give you an opportunity to demonstrate your achievement of the grading criteria:

page 77   **P1, M1**

page 87   **P2, P3, P4, M2, M3**

page 97   **P5, M4, D1**

To achieve a pass grade the evidence must show that the learner is able to...	To achieve a merit grade the evidence must show that, in addition to the pass criteria, the learner is able to...	To achieve a distinction grade the evidence must show that, in addition to the pass and merit criteria, the learner is able to...
P1 Describe the concept of the unequal society	**M1** Explain the concept of the unequal society	**D1** Evaluate potential links between social inequalities and the health of the population.
P2 Describe recent demographic changes in home country	**M2** Explain recent demographic changes in home country	
P3 Use examples to describe the application of demography to health and social care service provision	**M3** Explain the value of the application of demography to health and social care service provision	
P4 Describe two examples of social inequalities in home country	**M4** Use six examples to explain potential links between social inequalities and the health of the population.	
P5 Use six examples to describe potential links between social inequalities and the health of the population.		

19.1 *Understand the concept of an unequal society*

SOCIAL INEQUALITIES

The UK remains an unequal society and there is evidence that it has become more unequal in terms of wealth distribution. A report issued in July 2007 by the Joseph Rowntree Foundation showed that households in already wealthy areas have become disproportionately wealthier, while at the same time more households have become poor over the past 15 years, but fewer are very poor. This has meant that there are fewer 'average' (i.e. neither poor nor wealthy) households in the UK.

Example

The Joseph Rowntree Foundation is one of the largest social policy research and development charities in the UK. It seeks to better understand the causes of social difficulties and explore ways of overcoming them.

Research tip

You can read more about the research undertaken by the Joseph Rowntree Foundation by going to www.jrf.org.uk.

So does it matter if society is unequal?

These are some of the consequences for children:

- there are 3.8 million children living in poverty in the UK

- one in five children live in a family where nobody is in employment

- if you are born into a poor family you are more likely to remain poor

- children from poor backgrounds are more likely to lag behind educationally than those from well-off families

- children whose fathers are unskilled are twice as likely to die early compared with children from professional families.

Source: Child Poverty Action Group

Research tip

Find out more about the Child Poverty Action Group. Go to www.cpag.org.uk.

Social class

What factors can cause social inequalities? In Unit 7 we looked at a number of the main social structures in society and the influences of social class, age, gender, culture, ethnicity, disability and sexuality. Any or all of these factors can lead to social inequalities and have profound influences on the experiences and life chances of individuals or groups. Life chances are the opportunities that an individual has to improve their quality of life.

Key words

social class – a collection of people with similar positions; usually measured by education, occupation, and income

Social class refers to an individual's social and economic standing in society. The Office of National Statistics uses a social class scale consisting of eight social classes (see Table 19.1). This was first used in for the analysis of the 2001 census. Those in the same social class share many of the same characteristics; for example, the same educational background, similar housing etc. Occupation (job or employment) is closely linked with the level of income and also with how secure and regular that income is. However, in addition to earning money, another important source of wealth is the inheritance of wealth, which falls outside the social class classifications, and there is no category for the highly-paid sports personalities and other celebrities.

Level	Social Class	Examples of types of jobs
1	Higher managerial and professional	Managing director, doctor, judge, solicitor
2	Lower managerial and professional	Nurse, school teacher, journalist
3	Intermediate occupations	Clerical worker, secretary, airline cabin crew, auxiliary nurse
4	Small employers and own account holders	Self-employed builder, taxi driver
5	Lower supervisory, craft and related occupations	Employed craftsman, plumber, train driver
6	Semi-routine occupations	Shop assistant, postman, security guard
7	Routine occupations	Cleaner
8	Not in paid employment	Student, people not classifiable

Table 19.1 Social classification Source: The Office for National Statistics

Social inequality is reflected in the social class structure which defines the unequal distribution of wealth and income. There are very wealthy individuals and groups of people and other members of society who are living in poverty. High social status and wealth provides the advantages that go with financial resources such as good housing, access to good schools, ability to afford healthy, nourishing food, taking holidays and using high-quality health care.

closely reflects the amount that an individual has earned during their working life. So those that have been in regular well-paid employment are likely to be better off in retirement as well.

> **Think** Why has it been necessary to pass a law making it unlawful to discriminate on the grounds of age? What advantages may it bring to older people?

Age

There are more and more older people in society as individuals live longer. In some societies older people are considered of greater worth, as they are seen as wise and are therefore respected. However, in our society the elderly have lost much of their status as they are generally poorer and have less influence and power. Nevertheless, many people in retirement remain very fit and active. In October 2006 a new law came into force which makes it unlawful to discriminate against workers under the age of 65. It will be illegal to make someone redundant or bar workers from training or promotion because they are too old – or too young. As they approach 65, workers will have to be given six months' notice that their employer wants them to give up their job and retire. The employee will be allowed to request to continue working. Research has shown that older people who have stopped working are more likely to be poor compared to the population as a whole. In retirement people are usually reliant on their pensions or savings for an income. The level of income in retirement

Gender

Gender refers to the social and cultural expectations that are associated with being a male or female in society. So how equal are men and women in society? Gender can have an effect on the social status and identity of an individual, define their role and responsibilities, affect their health and influence the opportunities for promotion, power and high salaries.

Here are some facts illustrating inequalities that are associated with gender:

- young men are at greater risk of dying compared with young women

- women are more likely to have breaks in employment

- most company directors are male

- most nurses are female

- women in full-time employment earned 12.6 per cent less than men in 2006.

In the UK a number of measures have been taken to try to reduce the inequalities associated with gender. These have included: setting up the Equality and Human Rights Commission and the Women and Equality unit, and passing legislation such as the Equal Pay Act and the Sex Discrimination Act.

Culture

The ideas, beliefs, customs and way of life of a group of people are referred to as their culture. These may lead to inequalities for men or women. For example, different cultures may require different forms of dress which can lead to inequalities in the way in which individuals are treated. Other cultures have particularly strict rules governing the roles that women are allowed to play and the choices they can make.

Ethnicity

Ethnicity refers to the way in which people are classified based on their genetic heritage as well as their social and cultural background. They may share a common language, religion and geographical location. In the UK, the National Office for Statistics has identified 12 ethnic groups and undertakes a wide range of analysis based on these cultural groups. There are certain inequalities which are linked with ethnicity, such as employment.

The bar chart below shows unemployment rates by ethnic group and gender.

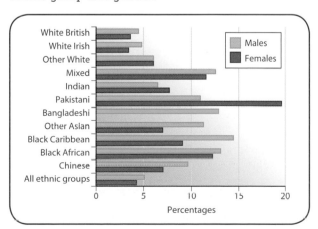

Figure 19.1 UK unemployment: by ethnic group and sex (2004) Source: Office for National Statistics

Unemployment rates for people from non-white ethnic groups were generally higher than those from white ethnic groups. However, Indian men had a similar level of unemployment to white men, at 7 per cent and 6 per cent respectively.

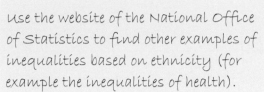

Research tip

Use the website of the National Office of Statistics to find other examples of inequalities based on ethnicity (for example the inequalities of health). Go to www.statistics.gov.uk.

Disability

In the UK up to one in five adults and one in twenty children is disabled. This means that they are not able to access the range of opportunities that others enjoy. They are more likely to live in poverty, have fewer educational qualifications, be unemployed and experience prejudice. In 2005 the government published a report called 'Improving the life chances of disabled people', in which it was pledged that:

> 'by 2025 disabled people in Britain should have full opportunities and choices to improve their quality of life and will be respected and included as equal members of society.'

Figure 19.2 A disability should not be a bar to a full working life

Research tip

You can read the report 'Improving the life chances of disabled people' (2005) by going to the Cabinet Office website: www.cabinetoffice.gov.uk .

Sexuality

The sexuality of an individual comprises a number of factors, including physical, psychological, emotional and spiritual aspects of their makeup. It includes their gender, sexual orientation and sexual preferences. Individuals and groups have experienced inequalities because of their sexual orientation – for example, at work. Discrimination against any employee on the grounds of their sexual orientation is unlawful. The Employment Equality (sexual orientation) regulations cover orientation towards persons of the same sex (lesbians or gays), the opposite sex (heterosexuals) and the same and opposite sex (bisexual). However 'genuine occupational requirements' are allowed if an employer can demonstrate that the job has to be done by a person of a particular sexual orientation.

Although steps have been taken to eliminate inequalities in employment and to provide redress for any bullying or harassment in the workplace, there are still many areas in society where individuals experience unfair treatment because of their sexuality. For example, in 2005 the Football Association announced that it was to make the eradication of homophobia one of its targets, having recognised that players, referees and opposing fans are often subjected to homophobic abuse. In other cases the discrimination may not be so open and obvious, but it is often the basis of bullying and harassment at school.

ASSOCIATED CONCEPTS

All the aspects that have been considered are areas where inequalities occur in society. They may be linked with income, health, education, employment and include the psychological and emotional experiences of individuals or groups.

However, it could be argued that would be impossible to eliminate all inequalities. In the UK it is expected that people should be treated equally and fairly. Much legislation has been passed to try to ensure that this is so. But this is not the experience of certain members of our society. So what problems are associated with the continued existence of such inequalities?

Stereotyping and labelling

Individuals and groups may find that they are stereotyped. Stereotyping is the process of describing all members of a certain group with a set of characteristics, regardless of their individual differences. We develop stereotypes when we are unable or unwilling to obtain enough information to make a fair assessment about a person or situation. For example, women may be stereotyped as being good at childcare, those who wear glasses as being clever or those with disabilities as unable to make decisions for themselves. People may be stereotyped according to their race or ethnicity, sexual orientation, gender, age, disability or nationality.

When the characteristics associated with a particular stereotype are applied to an individual or group it is known as 'labelling'. This may mean that negative characteristics are then assumed of all people who fall into the group. For example, young black men are negatively labelled as possible criminals, leading to a much higher number of 'stop and searches' by the police.

Example

Look at the list below. What stereotypes spring to mind? Write down your first thoughts:

- teenagers
- footballers
- nurses
- fashion models
- lorry drivers
- doctors
- Australians.

Now have a second look at what you have described. Suggest alternatives to your first 'stereotype' and explain what influenced your descriptions.

Prejudice

A stereotype may lead to the holding of an unfavourable opinion about an individual or a group. This is known as prejudice. Prejudice can be expressed through strongly held views, feelings or attitudes of dislike. It is difficult to prevent people from forming prejudices. They are often based on inaccurate information and are unfair. People who are at the receiving end of the prejudices of others are then treated unfairly and unequally. Prejudices are often directed at certain groups of people; for example, some minority ethnic groups, homosexual men and women, people with disabilities and those with mental health problems. Someone holding a prejudice about an individual will display certain attitudes to that person. This leads to them treating people differently based on their prejudices. The law cannot prevent people holding a prejudice but does seek to stop people acting on them. Society can exert influences on its members to indicate what is unacceptable.

Think Know yourself! What might your attitudes and prejudices be to the following?
- young men with skinhead haircuts
- individuals with multiple piercings
- a single mother with 3 children from different relationships
- a male ballet dancer
- an asylum seeker.

Discrimination

When individuals experience unfair treatment they are victims of discrimination. Unfair discrimination can be experienced either directly or indirectly. Direct discrimination occurs when one person is deliberately treated less favourably than another – for example, if a job is offered to a white person rather than a black person because of their skin colour rather than on the grounds of their qualifications for the job. Indirect discrimination occurs when the effect of certain requirements has a disproportionallly greater impact on one individual or group than another – for example, an employer requiring that all people who apply for a job must sit a test in a particular language although that language is not necessary for the job.

It is also clear that sometimes whole organisations impose types of discrimination. This is known as institutional discrimination. This can happen through the policies, procedures and attitudes which are followed by all members of an organisation, as illustrated by the Stephen Lawrence case study overleaf.

Discrimination can be experienced through prejudice based on race, ethnicity or skin colour, gender, sexual orientation, religion or faith, age or disability.

Marginalisation and social exclusion

When we judge people and groups based on prejudices and stereotypes and treat them differently, we are engaging in discrimination. This discrimination can take many forms. We may create subtle or overt pressures which will discourage persons of certain minority groups from living in a certain area. People with mental illness may find that people express fear of being with them. Individuals who are the recipients of prejudice, and are stereotyped into a certain group, frequently have a social stigma attached to them. This marks them out as being different and of less social worth than others. They may therefore be excluded from society or ostracised. This leads to marginalisation. This prevents people from accessing social resources and enjoying equal rights in society. One of the most extreme examples of marginalisation can be seen in what happened to German Jews under the rule of the Nazis. In Germany in the 1930s and 1940s the Jews were progressively marginalised. They were forced to wear a yellow Star of David and lost more and more of their rights as citizens. Eventually Hitler was able to convince his followers that the Jews were to blame for Germany's troubles. Six million Jews were murdered in the Holocaust.

CASE STUDY:
THE CASE OF STEPHEN LAWRENCE

In 1993 Stephen Lawrence, a black British student aged 18, was murdered. The prosecution of his alleged attackers was, however, dropped because of lack of evidence. In 1997 Stephen's family made a complaint to the Police Complaints Authority about the way in which their son's death had been investigated. Following widespread concern about the case, a public inquiry was ordered by the Home Secretary. This was conducted by Sir William Macpherson and it found that the Metropolitan Police Service had been incompetent in several ways, including failing to give first aid, not following up obvious leads and failing to arrest suspects. Senior police officers had also failed to give leadership and recommendations of earlier reports that had investigated race-related incidents had been ignored. Macpherson found that the police were institutionally racist. He also called for reform of the Civil Service, local government, the NHS, schools and the judicial system in the UK to ensure that institutional racism does not continue.

Institutional racism is described as:
'the collective failure of an organisation to provide an appropriate and professional service to people because of their colour, culture or ethnic origin. It can be detected in processes, attitudes and behaviour which amount to discrimination through unwitting prejudice, ignorance, thoughtlessness and racist stereotyping which disadvantage minority ethnic people'.

QUESTION

1 How might institutional racism occur in a care or educational setting?

2 What steps could be taken by an organisation to prevent it occurring?

This marginalisation means that people experience social exclusion. This is what can happen when individuals, groups or communities suffer a number of problems such as unemployment, poor skills, low incomes, poor housing, high crime environments, bad health and family breakdown. They are excluded from employment, income, social networks and an adequate quality of life. They are unable to access the benefits of full citizenship and cannot participate in normal social and economic activity.

In 1997 the government set up the Social Exclusion Unit to try to address some of the most difficult problems in society. It seeks to promote social inclusion, correcting the negative effects through a series of projects, such as supporting children who are in care, teenage pregnancy or adults facing chronic exclusion.

CASE STUDY: AMINA

Amina, her sister and her mother are asylum seekers. They fled from their own country when the beatings and oppression of her mother by her father and other family members started to include Amina and her sister. The final straw came when they heard that their father had agreed to marry them to two older men. On arrival in the UK they were housed on a very run-down housing estate in the north of England. They found it very cold and very different from their homeland, where they had a good standard of living. Despite being qualified as a teacher, Amina's mother was not allowed to work while her asylum application was considered. The girls enrolled in the local school, but it was quite a distance to travel. They found that they were teased about their accents and their ethnicity. They are anxious as to whether they will be able to keep up with the work and get qualifications that will enable them to go to university. They are unable to find a local religious place of worship. The local neighbourhood does not have any community groups and they are all unsure as to how they can gain a better understanding of life in the UK.

QUESTION

1 In what ways are Amina and her sister suffering social exclusion?

2 How might Amina and her sister be supported in integrating into life in the UK?

EVIDENCE ACTIVITY

P1 – M1

For **P1**, you have to describe the concept of the unequal society.

Using the case study of Amina, identify three ways in which she has experienced social inequality. Describe how age, gender, ethnicity, social class, religion, disability and sexuality can all contribute to social inequalities. You may have examples from your work experience that you can use.

For **M1**, you must explain the concept of the unequal society.

You should explain the concepts that you have described and the ways in which individuals experience inequality.

19.2 Understand the nature of demographic change within the unequal society

DEMOGRAPHIC CHANGE

Human society changes over time for a number of reasons. Natural disasters and disease can cause huge loss of life and change the make-up of a population. In the past, illnesses such as the Plague or Black Death might wipe out whole communities, while earthquakes and volcanic eruptions also caused widespread injury and death (and still do in some areas – for example, the devastating effect of cyclones in Bangladesh in autumn 2007). So what about changes affecting us in the 21st century? Wars have led to large numbers of people being forced to leave their homes, with many refugees living in camps for many years. In sub-Saharan Africa the impact of HIV/AIDS has led to high death rates, particularly amongst the most economically active members of society. More than 12 million children have been orphaned as a result of AIDS. In the UK, social trends have also influenced changes in society.

Demography is the systematic study of the growth, size distribution, movement and composition of human populations. The statistics can illustrate the changes occurring in society and can be used to help plan services to meet educational, health and other social needs. Information is collected on birth and death rates as well as patterns of migration and changes in life expectancy. The Office for National Statistics (ONS) collects and publishes a very wide range of demographic data. Although the ONS holds some information for Scotland and Northern Ireland, further information for can be found at the General Register for Scotland (GROS) and the Northern Ireland Statistics and Research Agency (NISRA).

The government set up the Public Health Observatories to oversee issues of public health. There are 12 observatories which provide a network that links with equivalent organisations in Europe. Each Public Health Observatory takes, as well as its regional role, lead responsibility for certain topics. For example, the London Public Health Observatory provides national information on tobacco, ethnic minorities and health inequalities in addition to local information.

Research tip

Find out about the public health observatory for your region. Look at the website for the Association of Public Health Observatories: www.apho.org.uk.

The Department of Health publishes community health profiles which give a snapshot of the health status of the local population. Local Authority Health Profiles are designed to show the health of people in local authorities across England. These cover all but two of the 388 local authorities, including county councils, district councils, unitary councils and London boroughs. The first local authority Health Profiles covering the whole of England were released in 2006. They are produced by Public Health Observatories and will be updated every year.

These health profiles can be used by local authorities and the health service to highlight the health issues for their local authority area and to compare them with other areas. The profiles are designed to show where there are important problems with health or health inequalities. The profiles can be used with other local information, to target action to improve the health of local people.

Research tip

You can find out more by accessing the website of the Office for National Statistics at www.statistics.gov.uk.

Research tip

Find out more about community health profiles: www.communityhealthprofiles.info.

CASE STUDY: HAMPSHIRE AND HACKNEY

Read the two health profile summaries for Hampshire (a generally prosperous county in southern England) and Hackney – a borough in London. Statistics are based on averages for the population of England.

Hampshire at a glance	Hackney at a glance
• Indicators of health are good when compared to other parts of the South East and to England.	
• On average, men and women residing in Hampshire will live longer than average.	• Men live almost two years less than average. Overall women live to the average age. However, women in the most deprived areas of the borough live 4.5 years less than average.
• Overall poverty is low. However, 81,800 people are dependent on means-tested benefits and more than 27,500 children are living in low income households.	• There is more than double the level of statutorily homeless households and children living in households dependent on means-tested benefit. More people in the Black African and Clack Caribbean populations are in routine manual occupations compared to the White British population.
• Most residents lead healthy lifestyles with lower than average rates of smoking and binge drinking. Physical exercise rates are higher than average. Almost 1 in 4 are obese.	• The estimated proportion of adults who smoke is higher than average, as is the rate of deaths due to smoking.
• Early death rates from heart disease, stroke and cancer are lower than average, and continuing to fall. Although the death rate from smoking is low, it still accounts for nearly 2,000 deaths each year.	• The rate of early deaths from heart disease and stroke is higher than average. The rate of diabetes is higher than average. There are fewer obese adults and binge drinkers than average.
• Hip fracture in the 65 and over age group is higher than average.	• Hip fracture in the 65 and over age group is lower than average.
• Local priorities are to reduce smoking and obesity and improve sexual health.	• Local priorities include reducing heart disease, stroke, diabetes, teenage pregnancy and infant mortality.
• More information can be found at: www.farehamandgosport,nhs.uk/ www.southamptonhealth.nhs.uk/ www.rushmore.gov.uk/media/ www.hampshirepct.nhs.uk/	
• Hampshire Local Health Comparisons is available from: www.shouthamptonhealth.nhs.uk/	• Hackney's Annual Public Health Report is available from: www.chpct.nhs.uk

Birth and death rates

There have been significant changes in the birth and death rates of the population. The birth and death rate refers to the number of live births or deaths per thousand of the population in a given year. The pattern for the 100 years between 1901 and 2000 is illustrated in the graph below. The number of births in the UK has declined throughout the century with two 'baby booms' after the world wars. In 1976 the number of deaths exceeded the number of births for the only time in the century.

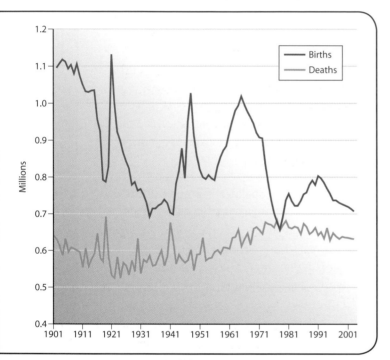

Figure 19.3 UK births & deaths 1901 to 2000
Source: Social Trends

A number of reasons may have contributed to the drop in the birth rate. For example, the contraceptive pill and other more reliable forms of contraception became more widely available from the 1960 onwards. Women are increasingly choosing to have careers and to work rather than have large families, and childcare costs are high. However, live births in England and Wales have been increasing since 2001. In 2006 there were 669,601 live births – an increase of 3.7 per cent on the previous year. Until the 1990s the population grew due to natural change as people lived longer.

Over the course of the 20th century, there were fairly steady falls in death rates which have continued. However, there have been some fluctuations; for example, when there has been a severe epidemic of flu or a particularly cold winter. These variations were especially marked during the early part of the last century. At that time nearly half of all deaths occurred under the age of 45 years. Infant mortality was high; for example, in 1901 25 per cent of deaths were those of children under one year old. By 2006 only 4 per cent of deaths occurred under age of 45.

The fall in the death rate reflects the advances in medical knowledge as well as the improved social and economic conditions in the UK. You can read more about these changes in Unit 12: Public Health.

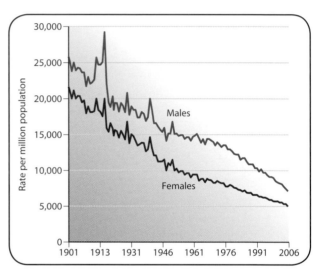

Figure 19.4 Age-standardised mortality rate for all causes by sex, England and Wales
Source: Office for National Statistics

Migration

One of the reasons why the UK population has continued to increase – despite the fall in the birth rate – is because of international migration into the UK. Immigration is people coming to live in a country from abroad, while emigration is the movement of people from one country to another. Net migration is the difference between the number of immigrants and the number of emigrants entering or leaving a country.

Patterns of migration have changed over the centuries according to a wide range of different factors. The UK has experienced migration over many centuries: for example, people escaping political or religious persecution, such as the Jews or Protestants from Europe, or workers from the Commonwealth, such as West Indians. British citizens have also emigrated to countries such as Spain, Australia, New Zealand or Canada.

In 2004 the European Union expanded to include a number of other countries in central and eastern Europe (Bulgaria, Czech Republic, Estonia, Hungary, Latvia, Lithuania, Poland, Romania, Slovakia, and Slovenia) as well as Cyprus and Malta. This has opened up the employment market in the UK to workers from these countries.

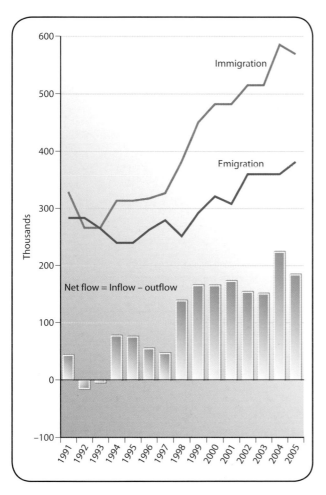

Figure 19.5 Total International Migration (TIM) to/ from the UK 1991-2005
Source: Office for National Statistics

In 2005 an estimated 565,000 migrants arrived to live in the UK for at least a year. In the same period 380,000 people emigrated from the UK for a year or more. Net migration was 185,000 – the equivalent of the population of the UK growing by 500 people a day. Of these people: 80,000 were from the group of central and eastern European countries which joined the EU in 2004; 70% were Polish.

CASE STUDY: HENRY'S STORY

'I was born in Jamaica and enjoyed a very happy childhood – growing up in the countryside and being free to roam. My life changed completely when I was 13 years old. My parents took me to Britain on a ship called The Empire Windrush. I did not understand at the time but the day we docked in Tilbury on 22 June 1948 marked the beginning of a movement of people from the Commonwealth to Britain. We were all British citizens, although we had never lived in Britain, but we were entitled to enter, work and settle in the UK if we wanted to. My parents thought that there would be better opportunities for the family. My father had been recruited to be a bus driver in London while my mother planned to work in a hospital.

'We got quite a shock when we arrived. We were not welcomed by everybody and we realised that people were unfriendly because of the colour of our skin. In fact when we tried to find somewhere to live we would see houses with notices in the windows saying 'Rooms to let. No dogs, no coloureds'. That upset me. We eventually found a house but it was in a very poor part of London, not at all like the home we had left. When I went to school I found that I was the only black kid in my class and I experienced a lot of hostility. I did not have any friends for several years.

However, we stuck it out and I have seen lots of changes over the years. There are many more black people in this country and people from all parts of the world. I am now 73 years old. This is my home. My wife, children and grandchildren are all here. They are making a good life. Both my children went to university and are in good jobs. Britain is my country now.'

QUESTION

In what ways have those who have immigrated to Britain experienced an unequal society?

As the number of people entering the UK from many different countries and cultures has increased, the idea of a multicultural society has developed. Multiculturalism acknowledges and promotes the recognition of varied and differing cultures in society. The size of the minority ethnic population was 4.6 million in 2001 or 7.9 per cent of the total population of the UK. Indians were the largest minority group, followed by Pakistanis, those of mixed ethnic backgrounds, black Caribbean, black Africans and Bangladeshis. The remaining minority ethnic groups each accounted for less than 0.5 per cent but together accounted for a further 1.4 per cent of the UK population.

Figure 19.6 *The UK is a multicultural society*

Think How can different cultures be promoted and celebrated?

Life expectancy

In most parts of the developed world there has been an increase in life expectancy. This is the term given to the statistical measure which predicts the number of years that a person is likely to live. Of the top 30 countries Japan has the longest life expectancy, with 79 years for men and 86 for women. The UK comes 22nd in the world rankings, with men expected to live for 77 years and women 81 years on average. At the other end of the table Swaziland has the lowest life expectancy at 39 years for both men and women, which is 40 per cent below the world average.

The World Health Organization has developed a more sophisticated form of measurement based on the number of 'healthy' years that can be expected (see the table below). The WHO rankings show that years lost to disability are substantially higher in poorer countries because some limitations – injury, blindness, paralysis and the debilitating effects of several tropical diseases such as malaria – strike children and young adults. People in the healthiest regions lose some 9 per cent of their lives to disability, compared with 14 percent in the worst-off countries.

Top ten countries		Bottom ten countries	
	No.years		No.years
Japan	74.5	Ethiopia	33.5
Australia	73.2	Mali	33.1
France	73.1	Zimbabwe	32.9
Sweden	73.0	Rwanda	32.8
Spain	72.8	Uganda	32.7
Italy	72.7	Botswana	32.3
Greece	72.5	Zambia	30.3
Switzerland	72.5	Malawi	29.4
Monaco	72.4	Niger	29.1
Andorra	72.3	Sierra Leone	25.9

Table 19.2 *Number of healthy years' life expectancy by country*
Source: www.who.int

So what about the differences in life expectancy within the UK? If you live in England you can expect to live for 76.9 years if you are male and 81.2 years if female; but in Wales the figures are 76.3 for males and 80.7 for females; in Scotland 74.2 and 79.0; and in Northern Ireland 76.0 and 80.8. Life expectancy for the UK increased over the period 1992 to 2004 by 3.2 years for males and 2.1 years for females. However, the differences are also tracked down to regional and local authority level. Life expectancies for both males and females are generally higher in the south, and lower towards the north of England and Scotland. The local authorities with some of the lowest life expectancies in 1992 improved less than other areas. For example, life expectancy in Glasgow

City increased between 1992 and 2004 by only 1.7 years for both sexes (from 68.2 years to 69.9 years for males, and from 75.0 years to 76.7 years for females). In 2004 life expectancy in Glasgow City was 6.7 years below the UK average for males and 4.2 years below the UK average for females.

Research tip

You can find details of life expectancy rates by region and local authority on the Office of National Statistics website: www.statistics.gov.uk

Infant mortality rates reflect the social, economic and medical development of a country. In developing countries the rates of death in children aged under one year are significantly higher than those in more developed countries. In the UK infant deaths have declined to less than one per cent. However there are still regional differences; for example, from 2002 to 2004, a baby born in Birmingham was eight times more likely to die before its first birthday than one born in Surrey.

An ageing population

The changes in life expectancy in the UK have led to an increase in the number of older people in the population. The implications of having an ageing population affect social, economic and medical resources of the country. For the individual, growing older may mean a reduction in their physical abilities, such as eyesight, hearing and mobility, and restrictions to their social activities as well as a reduction in their income on retirement. Illnesses and poor health make additional demands on social and medical services. However, there are also many retired people who live very full lives, undertaking a number of activities including voluntary work and additional leisure activities.

In 2005 there were more than 11 million people in the UK of state pension age and over, which was 19 per cent of the population. It is projected that by mid-2007 11,000 people will be aged 100 and over. These figures are based on population projections by the UK Government Actuaries Department.

Source: Projected populations at midyears by age last birthday, 2004-based, The Government Actuaries Department (GAD) © Crown Copyright 2005.)

Figure 19.7 Getting older does not mean you have to slow down

Research tip

Find out more about the Government Actuaries Department by visiting their website: www.gad.gov.uk/Population/2004/uk/wuk04singyear.xls.

The number of people over pensionable age is projected to increase from nearly 11.4 million in 2006 to 12.2 in 2011, then to increase further to over 13.9 million in 2026 and 15.3 million in 2031.

Source: National population projections 2004-based, National Statistics © Crown Copyright 2006 table 3.2 (Actual and projected population by age United Kingdom 2004-2031.)

The implications of all these changes have an effect on every aspect of society which must respond to the new demands that are made on its structures and the way in which services are provided. Health, education, transport, housing, and social and community needs all have to be regularly assessed and plans revised in the light of any change. In addition, the awareness of when and where certain groups are being marginalised may require additional investment in order to reduce inequalities.

DEMOGRAPHIC DATA

Demographic data can be obtained through a range of different sources. We have already used a number of them. Birth rates are the number of live births per thousand of the population in one year and death rates the number of deaths. There is a national system of registration of births, marriages and deaths in the UK. Relatives are required to notify their local registrar when a birth or death occurs. The certificate provided by a doctor indicates what conditions caused the death. In addition, doctors and hospitals provide statistics. The information is collected by the Office for National Statistics and other interested bodies which are then able to provide the data.

The census

The makeup of the population changes over time. Every ten years there is a national census which gives a detailed count of the population. This has occurred since 1801 and gives an interesting picture as to how society has changed over the past 200 years. It is a legal requirement that every

householder should complete the census form, which asks for information about everybody who is at the address on a specific night. The next national census is due in 2011.

The last national census took place on Sunday 29 April 2001. It aimed to include everybody so that a detailed picture of the population could be obtained. This enables comparisons to be made between different parts of the country as well as reviewing trends over time. In England and Wales, the census is planned and carried out by the Office for National Statistics. Elsewhere in the UK, responsibility lies with the General Register Office for Scotland and the Northern Ireland Statistics and Research Agency.

The form for a household in England asked questions which collected information on household accommodation, relationships, demographic characteristics (e.g. sex, age, marital status), migration, cultural characteristics, health and provision of care, qualifications, employment, workplace and journey to work. In Wales there was an additional question on the Welsh language. The forms for people who were living communally, such as in homes for the elderly, also collected information on each person.

Electoral register

A further source of data is collected through the electoral registers. The Electoral Register includes the names and addresses of almost every UK citizen over the age of eighteen. It lists the name and address of everyone who has registered to vote. Until 2002 the full electoral register could be sold to any commercial company for any purpose. Regulations were then introduced which allowed individuals to opt-out of having their information sold to commercial companies. The full register is available for use in elections, by credit companies undertaking credit checks and for purposes of security, law enforcement and crime prevention. The register is held at the local electoral registration office (generally, the local council office in England and Wales, the Valuation Joint Board in Scotland and the Electoral Office for Northern Ireland).

USING DEMOGRAPHIC DATA

Demographic data can be used for several purposes in health and social care. It can be used to identify needs, plan and target services, assess how effective any service is and to develop future policy objectives.

In order to plan any health or social care provision it is important to know what the needs are. This means understanding the composition of any population and identifying what services might be required. For example, in an area where there are large numbers of families with young children the needs are likely to be for maternity care, health visiting, nurseries, schools and other facilities for those age groups.

> ### CASE STUDY: HEALTH NEEDS
>
> In 2001 the local NHS undertook an analysis of the health needs of the population in order to plan where the major hospitals should be based. Although there were three District General Hospitals, this needed to be reduced to two. Demographic data indicated that the areas of greatest health need were in sites A and B, where there were greatest numbers of people with poor health and also higher levels of deprivation, such as low car ownership. Site A had a number of people who had retired and high numbers of single parent families. Site B had a large number of asylum seekers as well as an expanding population with many young families. Site C had two university colleges with large numbers of students. The local population was predominantly middle class, well educated and with good incomes. However all three communities lobbied to keep their hospitals open.
>
> ### QUESTION
>
> What information can be collected through demographic analysis that might affect the decision about health and social care provision?

> **Think** What health and social care provision would the following groups need?
> - mothers with young children
> - teenagers
> - 20-30 year old working adults
> - pensioners aged more than 85 years.

It is important that services are provided which are appropriate to the needs of the population. Demographic data can indicate not only the age of the local community but a number of other factors which can affect the way in which services are planned. For example, if an area is identified as having poor transport links and many members of the community do not have their own transport, then services may need to be provided close to them.

Services can be planned and targeted using the demographic data. The 2001 census asked about the following:

- age
- birthplace
- carers (unpaid)
- ethnic group
- health – general
- illness – limiting, long term
- marital status
- migrants
- children, school children and students
- qualifications – academic and professional
- working/not working
- hours worked
- means of travel to work
- occupation
- housing – type, bathroom facilities, central heating, number of rooms
- transport.

From the answers to these questions a large amount of information can be established, giving a picture of population in any specific location. By repeating the census every ten years trends can be observed and it can be seen if some of the decisions based on previous analyses have been successful. However, it is not necessary to wait for the ten-yearly census – the use of other data can provide much useful information.

Here are some more examples of information that has been collected (from the Office for National Statistics). As you can see, each set of facts could provide the basis for planning of services.

- Around 6 million people (11 per cent of the population aged five years and over) provided unpaid care in the UK in April 2001. While 45 per cent of carers were aged between 45 and 64, a number of the very young and very old also provided care.

- In 2000 one in six adults in the UK had a neurotic disorder (such as anxiety or depression), while one in seven had considered suicide at some point in their lives. One in 200 had a psychotic disorder such as psychosis and schizophrenia.

- GP home visits have declined as a proportion of all consultations, with an increase in telephone and surgery consultations. In 2003, 86 per cent of GP consultations in Great Britain took place in surgeries or health centres – compared with 73 per cent in 1971. The proportion of home visits declined by a fifth from 22 per cent in 1971 to 4 per cent in 2003.

- Between 2000 and 2004, the rate of new diagnoses of chlamydia among people who attended Genitourinary Medicine (GUM) clinics increased. Chlamydia is the most common sexually transmitted infection (STI) in the UK. The largest increases in chlamydia rates were seen in persons under the age of 16. However, the highest rates were in females aged 16 to 19 (1,339 per 100,000), and males aged 20 to 24 (1,034 per 100,000).

- New diagnoses of HIV among heterosexuals tripled between 1998 and 2003, reaching 3,800. The number of diagnosed HIV-infected patients receiving care in the UK in 2003 exceeded 37,000. Half lived in Greater London.

- The prevalence of obesity in England has increased markedly among both adults and children since the mid 1990s. In 2002 it was similar for both sexes; the rate for boys and girls was 17 per cent and for adults was 23 per cent. In 1995 the equivalent figures were 10 per cent for boys and 12 per cent for girls, 15 per cent for men and 18 per cent for women.

- Young drinkers aged 11 to 15 in England doubled their average weekly consumption of alcohol during the 1990s – from 5.3 in 1990 to 10.4 units in 2004. It has since stabilised for boys but continues to increase for girls. The greatest increase has been among girls aged 14, from 3.8 units in 1992 to 9.7 in 2004. In each year, among those who drank, boys consumed more alcohol than girls in every age group.

CASE STUDY: BINGE DRINKING

QUESTION

1 What services may be required by individuals who binge drink?

2 How might health and social care organisations respond to the increase in drinking amongst young people?

The government and other authorities use demographic data to develop future policy objectives. The government will use the facts discovered from the analysis of data along with other information as a base for many policy initiatives. For example, in 1998 the rates of teenage births – the number of births per 1,000 women aged 15 to 19 – were shown to be one of the highest in Europe. They were five times higher than those in the Netherlands, three times that of France and twice that of Germany. The government announced its ten-year Teenage Pregnancy Strategy to tackle both the causes and consequences of teenage pregnancy. It had targets to:

- halve the under-18 conception rate by 2010, and establish a firm downward trend in the under-16 rate

- increase the proportion of teenage parents in education, training or employment to 60 per cent by 2010, to reduce their risk of long-term social exclusion.

The Teenage Pregnancy Unit reports regularly on its progress in meeting its targets.

Research tip

You can find more information about teenage pregnancy rates on www.dfes.gov.uk/teenagepregnancy.

Many other policies for health, care and childcare are announced from time to time. You will find that they are all based in some way or another on demographic data.

EVIDENCE ACTIVITY

P2 – P3 – P4 – M2 – M3

For **P2** you are required to describe recent demographic changes in your home country.

For **P3** you must use examples to describe the application of demography to health and social care service provision.

P4 requires you to describe two examples of social inequalities in your home country.

Look back to the concepts of social inequalities you have described. Now find at least two examples in your own home country and describe them. Add this to your report.

For **M2** you have to explain recent demographic changes in your home country.

In order to find information about your home country, research some websites such as:

- ONS

- Public Health Observatories

- Community health profiles

- Age Concern

- Department of Health.

You should identify at least three types of recent demographic data that demonstrate changes over time. Prepare a report describing your findings, using appropriate graphs or charts. Explain the reasons behind the changes.

For **M3** you are required to explain the value of the application of demography to health and social care service provision.

You should research some of the decisions that have been taken on health and social care provision in your own area – for example, the development or reduction of health services, or the expansion of schools or pre-school places. Continuing your report, use these examples to describe how demography has been applied when making decisions about services (**P3**). Explain the value of using demographic data to health and social care provision (**M3**).

19.3 *Understand the potential links between social inequalities and the health and well-being of the population*

SOCIAL INEQUALITIES

At the beginning of the unit we looked at the different social inequalities that make up an unequal society. In this section we will examine them in more detail and see how the health and well-being of the population is linked to the inequalities that are experienced by individuals and groups within society.

Income and wealth distribution

The distribution of income and wealth is unequal. Income comes from factors such as wages and earnings from work, rent from ownership of land and interest from savings and share ownership. Wealth is the financial and other assets such as property, savings, land and rights to pensions etc. The poorest households in the UK rely on cash benefits from the state rather than income from employment. They have little or no income from investments. On the other hand the richest 20 per cent of households receive a high level of income from assets that they own.

Poverty can be difficult to define. Absolute poverty is recognised as a level of poverty where people have insufficient income and resources to meet their basic needs for food, clothing and shelter. While there are many parts of the world where this exists, in the developed world the concept of relative poverty is more commonly considered. This is an assessment of a degree of want that is relative to other people in society. For example, it is now expected that households in the UK should have a fridge, a television, a bathroom, are able to afford a holiday away from home etc. Another way of measuring relative poverty and inequality is the proportion of the population whose income falls below some pre-defined threshold. If income falls below 60 per cent of median income, this takes a

family below the European Union's official 'poverty line' or 'poverty threshold'.

Between 1979 and 1997 income inequality widened. The reasons include for this include the following:

- Differences in rates of pay in different jobs and industries – for example, the financial, business and information technology sectors have had high earnings potential partly due to shortages of skilled labour. Salaries in private sector service jobs have tended to be higher than those in the public sector. Many of the worst paid jobs are still found in low-skill service sector industries. The poorest households are most likely to have non-working individuals.

- Falling incomes for those dependent on state benefits; at present welfare benefits are increased in line with prices rather than earnings. This means that the relative income of those who depend on these benefits decreases over time. This has particularly affected pensioner households. There has a government promise to restore the linking of benefits with earnings in the future.

- Unemployment: although levels of unemployment have dropped for those who remain without work, it is a major cause of relative poverty.

- Changes to the tax system. Income tax rates have fallen, which means that those in work keep a greater proportion of their earned income. However, the top rate of income tax has been lowered as well as the basic rate. At the same time there has been a switch to indirect taxes such as VAT and higher duties on petrol, alcohol and cigarettes.

Figure 19.8 Absolute poverty

CASE STUDY: KAREN'S AND JESSICA'S STORIES

Karen Jones lives in Birmingham. She is a single mother with two sons aged 10 and 8 years old. They have been housed by the local council in a high-rise block of flats in a deprived area of the city. The flat is on the tenth floor but sometimes the lift is out of order because of vandalism by local youths. Karen is reluctant to let the boys go outside on their own and the only open space for recreation is about half a mile away. Karen finds it a struggle to make ends meet. The boys are growing quickly and often need new clothes or shoes. They have free school meals and Karen shops locally for the cheapest food she can afford. She also uses charity shops to get clothes for herself and the boys. The boys wanted to go on a school trip but were unable to do so because of the cost. The last holiday that they had was four years ago when they visited their grandparents in the country. Karen cannot remember the last time she went out for a meal or to the cinema.

Jessica Bukanza lives in Uganda. Her family came to the city of Kampala to seek work unsuccessfully and now live in a slum. Jessica's father died four years ago. The only shelter they have is a very cramped house made from mud and old cement sacks. There are six children in the family. They have to collect all their water from a stand pipe 400 metres away. Jessica is 12 years old and attends a school with one of her sisters, Helen. Both of them are small for their age. Their older brothers try to earn money from begging or casual work. They have not attended school. Their mother is living with HIV and most of the time is too sick to work. The family lives in extreme poverty. They have no money for food, clothing, medicines or schooling. A charity is paying for the school fees. The only regular meal that Jessica receives is at school.

QUESTIONS

1. Compare and contrast the stories of Jessica and Karen.

2. How do they illustrate the concepts of absolute and relative poverty?

There are large regional variations in average incomes. For example, the highest paid region is the south east of England and, in particular, London.

The distribution of wealth is more unequal than the distribution of income: 23 per cent of wealth is owned by 1 per cent of the population. The wealthiest 10 per cent own more than half the wealth in the UK; the wealthiest 50 per cent own 94 per cent of the wealth. The well-off have got wealthier over the past ten years. Inheritance is still an important source of wealth. However, overall the 20th century showed a gradual redistribution of wealth – in 1911 the richest 1 per cent owned 69 per cent of the wealth.

Example

Every year the *Sunday Times* publishes a 'UK Rich List'. These are some of the richest people in 2007:

Laskshmi Mittal and family – £19,250m
Roman Abramovich – £10,800m
The Duke of Westminster – £7000m
Sir Richard Branson – £3,100m.

Unemployment

Work is an important activity in the lives of most people. A job not only provides an income but contributes to an individual's self-esteem and gives a sense of purpose. Rates of unemployment are unevenly distributed in the population. You are more likely to be unemployed if you are unskilled, come from an ethnic minority or are aged between 16 and 19 years old. The employment rate for people of working age was 74.4 per cent for the three months ending in August 2007. The unemployment rate was 5.4 per cent, meaning that 1.65 million were out of work but had registered for employment.

Poverty

We have already seen that income and wealth are unequally distributed. At the other end of the scale, poverty is experienced unequally by different groups. The people who are most likely to experience poverty include the elderly, the sick and those with disabilities, single parents, children, the unemployed, the low paid, women and those from ethnic minorities.

Poverty can be considered to be anyone living on less than 60% of the UK average (median) income. According to the New Policy Institute, in 2007 for a single person this meant an income of less than £108 per week after tax, housing costs and benefits. For a family of two adults and two pre-school children, it means living on a weekly income of £301.

An ageing society

In October 2007 the number of people of pensionable age in the UK exceeded the number of children for the first time. As people get older, and retire from the labour market, their sources of income change. People aged in their fifties get most of their income from employment and self-employment (80 per cent). This falls to just 10 per cent for those in their seventies. State benefits (which include the state retirement pension) are the main source of income for pensioners. However, of these approximately one in five pensioners actually lives below the poverty line, with about 18 per cent living in persistent poverty. More than 1.6m pensioners entitled to pension credit do not receive it.

Disability

If you are sick or have a disability your opportunities for work are more likely to be limited. It is estimated that two-fifths of all adults aged 45 to 64, who are on below average incomes, have a limiting long-standing illness or disability. This is more than twice the rate for those on above-average incomes. Almost one-third of working age disabled adults live in income poverty. This means that people with disabilities are more likely to lack work or to be in low-paid work.

Mental illness and suicide

Mental illness can be both the cause and effect of experiencing unemployment. People who are experiencing mental health problems may have difficulty in gaining employment. Someone who becomes unemployed (because of redundancy or other problems) may experience psychological effects such as depression, low self-esteem, loss of identity and feelings of uselessness. These could lead eventually to suicide or other types of self-harm.

Example

- Adults in the poorest 20 per cent are around twice as likely to be at risk of developing a mental illness as those on average incomes. The differences by income are more pronounced for men than for women.
- People from manual working backgrounds are at a higher risk of developing a mental illness than those from non-manual backgrounds.
- In England, risk of mental illness is highest in the North East.

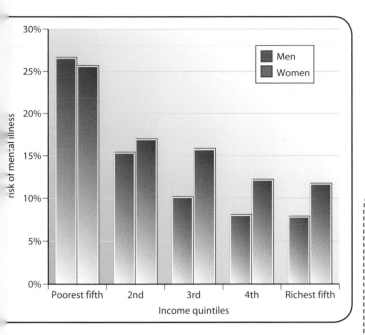

Figure 19.9 *The link between mental illness and income*
Source: Office for National Statistics

Research tip

You can find out more from The Poverty Site – the website of the New Policy Institute – on: www.poverty.org.uk.

FACTORS AFFECTING LIFE CHANCES

Life chances are the advantages and disadvantages that people have which can affect how well or badly they may do in society. The term was first used by Max Weber, a sociologist, writing at the beginning of the 20th century. He recognised that individuals had different opportunities to access certain resources such as food, clothing, money, education and health care. These may also affect their quality of life and influence their ability to acquire material goods, enter certain careers and obtain personal satisfaction. For example, a child who is born to well-off professional parents, lives in a large house in a 'good' neighbourhood, is sent to a good state or private school and enjoys many opportunities for sport and leisure, including travel, has higher life chances than one who is brought up on a council estate by a single parent and attends a local 'failing' school.

Family background

So we can see how family background influences the life chances of individuals, whether this is through the possibility of inheriting wealth or a family business, or by the expectations – whether high or low – of the family in which a child is brought up.

Example

In 1964 a television series called '7 Up' started, which followed the lives of 14 British children from the time they were 7 years old. It has continued to monitor their progress at intervals of 7 years. The children were selected from a range of different family backgrounds. In general, the children have continued in the same circles. For example, the three boys from elite prep schools continued at their elite level. The children from the working classes have by and large remained in those circles. (You may be able to access some of the episodes from your learning resource centre.)

Social class

Social class refers to a person's social and economic standing in society. The eight social classes which are used by the Office for National Statistics (see the table on page xxx <5 in script>) classify the different types of occupations in society, which in turn have an impact on the life chances of individuals. People in the same social class often share some of the same characteristics, including their experiences of health and illness. In broad terms, those in lower socio-economic groups are more likely to die prematurely and experience greater ill health during their life time. You can read more about social class and its links to health in Unit 7 and Unit 12.

Culture

Culture is the way of life associated with a particular society or group. Culture can affect individuals in several different ways. Certain cultures may influence the choice of food or the uptake of physical exercise which can affect physical growth.

Beliefs and practices may have a social and economic impact. For example, some cultures may not allow women to work, preventing them from gaining independence and raising their life chances. Some sociologists argue that the different social classes develop their own culture. The 'upper' classes tend to have distinctive language, mannerisms and attitudes which set them apart from other social classes. These are reinforced through the family, schooling and higher education at universities such as Oxford and Cambridge.

> **Think** How do the aspects of a person's culture affect their life chances?

Ethnicity

Ethnicity refers to the common genetic inheritance, culture, behaviour, language, or religion of a certain population. Studies that have compared a number of different life chances with ethnicity have found marked differences. For example, in education children in the UK from Indian backgrounds do as well, and often better, than white children. However boys from Afro-Caribbean homes do less well. The experience of health between different ethnic groups also showed variations.

Education

Education plays an important part in everybody's lives. It provides a method of socialising young people into the key cultural values of society, teaches knowledge and skills and prepares individuals for their working lives. The quality of educational experience is therefore crucial in ensuring that children reach their potential.

Housing

The environment in which you live can have a major impact on all aspects of development, including physical, intellectual, emotional and social. The quality of housing can affect the physical development of a child, for example through the amount of space available in which to play, whether or not the house is damp or overcrowded and the amenities such as baths or showers.

> **Think** Using the PIES (Physical, Intellectual, Emotional and Social) aspects of development, consider how each category could be affected by poor housing.

Employment

The employment status of an individual is very likely to affect them economically. The majority of people are only able to acquire material goods and services through the income they receive from their work. Employment can also affect health. While unemployment is linked with poor experiences of health, there are also some jobs which expose people to greater risks. For example, construction workers have higher rates of accidents at work. However, an individual also receives opportunities from being in employment, such as status and the possibility of promotion and career advancement, which can lead to enhanced self-esteem.

Nutritional status

'You are what you eat'! Nutrition plays an important part in our lives and particularly in our development. An individual needs to receive foods of the appropriate nutritional quality in order to grow, develop and remain healthy.

Social support network

Throughout our lives we receive support from different groups of people. These can be our family, friends, work colleagues and other groups, such as religious communities. The strength of these networks can help individuals in difficult times and also boost their self-confidence, allowing them to take opportunities.

Peer group influences

Very small children are influenced by their immediate family but as they grow older the role of the peer group becomes more important. A peer group is a group of people who share common characteristics – for example, they may be of the same age or share the same interests. The attitudes and values of the peer group may influence the ambitions of an individual.

Example

Jason is 11 years old and has just moved to his new secondary school. At his small primary school he was always top of his class and enjoyed working hard and getting praise from his teacher. Now he is trying to make new friends amongst a group of popular boys. However, they tend to 'play up' in lessons and call him 'teacher's pet' when he answers questions in class. At the end of the first term his report shows that he is in the bottom half of the class for academic achievement and it is suggested that he could do much better.

Think Looking at the example above, how might Jason's peer group affect his life chances?

Media influences

The media both reflects and influences public opinions and at some time or another every individual is affected by the messages that it conveys. There is evidence to show that people copy the attitudes and behaviours that they observe. For example, it has been suggested that prolonged exposure to violent TV programmes can cause children to become more aggressive. On the other hand, role models may influence the ambitions of individuals and messages about health, education and other activities can positively inform people and help to change attitudes.

Think How do you think some of the messages in the television programmes that you watch could influence the life chances of individuals viewing them?

Geographical area

Where we live can affect our lives. Looking at this in the widest terms, different parts of the world have very different lifestyles and opportunities. We already categorise the world into 'developed' and 'developing' countries and it is very obvious that the populations in certain countries are much more disadvantaged. Life expectancy is low and infant mortality very high in some countries, particularly in parts of Africa. Wars and conflicts disproportionally affect some areas while in others the terrain is difficult and this makes the growing of crops or the development of transport systems difficult. In the UK there are also geographical variations (e.g. the North-South divide, but there are exceptions within this). There are advantages and disadvantages of living either in a city or in the countryside. Statistics show regional variations in the experience of health.

Think What do you think are the advantages and disadvantages of living in a town or city compared with the countryside in terms of life chances?

Access to services

Access to jobs or services, such as health services, or to amenities, such as leisure or shopping facilities, can also affect an individual's life chances – for example, if hospital care is not easy to reach, a heart attack victim may have a poorer chance of survival. If a large firm closes down there may not be other job opportunities for those made redundant. Physical health, growth and development can be affected by the availability of appropriate facilities.

Potential effects

So what are the potential affects of social inequalities? We have looked at some of them as we have gone along. Some individuals, such as Alison Lapper, experience a range of social inequalities. You may know her from the statue that has been set up in London's Trafalgar Square.

CASE STUDY: ALISON LAPPER

Alison Lapper was born in 1965 with a congenital disorder called phocomelia which caused her to have no arms and truncated legs. Her mother rejected her and she was sent to a children's home where she remained for the whole of her childhood. There were about 250 children with a variety of impairments on one large residential site. The nursing staff had been taught that it was inadvisable to get close to the children so she experienced little affection or love and felt abandoned. The dormitory in which she lived did not have heating and accommodated about 20 children in cots with high sides, like being in a cage.

Attempts were made to try to fit Alison with artificial limbs, but these were unsuccessful and it was decided that she should try to live without external aids.

While she was in the residential home she began, during the holidays, to visit a family in Norfolk who had a farm. She loved going to the farm and became very settled with the family, who tried to adopt her. When the authorities contacted her mother for permission, her mother refused – despite the fact that she had had no contact for nearly four years. Her mother then visited her and took her back to her home in Birmingham, where she lived at the very top of a council high-rise building.

Alison made good progress at school, becoming head girl and winning awards. At 16 she followed her interest in art and eventually studied at the University of Brighton, graduating with a first-class honours degree in 1993. Since then she has pursued an artistic career using photography, digital imaging and painting, which she does with her mouth.

In 1999 Alison had a son, Parys, who was born without a disability. They have featured in the BBC documentary series 'Child of our Time'. In 2003 Alison was awarded the MBE for her services to art.

QUESTIONS

1. What inequalities has Alison experienced during her life?

2 How have these inequalities affected her life chances?

At the beginning of the unit there is a list giving some examples of the inequalities that certain groups may experience and the effects (see page xxx).

Here are some more facts.

Health:

- more babies are born with low birthweights in deprived areas

- in 2000 84 per cent of women with partners in non-manual occupations breastfed their babies, compared with 64 per cent of those with partners in manual occupations

- Indian and Pakastani boys are more likely to be overweight than boys in the general population.

Education:

- social class influences GCSE attainment. In 2002, 77 per cent of children in year 11 with parents in higher professional occupations gained 5 or more A* to C grade GCSEs

- participation in higher education is influenced by social class. In 2002, 87 per cent of 16 year olds with parents in higher professional occupations were in full-time education. This compares with 60 per cent of those with parents in routine occupations, and 58 per cent with parents in lower supervisory occupations.

- the likelihood of being employed is also higher for those with higher qualifications. In spring 2003, 88 per cent of working-age adults with a degree were in full-time employment, compared with 50 per cent of those with no qualifications. Education is also a key factor in explaining the inequality gaps between advantaged and disadvantaged groups in terms of health, living standards and social participation.

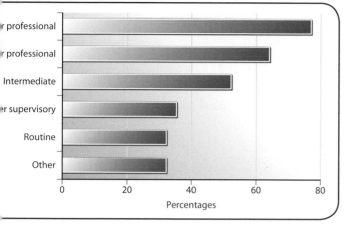

Figure 19.10 Attainment of five or more GCSE grades A* to C: by parental occupation
Source: NS-SEC, 2002, England & Wales

Living standards:

- on average, 91 per cent of households had central heating in their homes in 2001/02. However, single pensioner households are the least likely to have central heating, despite being one of the groups most vulnerable to the effects of cold indoor temperatures.

- car ownership is closely related to income, as well as to sex, age, stage of lifecycle and location. In 2002, 59 per cent of households on the lowest incomes did not have access to a car. High proportions of households without access to a car were found among single pensioners (69 per cent), student households (44 per cent) and lone parents (43 per cent). For many people, lack of access to a car can cause difficulties in getting to the shops or health services.

Research tip

You will find many more examples of the impact of social inequalities by researching information from the Office of National Statistics. Go to www.statistics.gov.uk

Amongst the many factors that can affect the life chances of an individual, some particular factors have been carefully researched. We will now look at some of these specific issues, but don't forget that for each individual there may be others which are specific to them.

Teenage pregnancy

The UK has the highest rate of teenage births in western Europe. Being a young mother can affect a girl's schooling, leading to low educational achievement. A study of 150 teenage mothers in South London found that 40 per cent had left school with no qualifications compared with national average of 6.6 per cent. There are higher rates of poverty amongst teenage mothers and poorer outcomes for their children.

Teenage pregnancies are more common among young people who have been disadvantaged or those who have low expectations for themselves in terms of education or careers. Girls from families in social class 5 are ten times more likely to become pregnant than those from professional backgrounds. Children who are, or who have been, in care, are also at higher risk of teenage pregnancy.

Drug misuse, alcohol and crime

Substance misuse is the term used to describe the continual misuse of any mind-altering substance which severely interferes with an individual's physical and mental health, or their social circumstances. The most common substances that are misused in this way are alcohol, glue or aerosols and a range of different drugs, including cannabis, cocaine and ecstasy. The need to purchase drugs to feed an addiction can lead an individual into crime as well as affecting all aspects of health, including physical, mental, social and emotional health.

Criminal activities not only affect the individual and his or her victim but reach out to damage families, communities and society.

Mental illness

Mental health problems are estimated to affect approximately between one in four and one in six of the population at any one time. The types of mental illness range from mild depression, caused by negative life events such as bereavement, divorce or redundancy, to complex problems that require ongoing specialised psychiatric care.

Suicides which are linked with mental illness have been decreasing, but still three times more men than women commit suicide. One in ten children in Britain aged 5 to 16 had a clinically recognisable mental disorder in 2004. Children from lone parent families, or where both parents are unemployed or have no educational qualifications, are more likely to be diagnosed with a mental disorder.

Eating disorders

At least 1.1 million people in the UK are affected by an eating disorder. The main types are anorexia nervosa, bulimia nervosa and binge eating disorder. Young people between the ages of 14 and 25 are most at risk, with girls ten times more likely to suffer than boys.

Physical health

The links between all types of physical health and social inequalities have been demonstrated in many studies. The rates of heart disease, strokes, cancers and accidents all show health inequalities which can in turn be linked with social inequality.

Research tip

Find out more about the links between physical health and social inequality. You could start by looking at Saving lives – Our Healthier Nation. Go to www.official-documents.co.uk.

Abuse

Different types of abuse may be experienced by individuals. The most common forms of abuse include child abuse, elder abuse and domestic violence. Bullying may be closely linked with abuse and may take place in a school, the workplace or in institutions including residential or nursing homes. The effects of abuse and bullying can be very serious for the individual, making them feel anxious and lowering their self-confidence, possibly leading to mental illness or even suicide.

You can remind yourself about abuse, bullying and other forms of discriminatory behaviours by looking back at Unit 2: Equality, diversity and rights.

Truancy and bullying

We have already seen how good educational achievement can positively affect the life chances of the individual, so truancy from school will inevitably have a negative effect. There are many reasons why children truant from school; however bullying by their peers is certainly one factor. Children who are absent from school not only miss out on educational opportunities but are often at greater risk as they wander the streets.

Motivation and talent

The life chances of individuals can however be improved in different ways. If someone is motivated to succeed, and is given the opportunity, then their health and well-being can be positively affected. The possibility of acquiring skills and developing other abilities may open up new pathways to success which in itself will bring financial, social and emotional rewards. The discovery of a talent, such as playing football or singing, may allow an individual to move away from the influences of their background.

CASE STUDY: DAVID BECKHAM

David Beckham was born in East London. His father was a kitchen fitter and his mother a hairdresser. The whole family supported  Manchester United. David was discovered to be an outstanding footballer and got the opportunity to attend special training with top clubs. He signed for Manchester United on his fourteenth birthday. He is now the fifth most-capped England player of all time. Married to former 'Posh Spice' Victoria, David Beckham has also become a media celebrity and is now a very wealthy man. He is thought to be worth at least £120 million and in 2006 earned more than £11 million from advertising endorsements alone.

QUESTION

How did David Beckham's life chances change through the discovery of his talents?

EVIDENCE ACTIVITY

P5 – M4 – D1

This section has given you many examples where social inequalities are linked to the health and well-being of the population. Undertake research in small groups to identify different examples under each heading. Share the information and then present individual accounts of your findings.

For **P5** you must use six examples to describe potential links between social inequalities and the health of the population.

For **M4** you should use the six examples you have identified for P5 and explain how social inequalities and the health of the population are linked.

For **D1** you have to evaluate potential links between social inequalities and the health of the population.

In your group, discuss and evaluate the impact, range and other effects of the links between social inequalities and health. Write an individual evaluation of your findings.

Nutrition for Health and Social Care

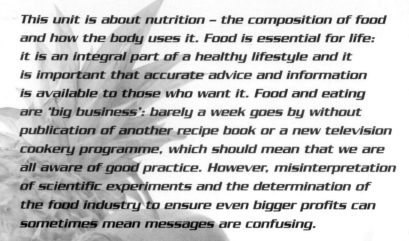

This unit is about nutrition – the composition of food and how the body uses it. Food is essential for life: it is an integral part of a healthy lifestyle and it is important that accurate advice and information is available to those who want it. Food and eating are 'big business': barely a week goes by without publication of another recipe book or a new television cookery programme, which should mean that we are all aware of good practice. However, misinterpretation of scientific experiments and the determination of the food industry to ensure even bigger profits can sometimes mean messages are confusing.

In this unit you will look at the role of food in a social context, and develop an understanding of food from a science-based perspective. Having examined the principles of nutrition, you will apply your understanding to the diet and lifestyle of a chosen individual and prepare a plan to improve nutritional intake.

Learning outcomes

By the end of this unit, you will:

So you want to be a...

Dietitian in the NHS

My name Tracey Greensmith
Age 24
Income £22,000

Being a good listener and the ability to help people to make difficult changes are essential requirements for this type of work.

What do you do?

I work on the hospital wards and in the clinics advising people on how to make positive changes to maintain or improve their health.

What responsibilities do you have?

I take a diet history, then provide advice specific to personal needs and circumstances. I support the family, or carer, responsible for providing the meals. I monitor how well the patient complies with their diet, then I assess the impact that it has on their health.

How did you get the job?

I did a vocational qualification in care which included sciences and a work placement with a dietitian. My part-time job as a carer in a residential home showed me the impact of diet on health and well-being. Maths and English GCSE are required for entry to the dietetics degree course; I was able to improve my grades and went to university where I took a degree in dietetics. This included a placement at a hospital that later had a vacancy just when I needed it!

What training did you get?

The degree course took three years, a mixture of academic study and 28 weeks practical work experience placements in the NHS. I then registered with the Health Professions Council. Since starting work I have been able to continue training and development.

What are the hours like?

I normally work a 36.5 hour week; I am part of the on-call team to cover evenings, weekends and bank holidays.

> **" I'm never bored and there are always new challenges. "**

What skills do you need?

Interpersonal and communication skills are really important as I have to listen carefully and give easy-to-understand advice in an acceptable manner. As I meet so many different people I must be non-judgemental and treat everyone appropriately. I have found it useful to have my driving licence as the hospital has clinics on more than one site.

What about the future?

I enjoy working in the NHS, but there are also opportunities in food and drug companies, sports and fitness clubs, supermarket chains and private healthcare providers. I might investigate working as a dietitian in the media. There are many areas for career development as dietetics is one of the fastest growing healthcare professions.

Grading criteria

The table below shows what you need to do to gain a pass, merit or distinction in this part of the qualification. Make sure you refer back to it when you are completing work so that you can judge whether you are meeting the criteria and what you need to do to fill in gaps in your knowledge or experience.

In this unit there are four evidence activities to give you an opportunity to demonstrate your achievement of the grading criteria:

page 109   **P1, M1**

page 122   **P2**

page 130   **P3, M2, D1**

page 133   **P4, P5, M3, D2**

To achieve a pass grade the evidence must show that the learner is able to...	To achieve a merit grade the evidence must show that, in addition to the pass criteria, the learner is able to...	To achieve a distinction grade the evidence must show that, in addition to the pass and merit criteria, the learner is able to...
P1 Explain concepts of nutritional health	**M1** Explain the potential risks to health of inappropriate nutrition	**D1** Evaluate the relative importance of different factors affecting the nutritional health and well-being of two different groups of individuals
P2 Describe the characteristics of nutrients and their benefits to the body	**M2** Explain the factors affecting the nutritional health and well-being of different groups of individuals	**D2** Evaluate how the nutritional plan will improve the health of the chosen individual.
P3 Identify the different factors that influence dietary intake for different population groups	**M3** Explain how the nutritional plan will meet the needs of the chosen individual.	
P4 Carry out a quantitative nutrient analysis of the diet of one individual		
P5 Prepare a nutritional plan for the chosen individual.		

21.1 *Understand concepts of nutritional health*

NUTRITION
FOOD AND DIET

Nutrition examines the relationship between **diet** and health; it is the scientific study of the processes of growth, maintenance and repair of the living body which depend upon the digestion of **food**, and the study of that food.

> ### Key words
> **diet** – the foods and drinks that are regularly consumed by individuals
> **food** – any substance containing nutrients that can be taken into the system by a living organism and metabolised into energy and body tissue to maintain life and growth

Figure 21.1 You are what you eat

Figure 21.1 shows a typical 'English breakfast' – served in restaurants, canteens and hotels all over the country – examine it closely!

> **Think** Food is what we eat, but not everything we eat is food. Of all the items in the breakfast picture which do you think are food? Which are not? Why?

There a many definitions of 'food' but for our purposes food is any substance taken into the body to maintain life and growth. Eggs, bacon, sausage, tomatoes, mushrooms and toast obviously fit this criteria, but what about salt and pepper? Tea and coffee?

Salt is a food as it acts as a regulator of body function, but pepper has no function except as a flavouring agent, so is therefore not a food! Tea and coffee provide no nutritional value unless milk (and perhaps sugar) is added; in fact, tea and coffee are drugs – they have mild **stimulant** actions which act through the nervous system, not the digestive system. (However, a drink of cocoa is a food! It contains nutrients from the crushed cocoa bean.)

> ### Key words
> **stimulant** – drug that temporarily increases alertness and awareness, and has various side effects including increased heart rate and addiction

There is really is no such thing as an 'unhealthy' food. But there are 'unhealthy' diets; and, of course, diet is only one factor in our lifestyle.

We have already stated that food is any substance taken in to the body to maintain life and growth. Food can provide the following:

- material from which the body can produce movement, heat or other form of energy

- material for growth, reproduction and repair

- materials necessary to regulate the production of energy or the process of repair and growth.

Nutrients

Our food is composed of **nutrients** – the chemical substances present in food which are essential to health. Most foods contain a variety of nutrients that perform various functions; an exception is glucose which is composed of a single nutrient and has a single function. The majority of foods supply a mixture of nutrients that fulfil a variety of roles. For example, milk contains protein, fat, vitamins and minerals; an apple will provide carbohydrate, a variety of minerals, some vitamins, very small amounts of protein and fat, and non-starch polysaccharides (dietary fibre).

Key words

nutrients – the chemical components of food that produce energy and promote or regulate the growth or repair of tissues

A nutrient is essential to an organism if it cannot be synthesised by the organism in sufficient quantities and must be obtained from an external source. Nutrients needed in relatively large quantities are called macronutrients and those needed in relatively small quantities are called micronutrients.

The nutrients to be considered in this unit are: carbohydrates, proteins, lipids (fats and oils)(macronutrients); and vitamins and minerals (micronutrients). Water and dietary fibre will also be investigated; they are essential for health but it is still debated whether they should be listed as nutrients.

> **Think** Think about the definitions of food, nutrients and nutrition; would you consider wine, beer and spirits to fit in any of these categories? Justify your answer!

Nutritional supplements

A bad diet is a bad diet – no matter how many vitamin and mineral supplements are added! For the majority of the population a well-balanced diet is sufficient for good health and no supplements are required. In fact, research shows that people who eat at least five portions of fruit and vegetables a day have much lower rates of coronary heart disease and cancer, while the same benefits have not been demonstrated for vitamin supplements. It is not just the **antioxidant** vitamins that protect our health – fruit and vegetables also contain a whole range of other natural and bio-active substances known as **phytochemicals**.

Key words

antioxidant – natural substances which decrease the chance of oils and fats in foods from combining with oxygen and changing colour or turning rancid. Rancid fats smell and taste unpleasant and are a health risk. Antioxidants are also used in fruits, vegetables and juice to extend the shelf life. Vitamin C (ascorbic acid) is one of the most widely used antioxidants.

phytochemicals – also known as bioactive substances, these are compounds commonly found in plant foods. They are not considered to be nutrients but may have beneficial effects on health, helping to protect against a number of illnesses such as heart disease and cancer.

> **Think** Who should take additives or food supplements? When and why are they necessary?

Taking large quantities of certain vitamins and minerals can be harmful to the body. For example, large quantities of vitamin A can be toxic, and large doses of zinc can interfere with the body's balance of copper – which is only required in trace amounts but is essential for efficient action of enzymes.

Nutritional supplements are sometimes prescribed for those who are deficient in specific nutrients; these might include vitamins, minerals, proteins or fibre. Supplements are sometimes given to improve the nutritional status of individuals – for example, protein supplements when recovering from illness or surgery, or folic acid (one of the B vitamins) for women planning to become pregnant. Supplements are also advised for **vegans** who might eat a limited variety of food.

> **Example**
>
> Those who smoke heavily might require additional vitamin C.

Key words

vegans – those who eat no meat, fish, dairy products or eggs. Non-food animal products, such as leather, may also be avoided.

Supplements are also sometimes taken by athletes to try to enhance physical performance and the sports supplement industry is worth billions. However these supplements have been known to contain banned substances which are illegal.

CASE STUDY: BILLY AND DONNA

Billy and Donna are training for the inter-school mini-marathon championships. Billy has decided to obtain some over-the-counter supplements to ensure that he comes well in front of Donna in the race. The supplements contain a variety of vitamins and minerals.

QUESTIONS

1. Do you think Billy's supplements will enhance his performance in the race?

2. How can Donna ensure that she is getting sufficient vitamins and minerals without resorting to supplements?

Additives

Some food additives are natural products – for example, beetroot is sometimes used for red colouring. Just because an additive has an E number does not mean that it is artificial. The addition of E numbers is a requirement of European Union (EU) legislation. Most additives used in foods must be labelled clearly in the list of ingredients, either by name or by an E number. This allows you to avoid foods containing specific additives if you wish. The addition of an E number means that the additive has passed safety tests and has been approved for use in the UK and also in the rest of the EU.

Additives have been used since the Middle Ages, when saltpetre was used to prevent meat going bad. Nowadays, nitrite, the active ingredient in saltpetre, is used. It prevents meat becoming contaminated with the organism that causes botulism.

As so much of the food we purchase now is either partially or fully prepared, it must contain additives in order to allow for storage and to prevent it spoiling. Additives also prevent 'caking' – the compacting of powder products like flour, gravy granules and custard powder.

Food additives are grouped by what they do. The additives that you are most likely to come across on food labels are:

- antioxidants – prevent oxidation of foods
- colours
- emulsifiers, stabilisers, gelling agents and thickeners
- flavour enhancers
- preservatives
- sweeteners.

Key words

oxidation – a destructive process that causes loss of nutritional value and changes in chemical composition. Oxidation of fats and oils leads to rancidity and, in fruits such as apples, it can result in the formation of compounds which discolour the fruit.

Figure 21.2 Oxidation can lead to discoloration

Fortification of food

Fortification involves the addition of nutrients to foods, irrespective of whether or not the nutrients were originally present in the food. It is a means of improving the nutritional status of a population (or potentially a sub-population). Some foods are fortified by law (e.g. margarine has the addition of vitamin D), others voluntarily (e.g. some breakfast cereals – particularly for children – are fortified with iron and vitamins, usually from the 'B' group).

> **Think** Which foods and drinks in your diet contain additives or are fortified?

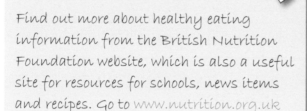

Research tip

Find out more about healthy eating information from the British Nutrition Foundation website, which is also a useful site for resources for schools, news items and recipes. Go to www.nutrition.org.uk

Malnutrition, undernutrition and nutrition deficiency

Malnutrition does not just refer to people who do not have enough to eat, it includes all who are poorly nourished – both undernourished and over-nourished.

Deficiency of nutrition occurs in times of starvation, whether caused through environmental conditions or civil insurrection; intentionally, as in anorexia or bulimia nervosa; or through illness.

> **Think** Which type of people would you describe as suffering from malnutrition?

Figure 21.3 Many different people can suffer from malnutrition

Example

Undernutrition is a deficiency in one or more nutrients. In the UK, undernutrition is reported in approximately 40 per cent of people admitted to hospital and the nutritional status of these people continues to deteriorate during the hospital stay. Weight loss often continues in many patients for a variety of reasons; surgery or treatments can lead to an inability to eat or to loss of appetite, although parenteral or enteral feeding might compensate for some loss of nutrition. It is also considered that inadequacy of catering and feeding practices are major contributors to worsening nutritional status.

Key words

parenteral – the practice of feeding a person intravenously, bypassing the usual process of eating and digestion. The person receives nutritional formulas containing salts, glucose, amino acids, lipids and added vitamins.

enteral – administration of nutrients through a gastric or duodenal feeding tube.

While marasmus and kwashiorkor are most commonly seen in developing countries, babies and children suffering from these dietary deficiency disorders caused by protein and energy malnutrition are often depicted by the media on UK television. The word *marasmus* comes from the Greek word meaning 'wasting' and it affects mainly babies under one year old. The symptoms are stunted growth, considerable weight loss, muscle wasting, diarrhoea and irritability. The body adapts to the shortage of food by the wasting of muscles and the depletion of fat stores. Babies appear wizened, with stick-like arms and legs, extremely underweight, with wrinkled skin and an 'old man's face'. The child will appear alert and have no loss of appetite. Marasmus is caused by deficiency of protein and energy in the diet.

Kwashiorkor is caused by a deficiency of protein in the diet and affects children of one to three years old. The symptoms are poor growth, muscle wastage, chronic diarrhoea and infections, deterioration of hair, skin and nails, a swollen liver and abdomen and oedema (swelling) of the face, hands and feet. The child will appear apathetic, with a bloated abdomen resulting from a swollen liver, and will have no appetite.

Obesity, energy balance and BMI

Worldwide, the prevalence of people who are overweight and obese is increasing, both adults and children. Increasing levels of obesity are associated with increased risk of developing cancer, cardiovascular disease and type 2 diabetes.

If a person regularly consumes more energy (calories) than they use up, they will start to gain weight and eventually become overweight or obese. On the other hand, if a person regularly consumes less energy than they use up they will lose weight.

Extra energy is stored in the body as fat. Energy balance is achieved when intake of energy matches the energy used and body weight remains constant. Balancing energy intake and output to maintain a healthy weight has many benefits.

> **Think** Think about all you have had to eat and drink over a 24-hour period and the exercise that you have taken. Do you think you have a satisfactory energy balance?

Body weight can be classified by using the body mass index (BMI) which is a useful guide to finding out if you are a healthy weight for your height. The BMI assumes that there is not a single weight for a person of a specific height, but there is a weight range within which a person will have good health.

Your BMI can be calculated by dividing your weight in kilograms by your height in metres squared:

$$BMI = \frac{\text{Weight in Kg}}{(\text{Height in metres})^2}$$

Estimate your own body mass index using the calculation above.

Example

Body Mass Index is used to classify different categories of weight. The Department of Health use the following BMI classifications:

- less than 18.5 = underweight
- 18.5-24.9 = normal healthy weight
- 25-29.9 = pre-obese
- 30-34.9 = obese class 1
- 35-39.9 = obese class 11
- Greater than 40 = morbidly obese class 111.

Most of us store fat either around our hips and thighs, or around our tummies. Those who store fat around the middle can be labelled as having an 'apple shape', while those who store fat around the hips and thighs have a 'pear shape'. The shape of your body is directly linked to your risk of poor health. In adults, waist measurements also provide a good obesity indicator. A report by the World Health Organization suggests that increased risk is present when the waist measurement exceeds 94cm (37 inches) for men or 80cm (32 inches) for women.

Example

Apples and Pears

Measure your waist-hip ratio while standing relaxed and naked. Measure your waist at its narrowest point. This is usually around your navel. Next, measure your hips at their widest point. This is usually around the buttocks. Do not pull the tape tight when doing either of these measurements. Finally, divide your waist measurement by your hip measurement. The figure you get from this calculation is your waist-hip ratio. For example, if your waist is 85cm (33in) and your hips are 100cm (39in), your waist-hip ratio is 0.85. If you're a man and your ratio is more than 1.0, or a woman and your waist-hip ratio is more than 0.8, it means you're an apple shape and at greater risk of health problems.

Think Are you an apple or a pear?

Research tip

You could use a BMI calculator like those on the NHS Direct and the Department of Health websites: http://www.nhsdirect.nhs.uk/articles/article.aspx?articleId=850 or http://www.bdaweightwise.com/lose/lose_bmi.aspx

Dietary Reference Values and Reference Nutrient Intakes

Dietary Reference Values (DRVs) are estimates made by nutritionists of the energy and nutrients required by healthy individuals and groups of healthy people in the UK population. The Scientific Advisory Committee on Nutrition (SACN) focuses on nutrients about which there is cause for concern, such as iron, folate and selenium.

Population groups for which dietary reference values have been set include:

- boys and girls (aged 0-3 months; 4-6 months; 7-9 months; 10-12 months; 1-3 years; 4-6 years; 7-10 years)

- males (aged 11-14 years; 15-18 years; 19-50 years; 50+ years)

- females (aged 11-14 years; 15-18 years; 19-50 years; 50+ years; those pregnant and breastfeeding).

DRVs include four types of estimates:

- Reference Nutrient Intakes – RNIs are used for protein, vitamins and minerals, and are an estimate of the amount that should meet the needs of most of the group to which they apply. They are not minimum or recommended targets.

- Estimated Average Requirement – EARs are estimates of the average requirement for food energy or for a nutrient. Some people will need more, many will need less.

- Lower Reference Nutrient Intake – LRNI is the amount of a nutrient that is enough for only the small number of people who have low requirements (2.5 per cent). The majority of people need more.

- Safe intake: this is used where there is insufficient evidence to set an EAR, RNI or LRNI. The safe intake is the amount judged to be a level or range of intake at which there is no risk of deficiency and which is below the level where there is a risk of undesirable effects. There is no evidence that intakes above this level have any benefits – in some instances they could have toxic effects.

DIETARY INTAKE

Your dietary intake refers to the amount of nutrients that are required in one day for good health. This will depend on your age, gender, physical activity and body size. It will also differ if you are pregnant or breastfeeding.

To help individuals understand which foods to eat in order to obtain the necessary nutrients, government bodies have published information which suggests the variety and quantities of foods to eat each day.

Balance of Good Health

The Balance of Good Health is consistent with the government's 'Eight tips for eating well', published in October 2005, which are:

1. Base your meals on starchy foods

2. Eat lots of fruit and vegetables

3. Eat more fish

4. Cut down on saturated fat and sugar

5. Try to eat less salt – no more than 6g a day

6. Get active and try to be a healthy weight

7. Drink plenty of water

8. Don't skip breakfast.

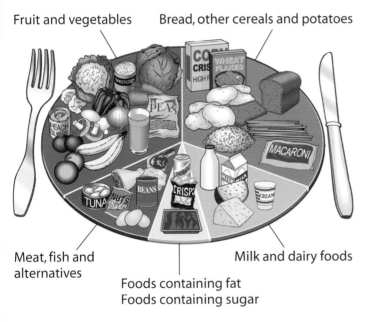

Figure 21.4 The Balance of Good Health plate
Source: British Nutrition Foundation

Food pyramid and food groups

The original version of the 'food pyramid' was published in Sweden in 1974. Following publication of nutrition studies, the pyramid has been developed and changed several times, until it was published in its current format by the USDA (United States Drugs Administration).

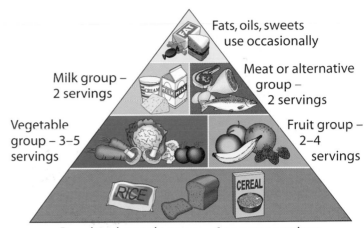

Figure 21.5 The food pyramid
Source: United States Department of Agriculture

The idea of the food pyramid has been criticised but it helps people to visualise the amount of food from each group that they should be eating.

In general terms, the food pyramid recommends the following intake of different food groups each day, although exact amounts of calorie intake depends on sex, age and lifestyle:

- 3-5 servings a day of vegetables, especially dark green vegetables and orange vegetables, e.g. spinach, peppers

- 2-4 servings of fruit a day, especially fresh and frozen fruits, e.g. apples, raspberries

- 2-3 servings of meat, poultry, fish, beans, eggs, or nuts a day, especially dry beans and peas, eggs, and nut and seeds

- 2-3 servings of milk, cheese, yogurt or milk substitutes a day

- occasional use of fats, oils, and sweets, especially oils

- 6-11 servings of grains a day, especially whole grains.

> **Think** Compare and contrast the Balance of Good Health and the Food Pyramid; which of these do you consider would be easier for group of 11-14 year-old children to understand? Why do think this?

'Five a Day' recommendations

The Government recommends an intake of at least five portions of fruit or vegetables per person per day to help reduce the risk of some cancers, heart disease and many other chronic conditions.

CASE STUDY: JIN AND JASMINE'S MEALS

Jin and Jasmine (aged 15 and 13 years) are always in a rush in the morning to catch the school bus, so grab some toast to eat on the way. At break time they will usually have crisps and cola. Lunch offers a choice: Jasmine will sometimes have a side salad with her meal but Jin does not like salad. The evening meal is eaten with the family, sometimes their mother makes home-made pies and puddings.

QUESTIONS

1. How could Jin and Jasmine ensure that they meet the 'Five a day' recommendations?

2. What could their mother include with the evening meal to help the family get their recommended 'Five a Day'?

Research tip

Find out more about 'Five a day' from the NHS website http://www.5aday.nhs.uk/ .There is much useful information including portion sizes, nutritional values, recipes, resources and games.

Effect of food preparation and processing

Most foods have to be prepared and cooked before they can be eaten. For some foods the process may be as simple as peeling an orange; for others, it may be more complex. For example, to make bread, grain has to be milled to produce flour, and it might require fortification or other treatment before it can be baked. At each stage of the process some nutrients will be discarded or destroyed; this will occur whether it takes place in a factory or at home. If the food has to be stored for a long period further nutrients may be lost.

The nutrients lost from foods will depend on the type of preparation, processing and storage. Heat causes chemical and physical changes in food which make the flavour, palatability and digestibility of the raw product more acceptable, and may improve its keeping quality. Cooking usually results in the loss of nutrients – the loss being greater the higher the temperature and the longer the cooking time. Using large quantities of liquid in the cooking will also cause loss of nutrients, although they can be retained if the liquid is used in the meal.

Whether the food is a wonderful four-course meal, or soup and a sandwich, we need to be sure that the ingredients are safe to eat and that they have been prepared in a hygienic and healthy environment.

Hidden ingredients

Hidden ingredients are of particular importance for people who are allergic or sensitive to specific foods, such as nuts or seeds, as even tiny amounts could make them ill or cause a life-threatening reaction. Other 'hidden ingredients' that we should all be aware of are the salts, sugars and lipids (fats) that are included in foods – often at very high levels. The American Stroke Association has identified that some cereals are particularly high in these nutrients.

Food producers are gradually making it easier for us to read the ingredients in their products, but that is of no help if we don't understand what the ingredients are or know the quantities we should

Example

The table below shows a summary of factors which may reduce the nutrients in food. (From: Manual of Nutrition. MAFF. 10th edition. 1995, The Stationery Office)

Nutrient	Heat	Light	Air	Water (by leaching)	Acid	Alkali	Other
Protein	✓ if prolonged						
Minerals				✓			
Vitamin A	✓ with air		✓ with heat				Metals
Thiamine	✓		✓	✓		✓	Sulphur dioxide
Riboflavin		✓		✓		✓	
Folate	✓		✓ but protected by vitamin C	✓		✓	
Vitamin C	✓	✓	✓ but protected by sulphur dioxide	✓		✓	Enzymes; metals

Table 21.1 Factors which may reduce the nutrients in food

be having. Genetically modified products, such as maize and soya (in their forms of flour and protein respectively), should be labelled so they can be avoided if necessary; however, their derivatives do not have to be labelled.

Research tip

The Food Standards Agency has a website for legislation related to food handling, safety and hygiene. Go to www.food.gov.uk to find out more. The British Dietetic Association website provides impartial advice about nutrition and health as well as advice about careers in Dietetics. Go to www.bda.uk.com.

The Department of Health has a useful website with up-to-date information about health and social care policy, health and nutrition-related publications and nutrition and illness. Go to www.dh.gov.uk

Another Food Standards Agency website considers 'ages and stages', 'keeping food safe' and 'food labels'. Go to http://www.eatwell.gov.uk/.

EVIDENCE ACTIVITY

P1 – M1

For **P1**, you should explain the different concepts of nutritional health, showing that you understand the need for satisfactory nutrient intake.

For **M1**, you must show a clear understanding of the potential risks to health of inappropriate nutrition. You should consider the risks of nutrient deficient diets.

P1 and **M1** require you to explain the basic theories of nutritional health and the risks to health of inappropriate nutrition. This could be achieved by writing an assignment supported by an illustrated presentation or posters.

21.2 *Know the characteristics of nutrients*

CHARACTERISTICS

Novel foods

The food that we eat and the liquids that we drink used to come from two main sources – animals or plants. A third category can be added to these – **novel foods**. Novel foods are of two types:

- those produced by processing plant foods, e.g. soya

- those produced from sources not previously used as food, including both plants and micro-organisms, e.g. Quorn.

However, other novel foods – including 'functional foods' – can also fall within the scope of this programme. A functional food is one that claims to have additional benefits other than nutritional value, for example a margarine that contains a cholesterol-lowering ingredient.

In addition to these three food sources can be added **genetically modified** (GM) foods.

Key words

novel foods – foods and food ingredients that have not been used (within the EU) for human consumption to a significant degree before 1997
genetically modified – when a plant is genetically modified, its genetic material is altered (or a gene is transferred from another organism) in order to produce certain characteristics

Soya beans are the most widely used novel food. Their proteins are of high biological value – unlike most vegetable proteins. Soya beans can be processed to assume a variety of meat-like appearances and can be added to pies, stews etc. Textured vegetable protein – TVP – has been developed by isolating proteins from a number of plants, especially soya beans, and converting them directly into soya 'mince' or 'chunks'.

Mycoprotein is another product that can be used as an alternative to meat. This is produced from fungal micro-organisms, processed and then used in the food industry or the home to be incorporated into recipes (for example, vegetarian meals).

Yeast is a micro-organism that can be grown on petroleum oil and used to provide protein-rich foods; at present this foodstuff is intended for animal use only.

The majority of foods supply a mixture of nutrients that fulfil a variety of roles: carbohydrates, proteins, lipids, vitamins and minerals; an exception is glucose, which is composed of a single nutrient and has a single function.

Requirements (Reference Nutrient Intakes for different groups)

The Reference Nutrient Intake (RNI) is the amount of a nutrient that is enough for almost every individual, even someone who has high needs for the nutrient. The RNI is much more than most people need and it is most unlikely that those consuming this amount will be deficient in that nutrient.

However, RNIs are not used for carbohydrates; these requirements are based on physical activity levels (PAL) multiplied by basal metabolic rates (BMR) which will give the EAR (Estimated Average Requirement) for energy. This is an estimate of the average requirement for energy or a nutrient (approximately 50 per cent of a group of people will require less, and 50 per cent will require more).

BMR is the energy required for life, i.e. breathing, heartbeat, maintenance of body temperature etc, so will vary according body size, growth rates, etc.

Some examples are shown in Table 21.2 opposite.

	Weight (Kg)	Basal metabolic rate (resting energy requirements in brackets)	
		MJ(Kcal)/day	MJ(Kcal)Kg/day
Infant, 1 year	10	2.3 (560)	0.23 (56)
Boy, 10 years	33	5.2 (1240)	0.16 (38)
Man, 40 years	76	7.3 (1750)	0.10 (23)
Woman, 40 years	62	5.7 (1360)	0.09 (22)
Man, 75+ years	69	5.8 (1400)	0.08 (20)

Table 21.2 Some examples of basal metabolic rate

A physical activity level (PAL) of 1.4 applies to most people in the UK; it represents very little physical activity at work or in leisure time. A PAL of 1.6 for women and 1.7 for men represents moderate activity during both work and leisure time. Women who have a high level of physical activity at work and leisure would have a PAL of 1.8, and men would have 1.9.

Nutritional requirements vary throughout life according to the amount growth and development taking place, and the amount of energy used.

Infants

The first four to six months of life is a period of rapid growth and development. Recent Department of Health advice recommends exclusive breastfeeding until six months of age. Breast milk contains all the nutrients required during this period. Mothers should be encouraged to breastfeed and not to give solid foods to infants before the age of four months. During the early months of life, babies can draw upon iron stores they have accumulated before birth but these stores are rapidly used and it is important that the diet given during weaning contains enough iron to meet the baby's needs for growth and development. Requirements for protein, thiamin, niacin, vitamin B6, vitamin B12, magnesium, zinc, sodium and chloride also increase between six and twelve months.

Children 1-3 years

At this stage children are rapidly growing so energy requirements increase. Protein requirements do not increase as much. There is an increased need for all vitamins except vitamin D, as some of this will now be synthesised in the skin, following exposure to sunlight. Slightly lower amounts of calcium, phosphorus and iron are needed. There is an increased requirement for all the other minerals except for zinc.

During the second year of life, children continue to need energy-dense diets. They should be given whole milk, not skimmed or semi-skimmed, and care needs to be taken over the amount of fibre (non-starch polysaccharide or NSP) eaten. If the diet is too bulky, owing to too many high fibre foods, there is a danger that the child will be unable to eat enough food to satisfy his or her energy needs. This could happen on a vegetarian diet. After the age of 2 years, semi-skimmed milk may be given provided adequate energy intake is assured, although skimmed milk should not be introduced before 5 years of age.

4-6 years

Energy requirements continue to increase and there is a greater need for protein, all the vitamins (except C and D) and all the minerals (except iron). The RNI figure for vitamin C remains the same as for younger children. No value is given for vitamin D since the action of sunlight on the child's skin will now be the major source of this vitamin.

7-10 years

During this period of increased growth and activity there is a marked increase in requirements for energy and protein. There is no change in the requirement for thiamin, vitamin C or vitamin A, but the requirements for the other vitamins and minerals are increased.

11-14 years

Energy requirements continue to increase and protein requirements increase by approximately 50 per cent. By the age of 11, the vitamin and mineral requirements for boys and girls start to differ:

- boys: there is an increased requirement for all the vitamins and minerals

- girls: there is no change in the requirement for thiamin, niacin or vitamin B6, but there is an increased requirement for all the minerals. Girls have a much higher iron requirement than boys (once menstruation starts).

15-18 years

Boys: energy and protein requirements continue to increase, as do the requirements of a number of vitamins – thiamin, riboflavin, niacin, vitamins B6, B12, C and A; also magnesium, potassium, zinc, copper, selenium and iodine. Calcium requirements remain high as skeletal development is rapid.

Girls: requirements for energy, protein, thiamin, niacin, vitamins B6, B12 and C, phosphorus, magnesium, potassium, copper, selenium and iodine all increase.

Boys and girls have the same requirement for vitamin B12, folate, vitamin C, magnesium, sodium, potassium, chloride and copper. Girls have a higher requirement than boys for iron (due to menstruation) but a lower requirement for zinc and calcium.

Adults: 19-50 years

Energy requirements are lower for both men and women in comparison to adolescents, as are requirements for calcium and phosphorus. Women have a reduced requirement for magnesium, and men for iron. The requirements for protein and most of the vitamins and minerals remain virtually unchanged in comparison to adolescents (except for selenium in men, which increases slightly).

Pregnancy and lactation

During pregnancy, there are increased requirements for some, but not all, nutrients. Women intending to become pregnant, and during the first 12 weeks of pregnancy, are advised to take supplements of folic acid to help reduce the risk of their child having a neural tube defect, e.g. spina bifida. In addition, all women of childbearing age are advised to choose a diet that supplies adequate amounts of folate (Department of Health, 1992). Additional energy (kcal 200 per day) and thiamin are required only during the last three months of pregnancy. Mineral requirements do not increase.

During lactation (breastfeeding), there is an increased requirement for energy, protein, all the vitamins (except B6), calcium, phosphorus, magnesium, zinc, copper and selenium.

50+ years

Energy requirements decrease gradually after the age of 50 in women and age 60 in men as people typically become less active. Protein requirements decrease for men but continue to increase slightly in women. The requirements for vitamins and minerals remain virtually unchanged for both men and women. There is one exception – after the menopause, women's requirement for iron is reduced to the same level as that for men.

After the age of 65 the RNI for vitamin D is 10 mcg/day. The reduction in energy needs, coupled with unchanged requirements for vitamins and minerals, means that the nutrient density of the diet becomes even more important. Nutrient density means the quantity of vitamins and minerals in relation to the amount of energy supplied by the foods and drinks consumed.

Example

Using the following formula, estimate your energy requirements for 24 hours:

EAR = BMR x PAL

Using the formula below, calculate your RNI for protein each day:

Protein per day = 0.75g x kg(your body weight)

Nutrient & RNI	Source:	Function
Carbohydrates EAR = BMR x PAL	With the exception of milk, carbohydrates are only found in products of vegetable origin e.g. sugar (including drinks), flour (cereals, bread, cake etc.), beans, fruit.	Carbohydrates can be divided into available and unavailable; the available carbohydrates – sugars and starch are converted by the body to simple sugars to provide energy. The unavailable carbohydrates include dietary fibre or NSP (non-starch polysaccharide). The term 'unavailable' is used because the fibre cannot be digested so does not provide energy.
Proteins RNI for all adults over 19 yrs = 0.75g/kg/d Figures for children and pregnant and lactating women allow for growth in children, growth of foetal and maternal tissue, and breast milk production.	Animal proteins – milk, meat, eggs, fish Plant proteins – cereals, nuts and seeds, potatoes, legumes	Proteins are essential for growth and maintenance of body tissues. They also produce substances such as hormones and enzymes which help to control many functions within the body. If insufficient carbohydrate and fat are available in the diet, then protein may also be used to provide the body with energy.
Lipids For women, no more than 34.9% of the daily energy requirement should come from fat. For men this figure is 35.8%. This figure is total fats.	Lipids include fats and oils which can be divided into saturated – usually the hard fats, mainly animal products e.g. fat on meat, butter, lard, cream; and unsaturated – usually the liquid fats e.g. corn oil, olive oil, oily fish (pilchards, salmon, sardines etc.).	Fats are essential for many reasons: • as a source of energy • they are involved in forming cell membranes • as a vehicle for the provision of fat soluble vitamins such as Vitamins A, E, D and K • fats are involved in making hormones • they are involved in keeping us warm • they provide us with a shock-absorbing protective layer.
Vitamins	Vitamins are required in very small amounts and are known as micro-nutrients. The different vitamins are found in various foods.	Vitamins (with the exception of vitamin D) cannot be made in the body but are required for numerous functions in the body - deficiencies can lead to serious health problems. Vitamins can be divided into two groups; fat soluble and water soluble.
Minerals	Minerals and trace elements, like vitamins, are micro-nutrients. Minerals tend to be required in milligram (mg) quantities and trace elements in much smaller amounts – microgram (mcg). Some minerals are found in only a few foods, e.g. the main source of calcium is milk and dairy products, so must these be included in the diet on a regular basis.	Some foods are fortified with minerals, e.g. iron is added to some breakfast cereals. It is better to receive the recommended levels of vitamins, minerals and trace elements through a well-balanced diet, however sometimes supplements are necessary if an increased requirement of one or more nutrients is necessary e.g. older people who don't go outdoors may need additional vitamin D.

Table 21.3 Sources and function of nutrients

Effects of processing

Some of the effects of food processing have been looked at above; however it is useful to consider the effects of freezing, storage and shelf life.

> ***Think*** Consider the food and drinks you have at home: for how long will they be safe to consume? What different methods have been used to ensure they don't 'go off'?

The aim of freezing foods is to prevent multiplication of the micro-organisms that cause food spoilage and poisoning. This is achieved by the formation of ice crystals which draw away available water from the food, and the very low temperatures inhibiting growth of micro-organisms. Methods have been developed by the food industry to ensure that products are frozen in the shortest time possible, reducing the risk of micro-organism growth. If frozen foods are kept below -18°C there is little loss of nutritional value until the food is thawed. The differences between fresh and frozen food when cooked and served are minimal.

Different nutrients are affected to various degrees by different food processing and storage methods, depending on the physical properties of the nutrient. Some are fairly resistant to changes in temperature, light and atmosphere. Others, however, such as vitamin C and folate, are extremely sensitive and initial concentrations can rapidly decrease, depending on how the produce is treated. Scientific studies have shown that vitamin C levels in some vegetables are actually lower in raw vegetables that have been distributed and stored at ambient or chilled temperatures than in those that had been immediately frozen after harvest – when nutrient concentrations are at their highest. Other studies have shown that vegetables stored at room temperature over two to three days may lose 50 to 70 per cent of their folate content.

It is essential to follow labelling advice; many products should be kept in the fridge once opened, which will ensure that warm temperatures do not allow micro-organisms to multiply. To ensure that nutrient value deteriorates as little as possible the following points should be followed:

- fresh fruit and vegetables should be scrubbed or washed in preference to peeling as most of the vitamins are stored just beneath the surface

- vegetables should be prepared immediately before cooking – if they are left standing in water the soluble vitamins will leach out

- steaming vegetables is preferable to boiling, as fewer vitamins will be lost

- fruit and vegetables should be stored away from heat and daylight

- bottled milk should be removed from the doorstep as soon as possible; some vitamins are destroyed by direct sunlight

- vitamins in fruit and vegetables that are damaged can be attacked by damaging enzymes

- food should be served as soon as possible following cooking, as keeping it warm will lead to vitamin loss from oxidation.

Next time you cook frozen vegetables read the instructions carefully – the cooking time is often less than you think!

Shelf-life is a term used by the food industry to specify the period of time in which a product can be stored, under specified conditions, and remain in optimum condition and suitable for consumption.

> ***Think*** Apart from shelf-life, what other terms are used on product labels to indicate periods of time a food might remain fit for consumption?

Research tip

Look at the following website for useful information regarding public health, food safety, consumer affairs, legislation and much more – http://ec.europa.eu/food/food/biotechnology/novelfood/index_en.htm. The site of the Foods Standards Agency has valuable information regarding genetically modified and novel foods. Go to http://www.food.gov.uk/gmfoods/.

CARBOHYDRATES

There are three main groups of carbohydrates in food: sugars, starches and non-starch polysaccharides (NSP). All are compounds of carbon, hydrogen and oxygen only. Carbohydrates are made up of saccharide (sugar/glucose) units. Carbohydrate in food is found in one of the following three forms:

1. Mono-saccharides (simple sugars) – single units which occur alone or make up more complex sugars, for example:

- glucose (dextrose) – occurs naturally in fruit and plant juices and in the blood of living animals, including humans

- fructose – occurs naturally in some fruit and vegetables and especially in honey. It is the sweetest sugar known. It is also a component of sucrose.

2. Disaccharides – consist of two monosaccharides linked together, for example:

- lactose – occurs only in milk, including human milk

- maltose – a combination of two glucose units, formed when grain is germinated.

3. Polysaccharides (complex carbohydrates) starches – many saccharide units linked together. Starches are found naturally in cereals, cereal products, root vegetables, pulses and potatoes. Starch is converted by the body to glucose which, if eaten in excess, is stored as fat.

Non-starch polysaccharides (NSP), or dietary fibre, is found in the cell walls of vegetables, fruit, pulses and cereal grains. The NSP in wheat, maize and rice are mainly insoluble cellulose which cannot be digested by humans, but which are essential to add bulk to faecal material. The amount of NSP in the diet has been linked to a reduction in the risks of diseases such as bowel cancer, diverticulitis, and haemorrhoids; and in controlling diabetes by slowing the rate at which nutrients are absorbed through the intestinal wall.

Sugar substitutes

Sorbitol is made from sugars, it is sometimes used in diabetic foods as it is absorbed slowly.

Artificial sweeteners, saccharine and aspartame, have no relationship to sugars. They are about 200-500 times as sweet as sucrose, so they provide virtually no energy and can be used when restricting the amount of sugar in the diet. Sugar substitutes are mixtures of an intense sweetener and a carbohydrate and as such provide much less energy than the equivalent amount of sugar.

PROTEINS

Proteins are compounds of carbon, hydrogen, oxygen and nitrogen. Most proteins contain sulphur and some contain phosphorus. Protein molecules consist of chains of hundreds or thousands of amino acid units. When protein is eaten the chains of molecules are broken down by the digestive process and the amino acids are absorbed into the bloodstream.

About 20 different amino acids occur in the proteins found in foods – each amino acid molecule contains at least one amino group (-NH2) and at least one acidic group (-COOH). Of the 20 amino acids found in proteins, eight are essential and must be supplied by protein in the diet as they cannot be synthesised by the body. One additional amino acid is required by infants for growth. Non-essential amino acids can be synthesised by the body converting one amino acid into another within the body cells.

A typical protein molecule contains at least 500 amino acids joined together by peptide links. These links are formed when the amino group of one amino acid reacts with the acidic group of an adjacent amino acid. During the formation of the peptide link a molecule of water is eliminated. Two amino acids joined together form a dipeptide, and longer chains of amino acids are called polypeptides.

Proteins vary enormously in structure and complexity but can be classified according to the shape of their molecules:

- Globular proteins are rounded in shape and the molecules are not closely packed together, allowing water to easily penetrate the empty spaces. Examples include ovalbumin, found in egg white, and caseinogen, found in milk. Most of the proteins found in body cells are globular – for example, haemoglobin and myoglobin.

- Fibrous proteins are straighter (inelastic proteins), or coiled in a spiral (elastic proteins). The molecules of fibrous proteins are closely packed together making it difficult for water to penetrate. Gluten, the protein found in wheat is an elastic protein.

Proteins may have a high biological value – usually animal proteins – or a low biological value – generally vegetable proteins.

Key words

high biological value – a protein that can supply all the essential amino acids required that cannot be made in the body in sufficient amounts for health

Vitamin	Function	Source
A – fat soluble	Maintains healthy skin. Essential to prevent night blindness.	Liver, spinach, carrots, cheese, margarine
B1 Thiamin – water soluble	Helps release energy from food. Repairs and maintains the nervous system.	Brazil nuts, brown rice, wholemeal bread, pork
B2 Riboflavin – water soluble	Helps release energy from food. Necessary for production and repair of body tissues. Maintains healthy mucous membranes in the nose and throat.	Liver, kidneys, milk, breakfast cereals, yeast extract
Niacin – water soluble	Helps release energy from food. Essential for the brain, nervous and digestive systems to function properly.	Liver, peanuts, chicken, fish, cheese, breakfast cereals
B6 Pyridoxine – water soluble	Assists in the formation of antibodies and red blood cells. Necessary for growth and maintenance of the nervous system.	Herrings, kidneys, bananas
B12 Cobalamin – water soluble	Necessary for the formation of red blood cells. Necessary for building genetic material. Helps maintain a healthy nervous system.	Liver, tinned fish, lamb, eggs, turkey
C Ascorbic acid – water soluble	Helps maintain healthy skin, gums, teeth and blood vessels. Helps absorption of iron from food.	Citrus fruit, sprouts
Folic acid – water soluble	Works with B12 to form red blood cells and produce genetic material. Necessary for growth and maintenance of healthy nervous and digestive systems.	Liver, kidneys, spinach, sprouts
D – fat soluble	Helps the absorption of calcium and phosphorous which in turn maintain strong teeth and bones.	Cod liver oil, herring, tinned fish, margarine
E – fat soluble	Helps maintain the proper function of the body. A natural antioxidant – helps protect body tissues.	Peanuts, canned tuna, cooked spinach, vegetable oils
K – fat soluble	Essential for blood clotting.	Leafy green vegetables

Table 21.4 Function and source of vitamins

Mineral	Source	Function	Effect of deficiency
Calcium	Milk, cheese, yogurt, tinned fish, fortified bread	Normal function of nerves and muscles. Blood clotting.	In children – poor bone formation. In adults – weak bones and teeth.
Iron	Liver, eggs, green leafy vegetables, bread	Production of healthy red blood cells.	Iron deficiency anaemia
Magnesium	Milk, bread, cereal products, potatoes	Essential constituent of all cells, necessary for the functioning of some enzymes.	Deficiency is rare, resulting from diarrhoea rather than low intakes.
Sodium	Bacon, sausages, meat products. Salt is added to tinned vegetables, butter, cheese, savoury snack foods, breakfast cereals and many foods both by the food industry and at home.	Conduction of nerve impulses. Fluid balance in the tissues.	Unusual in Western society – over-consumption affects blood pressure and fluid balance, contributing to heart disease.
Potassium	Abundant in potatoes, vegetables, fruit (especially bananas)	Present in the fluid within body cells and has a complementary action with sodium in cell functioning.	Deficiency is unlikely as it is found so widely in foods. However, in protein energy malnutrition (kwashiorkor), losses may be large as tissue breakdown and diarrhoea occurs, and heart failure may result unless supplements are given.
Selenium	Meat, fish, cereal products	Necessary for enzymes in red blood cells.	Deficiency is rare, especially in the UK.
Zinc	Meat, wholewheat cereals	Assists energy release and wound healing.	Prolonged shortage of zinc can lead to retarded physical and mental development in adolescents.

Table 21.5 Function and source of minerals

VITAMINS

Vitamins are naturally occurring organic substances that are required for the correct functioning of the body and general good health. Vitamins can be produced synthetically, and will be used by the body in exactly the same manner.

Minerals

Minerals are inorganic substances which are found in the soil. The table above describes some of these minerals.

LIPIDS

Dietary fat is required only in small amounts. One gram of fat provides 9 kcal (37 kj) of energy. About a third of our energy should come from fat.

Fats and oils are made of carbon, hydrogen and oxygen and are insoluble in water. Fats which are liquid at room temperature are called oils (lipids). Lipids carry flavour, odour and fat soluble vitamins (A, D, E, K).

Lipids are esters of glycerol and fatty acids. Most dietary fats are triglycerides; consisting of one molecule of glycerol and three of fatty acids. The simplest triglyceride is one in which all three fatty acids are the same. However, most triglycerides contain two or three different fatty acids and are known as mixed triglycerides.

The body can make all the fatty acids it needs except for two – alpha linolenic acid and linoleic acid. These are essential fatty acids (EFAs) and must be supplied by the diet. EFAs have a vital role in the development of every cell in the body, as well as regulating blood pressure and immune responses.

Each fatty acid is made up of a chain of carbon atoms with hydrogen atoms attached. If the fatty acid has all the hydrogen atoms it can hold, it is said to be saturated. Fats containing a majority of saturated fatty acids are generally animal fats and are usually solid at room temperature.

If some of the hydrogen atoms are missing and have been replaced by a double bond between the carbon atoms, then the fatty acid is unsaturated. Unsaturated fats are generally liquid at room temperature and come from plants.

If there is one double bond, the fatty acid is known as monounsaturated; if there is more than one double bond, the fatty acid is known as polyunsaturated.

The position of the double bond within the polyunsaturated fatty acid structure will determine its type – whether it is an omega 3 (n-3) or an omega 6 (n-6). In polyunsaturated fatty acids the hydrogen atoms can be arranged in two different ways:

• Cis - the usual form found in nature, the two parts of the hydrocarbon chain on the same side of the double bond.

• Trans – seldom occur in nature, but can be found in milk and in ruminant fats.

Trans fatty acids arise when the two parts of the hydrocarbon chain are on opposite sides of the double bond. Trans fatty acids can be produced during the hardening of oils to manufacture margarine, a process known as hydrogenation (the addition of hydrogen across a double bond).

High levels of saturated fats in the diet have been linked with raised blood cholesterol levels, which in turn have been linked to coronary heart disease. Trans fatty acids are treated by the body as saturated fats, so they are also related to raised blood cholesterol levels.

Cholesterol is essential to good health and forms part of the membrane of every cell. Dietary cholesterol is found in egg yolk, offal and shell fish and has little effect on blood cholesterol levels. However, the body metabolises saturated fats into cholesterol and too much cholesterol in the blood can lead to coronary heart disease and artery disease.

There are two types of blood cholesterol:

• HDL – high density lipoprotein

• LDL – low density lipoprotein

HDL is thought to have a protective effect on the heart, but LDL is thought to form deposits on the artery walls, restricting blood flow and leading to angina and heart disease.

Key words

fatty acids – chains of carbon atoms. It is the combination of hydrogen atoms on the carbon chain that determines the type of fat.
essential fatty acids (EFAs) – fatty acids that cannot be made by the body and must be obtained through the diet, but which have a vital role in cell development.
saturated – a fatty acid with all the hydrogen atoms it can hold; generally derived from animal fats and usually solid at room temperature.
monounsaturated – fatty acids with one double bond.
polyunsaturated – fatty acids with more than one double bond.
ester – formed in a reaction between an acid and an alcohol with the elimination of water. Esters are responsible for some of the flavours and odours found in foods, especially fruit, and are important in wines as they add to the bouquet.

Think How could you reduce the amount of salt you eat in your diet?

OTHER DIET-RELATED CONSUMPTION

Dietary fibre

As we have seen above, dietary fibre adds bulk to the diet. The adult diet should contain 12-18g of fibre per day. Children need proportionally less, but pre-school children should be introduced to fibre-rich foods only gradually. Too much fibre can make the diet so bulky that young children become full before they have eaten sufficient food to satisfy their need for essential vitamins, minerals and energy.

Functions of fibre include:

- preventing constipation by adding bulk to the diet

- giving better control of conditions such as diabetes by slowing down the rate at which nutrients are absorbed across the intestine wall

There is also a link between the amount of fibre in the diet and a lower level of cholesterol and other fat in the blood.

Water

Water is essential to life; death will occur within days if water is not available. About two-thirds of the body weight is water, so it is essential that any water lost is replaced. It is recommended that an adult in the UK should drink 1.2 litres of water each day – about 6-8 glasses.

The functions of water are to:

- act as a solvent and transport system for nutrients, enzymes and hormones

- aid the removal of waste products which would be toxic to the system

- act as a lubricant around joints, the digestive tract, eyeballs etc.

- regulate body temperature and dispose of excess body heat (through perspiration) caused by activity.

Think Do you drink enough water? Over a 24-hour period calculate how much water you drink each day; do not include caffeinated drinks (e.g. coffee, tea, cola) as these are diuretics and will make the body produce more urine.

Alcohol

Alcohol is a drug which affects the nervous system; its effects range from mild stimulation to loss of coordination and even death. Alcohol is a depressant and will enhance your current emotional state. For example, if you are upset before you start drinking, at the end of the night your mood will be lower than it was at the beginning of the evening.

In moderation alcohol may have a beneficial effect on health. There is evidence to suggest that having between one and two units of alcohol a day can help protect against coronary heart disease. But this is only thought to work for men when they are aged over 40 and for women after the menopause. It is recommended that women have no more than 14 units of alcohol each week, and men no more than 21 units.

Alcohol is absorbed by the body through the stomach and the small intestine without needing digestion. Once absorbed, alcohol is metabolised in the liver to provide energy. The rate at which this happens depends on the person's age, gender, body weight and liver size, and also on the rate of drinking. 'Chugging' drinks and 'doing shots' results in a large amount of alcohol entering your body in a short amount of time. Your body cannot process alcohol at a fast pace, which results in a higher blood alcohol content (BAC).

On average, one unit of alcohol is metabolised every hour. Generally, symptoms of intoxication appear when blood levels reach about 100mg of alcohol per 100ml blood.

In excess, alcohol is linked with obesity, i.e. too much alcohol can make you put on weight. Alcohol is also a diuretic so you need to have more non-alcoholic drinks that are not diuretics, as it is easy to get dehydrated.

> **Think** One gram of alcohol contains seven calories. So how many calories are there in one pint of lager? What about one shot of vodka?

CASE STUDY: WAYNE AND JADE'S EVENING OUT

Wayne and Jade are on their way home from an evening spent clubbing. Both Wayne and Jade started the evening at home with three shots of vodka. When they arrived at the club Wayne decided to drink lager while Jade drank cocktails with her friends. By the end of the evening, Jade remembered drinking about eight cocktails plus the vodka, whereas Wayne had drunk five bottles of lager followed by three more shots of vodka.

QUESTIONS

1. How much of her daily energy requirement had Jade obtained from alcohol?

2. Wayne had only eaten a burger and chips at lunch time, so what nutrients would be missing from his diet?

Nutritional supplements and substitutes

Nutritional supplements have been considered above (page 102). It is worth remembering that the majority of people do not need to take supplements, as they get all the nutrients they need from a healthy balanced diet.

'Slimming' foods are a multi-million pound business; they are generally divided into meal replacement products and low-energy versions of ordinary products.

Meal replacement products replace one or two meals each day; they come in the form of biscuits or powder which is added to milk. These products contain a variety of nutrients plus ingredients to give a 'full-up' feeling. Carrageenan, methyl cellulose and bran are all used for this purpose. Carrageenan is extracted from red seaweed and acts as a thickening agent by binding water so giving a 'watery' drink a thick, satisfying texture. Meal replacements may be convenient, but they are expensive and do not help establish good eating habits.

Low-energy versions of ordinary foods have the energy-rich substances (fats, sugar) replaced with energy-free substances such as air, water, bran and sugar substitutes.

Many food companies now try to meet healthier eating needs by reducing sugars and fats, and also by reducing the salt content of products.

PHYSIOLOGICAL PRINCIPLES

Aspects of digestion

Physiology related to digestion and nutrition have been covered in Unit 5, so it is only necessary to review the principles at this point.

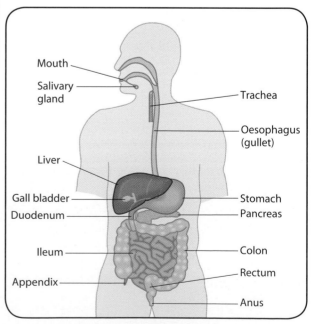

Figure 21.6 The digestive system

The process of digestion follows five steps: ingestion, mastication, digestion, absorption and egestion. The digestive system is lined with layers of tissue: the submucosa contains nerves, blood and lymph vessels, collagen and elastic fibres. The nerves regulate both the gut movements (peristalsis) – muscle contractions which force the food along and mix the food with secretions in a particular region – and the digestive secretions into the lumen of the gut.

Before food enters the mouth, the sight, smell and thought of the food stimulates a conditional reflex that results in the release of saliva into the mouth. You may have already heard of this reflex in psychology – the well-known Pavlov's dog!

Figure 21.7 The sight, smell and thought of food makes us want to eat

Digestion begins in the mouth with the mechanical processes of chewing and grinding of food to produce a larger surface area for the salivary enzymes to work on. When food enters the mouth saliva is released because the stimulation of the taste buds results in an unconditional reflex, whereby impulses are relayed to the brain via sensory neurones and then via motor neurones to the salivary glands.

> *Think* How much saliva do you think you release each day?

The saliva contains mucous, which lubricates the food. Saliva also contains: mineral salts which activate enzymes; lysozyme, which kills some bacteria that are ingested; and amylase, an enzyme that breaks down starch into shorter polysaccharides and then into maltose. The food and saliva mixture is pushed into a ball called a bolus and swallowed into the pharynx.

The muscular tube that leads to the stomach – the oesophagus – is lined with a squamous epithelium lining and mucus glands to lubricate the passageway for food. Peristalsis moves the food on towards the stomach where the circular muscle making up the cardiac sphincter relaxes and opens. With no food present, the sphincter (a muscular ring controlling the passage of food) remains closed so that no acid can enter and burn the oesophagus.

The gall bladder is a small sac attached to the liver which stores bile, a thick greenish fluid produced in the liver. The bile duct squirts alkaline bile into the duodenum. Bile is essential for the breakdown of fat. The pancreas also sends alkaline liquid into the duodenum. The pancreas lies behind the stomach and produces enzymes which help break down carbohydrates, fats and protein. The pancreas also contains the Islets of Langerhan which produce insulin.

Most chemical digestion by enzymes takes place in the duodenum (the small intestine) where the mucosa is folded and the millions of microscopic projections created by this folding of the inner surface of the wall are called villi. Between the villi are intestinal glands (or crypts of Leiberkuhn) which secrete intestinal juice.

The villi and the folds in the cell surface membranes of the epithelial cells lining the villi (microvilli) massively increase the surface area of the duodenum. Most absorption takes place in the small intestine – the villi absorb the nutrients and transport them to the bloodstream where they are circulated to their destination.

Renal function is considered at this point as the kidneys play a part in nutrition by reabsorbing glucose and sometimes reabsorbing water if the body is becoming dehydrated.

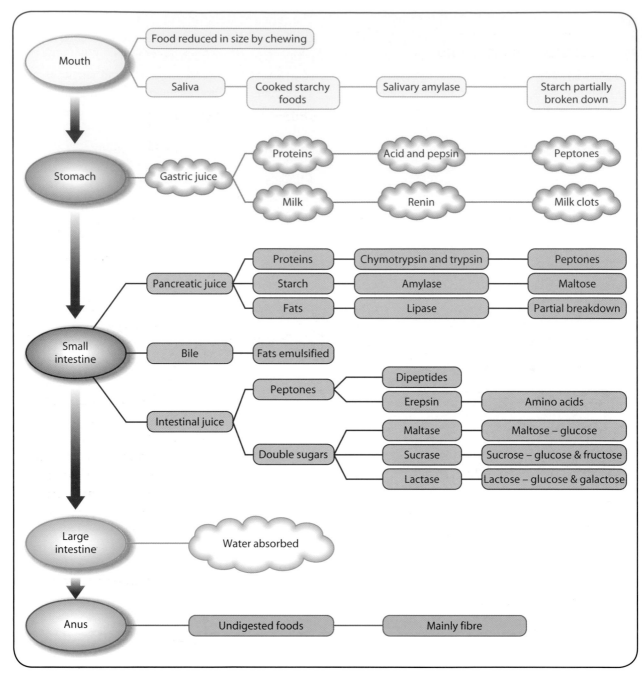

Figure 21.8 Summary of the digestive process

Research tip

The Institute of Food Research focuses on science, food and nutrition-related disciplines. Find out more by going to their website: www.ifr.ac.uk/

EVIDENCE ACTIVITY

P2

P2 requires you to describe the characteristics of nutrients and their benefits to the body. This could be achieved by tracing the path of a meal (for example, a burger with salad, chips and a milkshake) through the digestive process to the cells that will metabolise their chemical components.

21.3 *Understand influences on food intake and nutritional health*

POPULATION GROUPS

Developed world

In the developed world today there is rarely a problem with insufficient energy intake (except during or after war); however, people may suffer from diseases related to their lifestyle – overeating and unbalanced diets pose important questions and dilemmas for health professionals, and for the food industry!

Figure 21.9 Obesity is a growing problem

The causes and solutions appear to be simple – the balance of energy intake and expenditure. However, our society and environment complicate the problem. Malnutrition of the UK population is, quite literally, a growing problem!

The list of factors that influence the food we eat is quite long and at the top will be early experiences; the circumstances of birth and upbringing cannot be changed and it is here that lifestyle habits and choices might be formed. Not only are we in the UK and the rest of the 'developed world' provided with an enormous range of food products, but also we are provided with the knowledge with which to make healthy nutritional choices.

Less-developed world

In the developing world food choices and nutritional education might be limited, however this does not necessarily equate to a poorly nutritionally balanced diet. In many areas of the 'developing world' the diet is based mainly around plant food, which is high in fibre and low in fat. This could be a prime factor in the low rates of bowel cancer seen in these countries.

Unfortunately there are still many millions of people in the world who are starving and are malnourished because of poverty. Protein energy malnutrition (PEM), in the form of kwashiokor and marasmus, is a disorder seen in babies and young children in areas of the world where the population are starving. In areas of starvation or poor nutritional balance, micronutrients (vitamins and minerals) are often lacking. When a daily diet does not contain an adequate level of specific micronutrients the outcome can be serious – children might not reach their full intellectual capacity; growth can be stunted; blindness can occur.

Figure 21.10 Poverty leads to protein energy malnutrition (PEM)

Families and households

Families and households covers a range of people – adult men and women, children and young people, older people, and pregnant and breastfeeding mothers. All these people will have similar basic nutritional requirements; with variations according to age, gender and build, state of health, energy expenditure, cultural or religious dietary requirements, and of course, personal likes or dislikes!

Pregnant and lactating women

Pregnant women require a well-balanced diet containing a good supply of protein, iron and calcium – additional energy is not required until the last three months of pregnancy and then only an extra 200 calories are required daily. Health professionals might advise that folic acid supplements are taken pre- and post-conception to help prevent neural tube defects, such as spina bifida.

Pregnant women are advised to avoid alcohol, as are women who are breastfeeding (lactating). Whilst she is breastfeeding, the mother should have a varied diet (and plenty of liquids) to ensure that she has a sufficient intake of all nutrients required for herself and her baby.

Babies

The best food for babies is their mother's milk – it is designed especially for them. Breast milk requires no preparation; it comes at the correct temperature and will help give the baby some immunity from infectious diseases for the first few months of its life.

The baby should not start weaning until it is about six months old, when breast milk (or formula milk) will be insufficient to meet nutritional needs. Non-wheat cereals, fruit, vegetables and potatoes are suitable first weaning foods. Salt should not be added to any foods for babies. Between 6 and 9 months the amount and variety of foods should be increased to include meat, fish, eggs, all cereals and pulses. From the age of 6 months, infants receiving breast milk as their main drink should be given supplements of vitamins A, C and D.

> **Key words**
> weaning – the introduction of solid food to a baby's diet

Children

From one to two years the child is ready to eat mixed meals with the family. These should include foods for the baby to chew on to help the teeth erupt properly, e.g. pieces of rusk and sticks of carrot. Meals for the toddler should be small enough to prevent overfeeding and should be eaten with the family to help develop social skills. Young children have small stomachs and may not be able to obtain all the energy and nutrients they need if their diet contains too much fibre. Such diets can sometimes reduce the amount of minerals children can absorb, such as calcium and iron.

Healthy eating guidelines are not intended to apply in full to pre-school children (one to five years of age). A diet which is low in fat and high in fibre may not supply enough energy for a young child. However, a healthy family approach to diet and lifestyle will encourage a child to eat more healthily, as food preferences are often established during this early stage of life.

It is important to avoid having too many snacks and sweets, as this will help prevent the child getting fat and having poor dental health, but to encourage an eating pattern based on mini-meals and snacks selected from the four main food groups. At least one food from each of the four main groups should be eaten at each meal. During childhood milk should still form part of the diet as bones and teeth are developing. Whole cows' milk is recommended for children over the age of 12 months as a main drink as it is a rich source of a number of nutrients. Semi-skimmed milk can be introduced after the child is two, as long as the diet provides enough energy. Skimmed milk is not suitable for children under five years of age, as it does not provide enough energy and vitamin A for the growing child.

As children grow rapidly and become more active they have high energy requirements for their size. Children aged four to six years still have small stomachs which cannot cope with large meals, so energy and nutrient-dense foods eaten as part of small, frequent meals may be necessary. Despite this need for a high energy intake, however, the 2002 Health Survey for England found that about one in five boys (21.8 per cent) and more than one in four girls (27.5 per cent) were either overweight or obese. These children should not be expected to lose large amounts of weight. They should be encouraged to remain at a constant weight or increase weight slowly while their height increases, so that they grow to be an acceptable weight for their height.

Teenagers

As teenagers grow and develop rapidly their need for energy and most nutrients is high, however the need differs between boys and girls. Boys need more energy and protein than girls as they have a greater growth spurt which usually begins around the age of 12 years. The growth spurt for girls usually begins around the age of 10 years. Teenagers also require more calcium than adults as they have a rapid increase in bone mass. Boys should aim for 1000mg of calcium each day and girls should aim for 800mg.

> **Think** Where can good sources of calcium be found to ensure these requirements are met?

During adolescence iron requirements increase – especially when girls begin menstruation. The National Diet and Nutrition Survey of young people published in 2000 found that many teenage girls had intakes of iron below the lower reference nutrient intake (LRNI), implying that the numbers of teenage girls who were anaemic could be high.

> **Think** Which foods could help increase the iron intake for teenage girls? Remember that some foods are naturally high in iron and others are required by law to be fortified.

Amongst teenagers, especially girls, there is an increased tendency to control weight by unsuitable methods such as smoking or using very low calorie diets. These methods of weight loss can lead to serious health problems. It is often during the teenage years that anorexia nervosa or bulimia develops. These psychological illnesses are expressed by excessive concern about body shape or weight. Eating disorders are typically seen in girls and young women and less commonly in teenage boys.

In teenage girls (and women), anorexia may lead to menstrual abnormalities, including cessation of periods, which may have a serious effect on bone health. Bone loss is mainly due to low levels of estrogen. Therefore, if anorexia occurs before the menstrual cycle is fully established and bone formation has peaked, then it is more likely to cause long-term problems, including the risk of fragile and broken bones. A prolonged eating disorder can lead to permanent bone loss.

Bulimia sufferers also have an obsession with body weight and shape; they may use large quantities of laxatives, slimming pills or excessive exercise to try to control their weight. Many bulimics have poor dental health because they vomit so much and vomit is acidic and can erode teeth.

Key words

anorexia nervosa – a wasting disease often brought on by psychological distress; the causes are complex. Weight is lost through excessive dieting and the person with anorexia will consider themselves to be too fat even when their BMI is well below normal limits. The huge amount of weight lost can be life-threatening.
bulimia – is related to anorexia but does not always lead to life-threatening weight loss. Bingeing and purging are symptomatic of this disorder and put severe stresses on the physiology of the body.

Adults

The diet and nutritional requirements of adults do not vary much between the ages of 19 and 50 but energy requirements depend very much on age, gender and activity levels. Requirements for energy usually start to decrease after the age of 50 as activity levels fall. Adults should aim for a body weight that is appropriate for their height.

CASE STUDY: SAM'S DIET

Sam is a 40-year old office worker. He drives to work each day and takes no exercise. Sam's diet is high in processed foods – he enjoys doughnuts, beer and very large meals that are high in fats and sugar. He knows that he is overweight and is probably unhealthy, but struggles to come to terms with the problem.

QUESTIONS

1. What might influence Sam's choice of diet?

2. How could Sam's diet be changed in line with current healthy eating guidelines?

3. How might Sam be encouraged to maintain the change in diet?

Older people

The elderly in the population are a very mixed group; the 'young old' (those under 75 years), and the 'old' old. They also have different levels of health and fitness, and nutritional requirements will change with increasing age; energy needs will fall as lean body tissue decreases and the BMR falls. Older people tend to be less active but it is important that they do take exercise. Older people with poor dental health tend to eat a more restricted range of food in the belief that chewing hard or crunchy foods will be difficult. The diets of older people might also be restricted in order to control disorders such as diabetes, heart disease, osteoporosis or rheumatoid arthritis, all of which are common in the elderly.

Further influences on the diet of the elderly include mobility and physical ability to shop, prepare and cook meals; access to shops, and financial circumstances.

NUTRITIONAL HEALTH

BMI

On page 105 above we looked at the body mass index (BMI). You will remember that the BMI assumes there is not a single weight for a person of a specific height, but there is a weight range within which a person will have good health.
(BMI = weight (kg) divided by height $(m)^2$.) In Britain, 41 per cent of men and 33 per cent of women are overweight (BMI of 25 or more). Obesity is a growing problem, with 25 per cent of men and 20 per cent of women being obese (BMI over 30).

Think There are some groups of people whose BMI would put them in the overweight or obese categories despite them being extremely fit and healthy. Which groups of people would fit into these categories, and why?

Specific nutrient needs

You will remember that Reference Nutrient Intakes (RNIs – see page 106) are the amount of a nutrient that is enough for almost every individual, even someone who has high needs for the nutrient. However, there are some factors that affect food intake and have specific nutrient requirements. These include certain diseases or disorders, such as diabetes, lactose intolerance, loss of gastro-intestinal function and diet-related disease.

Diabetes is not a single disease but a group of disorders, but at this point we need only to concern ourselves with two: Type 1 (insulin-dependent diabetes) and Type 2 (maturity-onset diabetes). Diabetes develops when the body cannot metabolise glucose efficiently, either because there is no or insufficient insulin produced, or the insulin produced is ineffective.

Key words

insulin – a hormone produced by the pancreas that controls the level of glucose in the blood (blood sugar). Insulin removes glucose from the blood and helps it to enter the cells. Insulin must work efficiently as both high (hyperglycaemia) and low levels (hypoglycaemia) of blood sugar are harmful.

Type 1 diabetes often occurs in childhood and usually in people under the age of 40. It is important that the body's blood glucose is maintained in order to prevent symptoms and the long-term consequences of high blood-sugar. Type 1 diabetes is managed by injections of insulin and a healthy diet.

Type 2 diabetes (non-insulin dependent) usually develops in middle-aged people (over 40 years) but is being seen in younger adults. The insulin produced by the body is either insufficient or does not work properly. This type of diabetes can be managed by diet and exercise alone, or in combination with tablets. Type 2 diabetes is increasing dramatically in the UK and is thought to be linked to being overweight and obese. A diet high in fat (especially saturated fat) and low in fibre is a significant factor in the onset of type 2 diabetes.

People with diabetes are recommended to have the same healthy diet that is recommended for all people; i.e. a balanced diet based on starchy foods and plenty of fruit and vegetables, low in fat, salt and sugar. A small amount of sugar and sugar-containing foods can be eaten, preferably as part of a healthy meal. Special diabetic cakes, biscuits or pastries are of no particular benefit and they may contain a lot of fat.

Lactose intolerance is a disorder which occurs in humans who cannot synthesise the enzyme lactase which is needed to break down lactose. Those who are lactose intolerant suffer from severe stomach cramps, flatulence, diarrhoea and vomiting if they drink milk. Soya milk and lactose-reduced milk can be found in supermarkets and be used to replace cow's milk. Some people are able to tolerate moderate amounts of milk by taking it with meals or replacing fresh dairy products with fermented dairy products. Live yogurts are usually better tolerated as the live yogurt bacteria can help lactose digestion in the colon. Some cheeses, such as Edam, Emmental and Parmesan contain little or no lactose. However, lactose is widely used as an ingredient in many ready-made meals and other food products so food labels should be checked carefully.

Food allergies, sensitivities and intolerances are terms which are often confused. Food allergy and food intolerance are both types of food sensitivity. Food allergies affect relatively few people – estimated to be only 1.4 per cent of the UK population, but the reaction can be quite severe. Food allergies involve the immune system and most commonly affect young children; although they may outgrow allergies to milk or eggs before they go to school, they are less likely to outgrow an allergy to peanuts or fish.

Food intolerance does not involve the immune system and is not usually life-threatening. However, if food to which someone is intolerant is eaten it could make them feel ill or affect their long-term health.

INFLUENCES

Throughout this unit we have identified influences on food intake and nutritional health. Personal taste, lifestyle, habit and economic factors all play a large part in our choices of meals. Who we eat our meals with and when we eat will impact on the choice of food. Eating is often a social activity to be enjoyed with partners, in small family meals and at large community gatherings. The choice of food for a meal might be influenced by religious or cultural beliefs.

> **Think** When did you last eat a snack? What influenced your choice of food?

Reasons for our choice of food can include any or all of the following reasons:

- psychological reasons – eating for comfort, or food given as a reward

- social customs – parties, entertaining, business obligations

- budget and food availability

- pressure of advertising - new trends in diet

- lifestyle, time available and skill of the cook

- awareness of healthy eating guidelines and food health education

- desire to lose or gain weight

- sensory perception – appearance, aroma, texture, 'mouth feel', personal likes and dislikes

- ethical and cultural reasons – e.g. being vegetarian or vegan

- physiological factors – state of health

- peer group pressure.

The perceived role of food is what we expect when we buy the product – because it is healthy, luxurious, cheap, traditional, convenient, versatile etc. Food manufacturers and the media encourage consumers to dwell on one aspect of a food. We listen to the information that we want to hear and concentrate on the image that we want the food to fulfil.

> **Think** Next time you watch television make a note of all the food and drink advertisements. What are the main nutritional contents of the products advertised?

Legislation, regulations and policies

The Children Act 2004 provides the legal underpinning for Every Child Matters, which aims to improve the well-being of children. The Act provides a legislative spine for the wider strategy for improving children's lives. This covers the universal services which every child accesses, and more targeted services for those with additional needs.

> ### Research tip
>
> Find out more about the Children Act 2004 by going to www.opsi.gov.uk/ acts/acts2004/20040031.htm .This site provides a summary of the Act and links to related sites.

The UK has seen dramatic increases in childhood obesity in recent years. The government responded to the rise in obesity with a public service agreement (PSA) target, which it published in 2004. This target is jointly owned by the Department of Health (DH), the Department for Children, Schools and Families (DCSF), and the Department for Culture, Media and Sport.

The Food in Schools (FiS) programme is a joint venture between the Department for Children, Schools and Families and the Department of Health. A range of nutrition-related activities and projects is being developed as part of the programme, to complement and add value to existing healthier food initiatives in schools. The FiS Programme has strong links to the overall '5 a day' programme, including the National School Fruit Scheme and other Department of Health diet and nutrition priorities set out in the NHS Plan.

The Department of Health-led strand of the FiS Programme comprises eight pilot projects which follow the child through the school day. It complements but is outside the formal curriculum. The projects are healthier breakfast clubs, tuck shops, vending machines, lunch boxes and cookery clubs as well as water provision, growing clubs and the dining room environment.

The School Fruit and Vegetable Scheme is part of the 5 a day programme to increase fruit and vegetable consumption. All 4- to 6-year old children in LEA-maintained infant, primary and special schools are entitled to a free piece of fruit or vegetable each school day.

> ### Research tip
>
> Department of Health policy and guidance for the school fruit and vegetable scheme can be found at www.dh.gov.uk/en/PolicyAndGuidance/ HealthAndSocialCareTopics/FiveADay/ FiveADayGeneralInformation/DH_ 4002149

Nutrition Standards for School Lunches and other School Food 2006

The School Meals Review Panel (SMRP) endorsed two sets of standards for school lunches:

a. Food-based, which will define the types of food that children and young people should be offered in a school lunch and their frequency; and

b. Nutrient-based, which will set out the proportion of nutrients that children and young people should receive from a school lunch.

The standards that are being introduced to primary, secondary and special schools will be in place by 2009, and include the following:

a. no confectionery will be sold in schools;

b. no bagged savoury snacks other than nuts and seeds (without added salt or sugar) will be sold in schools;

c. a variety of fruit and vegetables should be available in all school food outlets. This could include fresh, dried, frozen, canned or juiced varieties;

d. children and young people must have easy access at all times to free, fresh drinking water in schools (in guidance, it will be clear that it would be preferable for this drinking water to be chilled; and for it to be located so that children do not have to depend on going to the lavatory to access it);

e. the only other drinks available will be:

   i) water (still or sparkling);

   ii) milk (skimmed or semi-skimmed);

   iii) pure fruit juices;

   iv) yoghurt and milk drinks (with less than 5% added sugar);

   v) drinks made from combinations of (i) to (iv) above;

   vi) low calorie hot chocolate;

   vii) tea; and

   viii) coffee.

Artificial sweeteners should be used only in yoghurt and milk drinks, or combinations containing yoghurt or milk.

Research tip

Find out more about Nutrition Standards for School Lunches and other School Food 2006. This is the direct link to the pdf document www.cnguk.org/dnlds/Nutritional%20Standards%20for%20School%20Lunches%20and%20other%20School%20Food.pdf .

Every Child Matters: Change for Children is a new approach to the well-being of children and young people from birth to age 19. The government's aim is for every child, whatever their background or their circumstances, to have the support they need to:

- be healthy

- stay safe

- enjoy and achieve

- make a positive contribution

- achieve economic well-being.

Research tip

Visit the home site for Every Child Matters with links to health, welfare and care: www.everychildmatters.gov.uk/.

RISKS TO HEALTH

In this section we have seen how food intake can affect the health of the individual. One of the major causes of death in the UK is cardiovascular disease (CVD); this includes both heart disease and stroke. CVD is the primary cause of premature death in the UK, and is a major cause of ill-health. Eating a healthy diet and keeping physically active, accompanied by not smoking, and drinking moderate amounts of alcohol, can all help reduce the risk of cardiovascular disease.

The most practical food-related advice to reduce the risk of cardiovascular disease is to follow the healthy eating guidelines: reduce salt intake; reduce fat, especially saturates; eat at least five portions of fruit and vegetables each day and at least two portions of fish each week, one of which should be oil-rich.

The risks to health from obesity have also been outlined. People who are obese have a higher risk of diabetes, heart disease, stroke and different types of cancer.

Research tip

The Cancer Research UK website provides a wealth of information and activities linked to food and health. Go to http://info.cancerresearchuk.org/healthyliving/dietandhealthyeating/

Alcohol-related disease

Alcohol is regarded as a food as it can be metabolised by the body to provide energy. Alcohol is quite high in energy, providing 7kcal per gram (carbohydrates & protein = 4kcal per gram; fat = 9 kcal per gram), so excessive alcohol will lead to weight increase if physical activity does not use the energy.

It has been suggested that drinking moderate amounts of alcohol can help protect against coronary heart disease; however, excessive intake of alcohol has a damaging effect on health including cirrhosis of the liver. It has also been linked to cancers of the mouth and liver in men and women, and to breast cancer in women. The Department of Health recommends that men should not consume more than 3-4 units of alcohol per day and women not more than 2-3 units; it also recommends that two days each week are alcohol-free. A unit of alcohol is half a pint of beer (although strong lagers and beers contain more), a small glass of wine or a single measure of spirits.

Alcohol can be absorbed by the body without being digested. Absorption takes place through the stomach walls and in the small intestine and will take from thirty minutes to two hours, depending on the concentration of alcohol, the amount taken and the amount and time of food consumption. Once food is absorbed it is distributed via the bloodstream throughout the body. Alcohol is removed from the bloodstream slowly so the effects of alcohol and the blood alcohol level will remain high for a considerable period of time.

Alcohol passes easily from the bloodstream to the brain and will cause intoxicating effects on the nervous system. The sedative effect of alcohol causes slowing of thought processes and reflexes, and high doses can lead to coma and death. The drinker will pass through stages of staggering and slurred speech, lack of judgement and a sense of bravado, and loss of emotional control.

The later stages of stupor, respiratory depression and death often occur after the drinker has passed out, and he or she may be found dead in bed. Death can also be caused by vomiting as excess alcohol triggers the vomiting centre in the body – if vomiting occurs while the drinker is asleep they have a high risk of choking or drowning in their own vomit.

> **Think** Are any of the news items in your local newspaper related to the intake of alcohol?

EVIDENCE ACTIVITY

P3 – M2 – D1

P3 requires you to identify the different factors that influence dietary intake for different population groups.

M2 requires you to explain the factors affecting the nutritional health and well-being of different groups of individuals.

D1 requires you to evaluate the relative importance of different factors affecting the nutritional health and well-being of two different groups of individuals.

For **P3** and **M2** case studies could be used to identify the influences on dietary intake, and to discuss the potential health/ill-health of those people, e.g. families from different cultures or of different composition (parents and children/student household/unemployed single adult).

For **D1**, two groups of individuals should be selected and the importance of the factors that affect their health and well-being should be compared and contrasted, e.g. teenage girls, gymnasts, rugby players, pregnant women, labourers etc.

21.4 *Be able to use dietary information from an individual to make recommendations to improve nutritional health*

RECORD OF FOOD INTAKE

In order to give advice on dietary changes it is first necessary to know what and how much is eaten over a period of time. There are several methods available for collecting information on food intake and eating habits including: 24-hour recall; daily food record; weighed food intake.

The 24-hour recall method is quick and easy to use. The interviewer collects information on what the client eats. This method relies entirely on an accurate memory so might not be completely reliable.

The daily food record gives a good overall guide to the types and quantities of food and drink consumed. At least three days' intake should be recorded; one of these days should be a weekend day to take into account the different food patterns present at a weekend. A seven-day record would give a far more detailed picture and is recommended.

If the diet of an athlete or sports person is being analysed it would be advisable to record rest and competition days as well as training days.

A food analysis diary should include details of food relevant to the analysis, e.g. whether it is cooked, raw, with/without skin, fried, steamed; all meals, snacks, drinks (including alcoholic drinks and mixers), confectionery and supplements.

A weighed food record of intake gives a useful account of the types and frequency of foods eaten and an estimation of quantity. According to this method the individual foods are weighed before consumption, which improves the accuracy of the analysis. However, this method is very time consuming and intrusive and could distort the pattern of foods consumed as the individual may be more selective by selecting foods that are easy to weigh.

> **Think** Can you list everything that you have eaten and drunk in the last 24 hours?

	Monday	Tuesday	Wednesday	Thursday	Friday	Saturday	Sunday
Breakfast							
Morning snacks							
Lunch							
Afternoon snacks							
Dinner							
Evening snack							

Figure 21.11 Food record diary

SOURCES OF NUTRITIONAL INFORMATION

Once the diet diary is complete, the food can be analysed for nutritional values. There are software computer programmes that will analyse the data, but there are also printed tables e.g. *Manual of Nutrition* (10th edition), MAFF.

QUANTITATIVE ANALYSIS

The analysis should include: energy, protein, fat, iron, vitamin C, fibre and the proportion of energy from fat. Much of this information can be found on food labels, but some will be found in the food tables.

LIFESTYLE NEEDS

To make sense of the data you have collected and analysed you will need to evaluate your findings. Your food record should enable you to examine normal eating patterns, and may show how your lifestyle dictates what you eat, when, where and why.

You might be able to find the answers to the following questions:

- Is there room for improvement, or is your diet better than you thought?

  - Are some days better than others?

  - Do you feel more tired towards the end of the week?

  - Which foods dominate your diet?

  - Which foods are eaten only occasionally?

  - Is there enough variety in your diet?

- Does your diet meet your nutritional requirements? Is this true for all of the nutrients?

- What constraints ate placed on your lifestyle that might prevent you making changes to your diet?

- Do you drink enough water?

Look back at page 105, where you should have estimated your BMI at the number of kilocalories you require each day. By looking at the RNI tables you should find out your requirements for specific nutrients.

With these figures and your analysis you are in a position to give an in-depth evaluation of the diet diary and to make recommendations that will improve your health – or the health of a chosen individual.

Research tip

The Health Canada database contains some food products that can be purchased in the UK. Go to www. hc-sc.gc.ca/fn-an/nutrition/fiche-nutri-data/nutrient_value-valeurs_nutritives_e.html#obtain . You could also look at the USDA (US Department of Agriculture) Agricultural Research Service 2007, USDA National Nutrient Database for Standard Reference, Release 20, Nutrient Data Laboratory Home Page. This is a comprehensive database but does not contain all of the UK food products: www.ars.usda.gov/ba/bhnrc/ndl .

EVIDENCE ACTIVITY

P4 – P5 – M3 – D2

P4 requires you to carry out a quantitative nutrient analysis of the diet of one individual.

To meet the requirements of the assessment criteria it might be easiest to analyse your own dietary intake; however any individual (real or fictional) can be selected, e.g. an obese person, a vegan or a person with a diet-related disorder.

A food diary should be kept for a period of time – long enough to include opportunity for different food events to occur, e.g. food eaten at weekends is often different from that eaten during the week, so the diary should include a weekend. The quantitative analysis will include the amount of specific nutrients eaten.

For **P5**, you are required to prepare a nutritional plan for the chosen individual.

The nutritional plan for the chosen individual should include acceptable changes. It should also identify the nutrients found in the foods, and quantities of liquids.

M3 requires you to explain how the nutritional plan will meet the needs of the chosen individual.

Explanation of the plan will indicate the importance of the nutrients for the chosen individual, and will point out any dietary deficiencies.

For **D2**, you should evaluate how the nutritional plan will improve the health of the chosen individual.

The evaluation of the plan continues from M3 by stating the improvements in health that might occur over a period of time.

Research Methodology for Health and Social Care

unit 22

This unit is about the ways in which research is carried out in health and social care. Research is used in order to gather the evidence on which much of the practice of health and social care is based. This is known as 'evidence-based practice' and it is important in demonstrating the effectiveness (or otherwise) of the work undertaken in healthcare settings.

The unit looks at the reasons for conducting research along with the main principles of research methodology. Some of the ethical issues which need to be considered will also be addressed.

The knowledge that is gained by studying this unit will enable you to undertake a small-scale research project of your own. It will help you plan, carry out and evaluate a project on a topic of your own choosing. This will form the major part of the assessment for this unit.

Learning outcomes

By the end of this unit, you will:

22.1 Understand the purpose and role of research within health and social care   page137

22.2 Understand the research methodologies relevant to health and social care   page 141

22.3 Be able to identify a suitable topic and produce a plan for a research proposal   page 149

22.4 Be able to conduct the research and present the findings   page 156

22.5 Be able to evaluate the research project   page 163

22.6 Understand the implications of and ethical issues related to using research in health and social care   page 165

So you want to be a...

Scientific laboratory technician

My name Ayesha Brown
Age 19
Income £17,000

Attention to detail and keeping accurate records are very important in this job.

What do you do?

I work as a technician in an NHS laboratory. My role is to do various scientific procedures which will allow the medical scientists to carry out the more complex analysis of samples that are sent to us. I also undertake some simple routine tests and report on them. I work as part of a team which I really enjoy. We all know that we are doing important work that can have a major impact on the care and treatment of patients.

What are your responsibilities?

Health and safety is of paramount importance in a laboratory so I need to take great care to follow all the correct procedures, as laid down in our guidelines. I am responsible for preparing specimens and samples. I collect the data from tests and need to make sure that it is accurate and reliable. I check the equipment regularly and ensure that it is kept clean and in good working order. I am also responsible for checking the stock and reordering if necessary.

How did you get your job?

At college I asked if I could do my work experience in a laboratory as I have always been interested in science. I was lucky enough to be given two weeks at my local hospital in their haematology lab. As I was coming to the end of my course I contacted the hospital trust again and was fortunate that they had some vacancies for laboratory technicians. The fact that I had had work experience certainly worked in my favour when I applied.

What training did you get?

The majority of training is on the job. There are also in-house courses on first aid, time management and health and safety. The team has been very good in ensuring that I develop all the skills I need and I will have the opportunity to take NVQ qualifications in the future.

What are the hours like?

The hours are mainly nine to five although occasionally there is some on-call work.

What skills do you need

You need to be practical and able to use technical equipment accurately. It is important to be thorough and keep accurate records – someone's life might depend on it! As we work as a team it is important to get on well with other people. An interest in science and previous laboratory experience is also useful.

> "Someone's life may depend on my doing my job properly."

Grading criteria

The table below shows what you need to do to gain a pass, merit or distinction in this part of the qualification. Make sure you refer back to it when you are completing work so that you can judge whether you are meeting the criteria and what you need to do to fill in gaps in your knowledge or experience.

In this unit there are six evidence activities to give you an opportunity to demonstrate your achievement of the grading criteria:

page 140	P1	page 162	P4, P5, M2, D1
page 148	P2	page 164	P6, M3, D2
page 155	P3, M1	page 167	P7, M4

To achieve a pass grade the evidence must show that the learner is able to...	To achieve a merit grade the evidence must show that, in addition to the pass criteria, the learner is able to...	To achieve a distinction grade the evidence must show that, in addition to the pass and merit criteria, the learner is able to...
P1 Explain the purpose and role of research for the health and social care sectors	**M1** Justify the choice of topic and hypothesis	**D1** Discuss how the methodology of the research project could be altered to reduce bias and error
P2 Describe the key elements of research methodologies	**M2** Review the research methods chosen in relation to the results obtained, any sources of bias or error and ethical considerations	**D2** Analyse the purpose and role of research in the sectors, drawing on the piece of research undertaken.
P3 Identify a research topic and carry out a literature search	**M3** Analyse the findings of the research in relation to the original hypothesis	
P4 Carry out the primary research and collect and record appropriate data	**M4** Discuss the possible implications that the research results may have on current practice.	
P5 Present and report findings in a relevant format, identifying sources of bias or error		
P6 Discuss the findings of the research in relation to the original hypothesis		
P7 Outline any possible improvements to the research, referring to any relevant implications and ethical issues.		

22.1 *Understand the purpose and role of research within health and social care*

WHAT IS RESEARCH?

Research describes the process of systematic investigation that is used to establish facts. It involves thorough inquiry in order to determine the best way of doing something. It is used in many different settings and can be on a large or small scale. For example, the government might commission very large scale research activities to determine the views of the public on whether Britain should have the euro; or a class in a school could find out what is the most popular school dinner in their group!

It is expected that properly conducted research should provide accurate information which can be confidently used as the basis for future plans. The foreword to the document 'Research Governance Framework for Health and Social Care' published in 2005 states:

'The government is committed to enhancing the contribution of research to health and social care. Research is essential to the successful promotion and protection of health and well-being, and also to modern, effective health and social care services.'

Research tip

Find out more about the Research Governance Framework for Health and Social Care by going to http://www.dh.gov.uk/en/ Publicationsandstatistics/Publications/ PublicationsPolicyAndGuidance/DH_ 4108962

PURPOSE

There are several reasons why research is undertaken. In order to plan any health provision it is important to know what the needs are. This means finding out what individuals, groups or communities already have or do not have. It will also show who might have the greatest need and therefore should be a priority. The results of research can be checked against certain norms to see if everybody is receiving health care at the accepted standards. Comparisons can be made between similar client groups which can lead to the identification of a need. For example, all women over 50 years old are entitled to free breast screening. In order to meet this target it will be necessary to know the number of women in any area who are entitled to this service. Therefore one type of research is demographic research. Demographic data is collected which can be used to identify the needs of the population.

Key words

demographic – to do with the population, including statistics of births, deaths, disease

CASE STUDY: SEATOWN

Seatown is a town near the south coast of England. It used to be a popular tourist attraction and has many hotels. However, since many people now choose to go on holiday abroad the hotels have been converted into flats and bed and breakfast accommodation. There is a high number of single parent families and 10 per cent of the adult population is unemployed. Many of the single mothers are teenagers and there is an increasing proportion of children under 5 years old.

QUESTION

How do the demographic characteristics of Seatown help to identify the health care needs of the local population?

Another way of identifying the needs of a population is by epidemiological research. This studies the patterns of disease within a population. You will find out more about epidemiology in Units 7 and 12. Studies of who gets ill, why they get ill and how they should be treated will show who needs to be treated and how. For example, in 2004 there was a sudden increase in the numbers of young people and children contracting mumps. Some cases were in those born before the MMR (Mumps, Measles and Rubella) vaccine became routine in 1988. Others were children who had not been vaccinated – possibly due to fears about the safety of the vaccine.

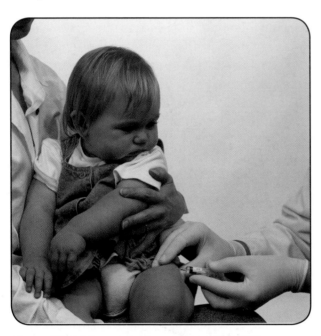

Figure 22.1 Young children receiving MMR vaccination

Research into the lifestyles and behaviours of individuals can indicate where there are unmet or possibly future needs. For example, the number of people who are smokers has a direct impact on the health of a population and so the need for health interventions can be identified.

Research helps to increase knowledge and understanding. Some research will be highly scientific and at the edge of current knowledge. For example, the research on stem cells from human embryos is hoped to lead to successful treatments for degenerative diseases, such as Parkinson's and Alzheimer's, or for those paralysed by spinal

CASE STUDY: SIR RICHARD DOLL'S RESEARCH

Sir Richard Doll was one of the first people to link smoking to health problems. In 1950 he studied a group of lung cancer patients and discovered that the one factor which they all had in common was smoking tobacco. He concluded (in the *British Medical Journal* in 1950) that:

'The risk of developing the disease increases in proportion to the amount smoked. It may be 50 times as great among those who smoke 25 or more cigarettes a day as among non-smokers.'

QUESTIONS

1. How has the research of Sir Richard Doll contributed to the knowledge about cancer?

2. What actions have been taken based on Sir Richard Doll's research?

injuries. Research can take place at every level. Small-scale research projects, as well as large-scale projects, can make a difference to the knowledge and understanding of healthcare practice. An individual's knowledge can be furthered by undertaking research. You have already undertaken research in studying for much of your health and social care qualification. The same rules apply in that research should be accurate, appropriate and have a useful application.

Research may be carried out to see if there are any gaps in the provision of healthcare. It may be part of a checking procedure, to see whether everybody has received the care they are entitled to, or whether care has been given at an appropriate standard. It may also identify where healthcare is not provided or if it is inappropriate to the needs of the client group.

CASE STUDY: SPEAKUP!

In 2005 the Mental Health Foundation launched a website that gave young people an opportunity to say what they thought of mental health services for those aged between 16 and 25 years old. Called SpeakUp!, it was organised in response to findings by the charity which indicated that there was a gap in the provision of care specifically for adolescents and young adults. This led to many of them feeling alienated, as most services were either for children or adults.

QUESTION

How might the gaps in mental health provision for adolescents and young adults have been identified?

Planning of provision relies heavily on knowing what the needs are – or will be – for a population. For example, demographic data can be used to show how many older people there are likely to be in a neighbourhood so health authorities can plan the care required by that age group. The number of new babies born in an area will be used for the planning of maternity services, health visiting, nurseries, schools and other facilities. Research can help in providing such information.

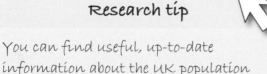

Research tip

You can find useful, up-to-date information about the UK population (national and local) from www.statistics.gov.uk.

ROLE

We have already seen some examples of the role of research in health and social care. The principle that is now widely held in health and social care is that practice should be 'evidence based'. It was not always like this. Certain practices used to be followed because 'that's the way we have always done things'. For example, patients used to be kept in bed for long periods after even minor operations. However, research showed that this was not always beneficial and nursing practice has now changed to encourage mobilisation (moving around) as early as possible. This is based on a large amount of research which showed that a number of complications were avoided by such practices. Organisations such as NICE (National Institute for Health and Clinical Excellence) provide national guidelines on promoting good health and preventing and treating ill health. The information is based on careful assessment of the evidence collected through research.

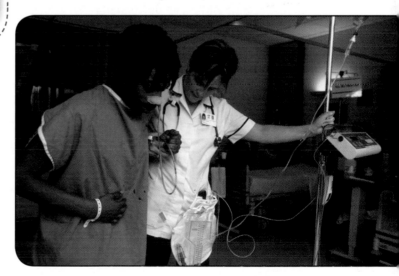

Figure 22.2 Early mobilisation of post-operative patients is based on research

As well as guiding practice, research can be used to improve practice. This may happen through making comparisons between different ways of doing things. Alternatively, it may be done through evaluations of certain practices to see whether there is improvement. For example, teachers working with young children want to ensure that their teaching practices are up to date. In order to do this they may research new methods of teaching and activities.

Reflection means thinking things over and considering whether things have gone well or badly or whether they could have been improved. Research can help this process by systematically reviewing the processes of a healthcare practice. It forms part of the learning cycle, allowing people to consider the factors that have influenced a certain situation. (See Kolb's learning cycle in Unit 44 on page xxx.) The outcomes of this reflection may lead to changes in behaviour or actions.

The role of research in monitoring progress is essential. Within research programmes it is essential to set up appropriate ways of monitoring or evaluating the impact of healthcare practices. For example, in 1999, children began to be immunised against Meningitis C. Before the introduction of the vaccine, Group C disease accounted for 40 per cent of cases. It is now the cause of less than 10 per cent. This reduction is evidenced through the ongoing monitoring research associated with meningitis and the immunisation programme by the NHS.

From time to time new and challenging issues arise which may require research. For example, the London Tube bombings of July 2005 led to a review of the work of the emergency services on that day and recommendations of changes to be made for the future when dealing with major incidents.

EVIDENCE ACTIVITY

For **P1**, you need to explain the purpose and role of research in health and social care.

Every day new research is published. Look in a health journal or a broadsheet newspaper and identify a piece of research linked with health or social care. What has been its role or purpose? Use the examples that you have identified to illustrate your explanation.

22.2 *Understand the research methodologies relevant to health and social care*

TYPES OF RESEARCH

There are different ways in which evidence may be collected. The most important differentiations are between qualitative and quantitative data and primary and secondary research. Each type can be used exclusively or in combination. The data can be used to draw conclusions and make evidence-based decisions.

> ### Key words
>
> qualitative – information that is collected which reflects opinions, attitudes or feelings
> quantitative – method of research which use data that is numerical or anything that measurable
> primary research – any method of obtaining original information that did not exist before from a source, e.g. by interviewing an individual
> secondary research – obtaining information from someone else's research

Quantitative data

Quantitative data can be analysed and presented using numbers. The results can therefore be displayed using graphs, pie charts, tables or other forms of display. This method is associated with a scientific approach. Sometimes it involves very large numbers of people. The chart below illustrates quantitative data.

Qualitative data

Qualitative data cannot be put into a numerical form. It involves trying to reflect the reasons that govern behaviour. The researcher tries to capture the views of the participants. This can be done by presenting extracts from interviews or a summary of what was said. Some analysis can be made by trying to categorise some of the replies to see if there is a common theme. Qualitative data is therefore not expressed in numbers or reported using statistical methods.

Primary research

Primary research is research that is carried out by the researcher themselves. Any data that is collected is known as primary data. It can be quantitative or qualitative. The researcher may use surveys, questionnaires, interviews, observation or experiments.

Secondary research

Secondary research uses information from other sources. It involves finding and analysing reports of research already carried out by others. It can be a very useful starting point when you want to find out what is already known about a topic. From there you can decide whether to repeat the work already carried out to see if there have been any changes or to follow a different line of enquiry. Secondary sources are also very important when using data such as government or official statistics. This type of information comes from very large-scale databases and provides a good point of comparison to some primary research.

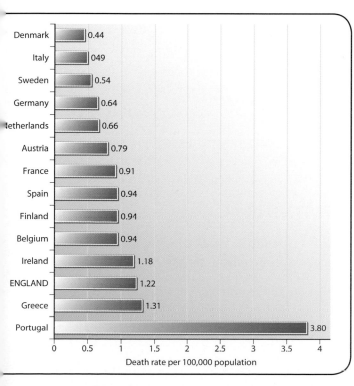

Figure 22.3 An example of quantitative data about child pedestrian deaths
Source: Saving Lives: Our Healthier Nation

PRIMARY SOURCES

Primary sources of research include questionnaires, interviews, scientific experiments and observation.

Questionnaires

Questionnaires can be used in different ways. Self-completion questionnaires ask the recipient or respondent to complete the questionnaire on their own. This may be done in the form of a postal questionnaire. On some occasions the interviewer might ask the questions from the questionnaire and complete the form for the respondent.

The questionnaire usually consists of a number of closed questions. These are questions requiring a 'yes' or 'no' answer. These answers can then be easily quantified. Sometimes the questions may be 'open' which allows respondents to elaborate or put down their own views.

There are several advantages and disadvantages to using questionnaires (see Table 22.1). These must be considered before deciding whether to use them as a method of research.

> **Think** Have you ever been asked to complete a questionnaire? If so, was it easy to answer the questions? If it wasn't, what made it difficult to answer them?

Questionnaires need to be carefully designed in order to get the required data. If possible they should be pre-tested or 'piloted' first. This can be done using a group of individuals who will not necessarily be part of the main group to be surveyed. The results from the pilot study allow adjustments to be made if there are any problems in the structure or wording of the questionnaire.

These are some questions which you should ask before starting to design your own questionnaire.

- What information is required and from whom?

- How is the information to be collected? Will the questionnaire be completed by the participant on their own or by interview?

- How many people will there be in the sample?

- When will the survey take place?

- Does the questionnaire need piloting or pre-testing?

- How will the data be analysed and reported?

CASE STUDY: RESEARCH INTO SMOKING

Jacquie is studying health and social care at college. She is interested to know about the smoking habits of her classmates. She undertakes a survey of the class to see how many of them smoke, how long they have been smoking for and whether any of them have tried to give up. Jacquie also explored the attitudes of those who smoked most heavily and those who have never smoked. She used the Department of Health website to look up the main effects of smoking on health. She also wants to know how the numbers in her class compare with the national averages of young people smoking.

QUESTIONS

1. What quantitative, qualitative, primary and secondary research did Jacquie use?

2. What are the reasons for your answer?

Advantages	Disadvantages
Information collected from a large sample	Low response rate
Can be relatively cheap	Cannot be sure right person completed form
Individuals have time to consider answers	Inflexible as questions may not 'fit' answer respondent wants to give
Respondents not influenced by interviewer	No check as to whether questions are understood
Easily quantifiable if closed questions used	Only those with strong opinions will complete questionnaire
Less intrusive than interview	Unable to observe reactions to questions
	Require a certain level of literacy – may not be suitable for all groups

Table 22.1 Using questionnaires

It must be clear at the start of any questionnaire exactly what its purpose and role is. This can be done in an introduction. For example, it should tell the participants the reasons for undertaking the survey and reassure them regarding confidentiality of their answers.

The content of the questionnaire needs thought. What are you trying to find out? What information is needed? For example, is it really necessary to know the age or gender of the participants? Do you need to know their ethnic background?

The way a question is worded is very important. Interesting questions will hold attention. They should be clear and as specific as possible, easy to understand and respond to. Any term that is used must have the same meaning for both the questioner and the subject. For example, 'being healthy' may mean different things to different people. Only one question should be asked at a time. For example, 'Do you plan to leave your car at home and walk to work?' asks two questions rather than one.

The way a question is worded will indicate whether it is a 'closed' or 'open' question. Closed questions give the respondent a choice of answers from which they select one; open questions give an opportunity to answer in their own words. Analysis of closed questions is simpler as they fit into a structure and are consistent, but may not show the breadth of responses.

Example

Open question
What is the most important issue facing a new mother?

Closed question
Which of the following is the most important problem facing a new mother?

- feeding the baby
- the baby's sleep pattern
- getting her figure back
- adjusting her lifestyle

Questions that might be sensitive should be avoided or handled in strict confidence. This would include questions regarding drug taking, breaking the law or personal issues such as abortion.

Questions should naturally flow from one to another and should not ask for the same information in a later context. Once the questionnaire has been carefully designed it can be reproduced ready for completion. Postal surveys can be sent off, although the inclusion of a stamped addressed envelope may help to get a better response.

Figure 22.4 You may have been involved in this type of research

Interviews

Interviews involve the researcher meeting with individuals or groups face to face and collecting information from them. There are two main types of interview: structured or formal and unstructured or in-depth. In the structured interview the researcher works through a questionnaire or

interview schedule which ensures that each person is asked the same questions. This is to ensure that as far as possible each interview is carried out in exactly the same manner. This helps to minimise the chances of bias and means that comparisons can be made between the answers given by different people. The advantages and disadvantages of structured interviews are outlined in the table below.

Advantages	Disadvantages
Good response rate	Sample size may be small
Questions can be explained	Bias because of interaction between interviewer and respondent
Large amount of information can be gathered	Time consuming
Important additional lines of inquiry can be followed up	
Reactions of interviewee can be observed	
It is known who is answering the questions	

Table 22.2 Using structured interviews

Unstructured interviews allow a range of issues to be explored. The interviewer asks open-ended questions about a topic and the respondent is encouraged to answer freely and in depth. This type of interview allows people to express what they really think. The respondent is not constrained and an atmosphere of trust can be built up, giving even more opportunities for the interviewer to gain information. It is a flexible approach which also facilitates the sharing of views on sensitive subjects. It often requires a high level of skill in interviewing. The table below outlines the advantages and disadvantages of unstructured interviews.

Advantages	Disadvantages
Large amounts of information can be collected	Can be very time consuming
Respondents are able to express themselves freely	Interviewers need well-developed skills
Sensitive subjects can be explored	Information cannot be standardised
Trust can be developed	Results may be biased because of interaction between interviewer and respondent
Flexible as conversation not restricted to set questions	

Table 22.3 Using unstructured interviews

Experiments

Experiments are usually associated with the testing of scientific theories. Medical experiments can be carried out by comparing how different groups of patients react to medical interventions, such as the use of drugs. In these cases some patients may be given a **placebo**, which is an inactive treatment. However, some patients may report feeling better although they have not received any active treatment. This is known as the 'placebo effect'. Medical experimentation is very tightly controlled and has to be approved by special committees. However, sometimes things can go very wrong; for example, in March 2006 a new drug was tested on some volunteers which left several people fighting for their lives and one man permanently injured.

Key words

placebo – a dummy pill used as a control in experiments, for example a sugar pill

Experiments are also used by social scientists, such as psychologists, who try to apply the experimental method to the study of how people behave. A successful result of an experiment relies on being able to control variables and to seek to change one of the variables in order to measure the effect. However, human behaviour is influenced by so many different variables that it can be difficult to ensure that a change to any one specific variable can be identified as the cause of a change in behaviour. At other times the subjects of the research may not be fully aware of the implications or content of the research; see the case study on page 150, for example. Table 22.4 outlines the advantages and disadvantages of using experiments as a research method.

Advantages	Disadvantages
Can measure cause and effect accurately, especially in clinical trials	Some research does not lend itself to experimental approach, especially social research
Tests can be repeated easily	May require very sophisticated equipment
Researcher controls the experiment	Ethical considerations may prevent use of experimental research
Provides quantitative data which can be analysed	

Table 22.4 Using experiments

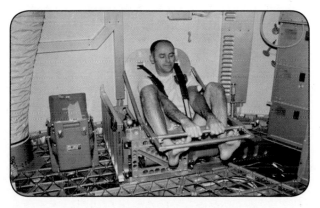

Figure 22.5 A medical experiment in space

CASE STUDY: MILGRAM'S OBEDIENCE EXPERIMENT

In 1961, Stanley Milgram, an American psychologist, set up a social psychology experiment to measure the willingness of individuals to obey an 'authority' figure who instructed them to do things that they would not normally consider doing. He told the participants that it was an experiment to test the effect of punishment on learning. The participants were required to play the part of a teacher and an actor was employed to play the part of a learner, but the participants did not know this. The 'teacher' was required to give the 'learner' an electric shock every time a wrong answer was given with the intensity of the shock increasing with every incorrect answer. The participants believed the shocks were real – although in fact the actor faked his reaction to the shocks with screams and protests. Whenever the 'teacher' expressed a desire to stop they were firmly encouraged to continue. Before the experiment a survey had predicted that only a very few people would continue to cause pain and distress. In fact, 65 per cent of the participants went on to administer the most powerful 'shock' despite showing signs of being uncomfortable doing so.

QUESTIONS

1. What are the advantages and disadvantages of testing the theory of obedience in this way?

2. Do you think this experiment would be conducted in the same way today? Why?

Observation

Observation is undertaken when the researcher watches people in their setting. There are different types of observation. *Direct observation* takes place when the researcher stays separate from the group or person they are watching and takes no part in their activities. The observation can be done in an open manner, when the participants are aware of the fact that they are being observed, or in a covert or secret way, for example using a one-way mirror. *Participant observation* involves the researcher joining in with the study group. Again this can be done in an open manner or covert manner. Open participant observation would entail the researcher discussing with the group their participation and gaining permission. If done secretly, the researcher would join the group but conceal their identity and their reasons for being there.

Observations have to be structured and organised in order to get useful information that can be used in research. Observation allows the researcher to see what people actually do and study their interactions. Both quantitative and qualitative data can be obtained; for example, by counting the number of people doing a certain activity or by recording how people behave with each other. It is not always easy to record the findings of observations as note taking can be distracting for the researcher while technological methods, such as videoing, can distract the participants.

Table 22.5 outlines the advantages and disadvantages of using observation.

Advantages	Disadvantages
People are studied in their own environment and are likely to act naturally	Presence of an observer may influence the behaviour of the group
Rapport between researcher and participants may produce more valid data	Researcher may become over-involved and lose objectivity
Can detect behaviours that people may be unaware of	Observation cannot be replicated
Can produce valid and accurate data	Covert observation may be unethical
May be only method to use with hostile groups or non-literate groups e.g children	Recording of data may be difficult
Looks at behaviour and interactions between members of a group	Behaviours may be misinterpreted

Table 22.5 Using observation

SECONDARY SOURCES

Secondary sources are information, data and research which have already been carried out. The sources of such data include research undertaken by the government, universities, the mass media and individuals. It can be looked at and used as a starting point by other researchers. Such information can be found on the internet, in journals, books or in the media. Whenever research that has been undertaken by others is used (whether by students or for publication), it must be acknowledged by a full **reference** to the source.

Key words

reference – precise direction to a page (or chapter etc.) of a book, journal or file where information may be found

Before starting a research project, it is necessary to undertake a literature review. This involves finding out what has already been published by other researchers on the topic.

Official statistics are published by the government and are published on the internet and in official documents. Data relating to demographic characteristics of the population, including births, marriages, deaths, health, education and crime etc., are available and, because they are collected at regular intervals, comparison of trends over time can be made.

The internet

The internet is increasingly used as a source of information. The amount of information is vast and readily available and can also be very confusing. There is a great temptation to download huge amounts of data and use it indiscriminately. But, just as when using other sources, careful consideration should be given to the relevance and accuracy of any data or information. Sources must be carefully referenced so that they can be found again by any subsequent reader.

Some websites are particularly relevant for research in health and social care. These include that of the Office for National Statistics for official government information and the Department of Health's website for details of policies about health.

Research tip

Make a start on your research by seeing what is available at the Department of Health – go to www.doh.gov.uk. The Office for National Statistics is at www.statistics.gov.uk/

Journals

Journals and professional publications are usually aimed at a specific group of people who share a specialist interest. Sometimes the reported research is highly technical. However, the fact that it is included in the journal is not always a guarantee of accuracy.

Books

Books include textbooks, reference books and other published work such as diaries, letters and autobiographies. You will find that librarians or staff in learning resource centres will be happy to give guidance and help in finding appropriate books on certain topics. It is important to make sure that the material in the book is up to date.

The media

The media may report research findings in newspaper and magazine articles or on the television and radio. Although it is a good way to highlight the findings of a project, the reporting may not always be completely accurate. At times the 'story' may be distorted to make headlines. For example, there may be a political reason behind the reporting and sometimes an aspect of research can be sensationalised. The specific source of any media report should be carefully investigated. The media may commission their own research by conducting opinion polls. When reviewing information published in the media it is important to be aware of the possibility of bias in the reporting.

CASE STUDY: WHAT'S IN A NAME?

An independent report for the government, Tackling Obesities: future Choices, issued in October 2007 was widely reported in the media. Here are some of the possible headlines summarizing aspects of the report

- Being fat can knock 13 years off your life

- 40% of Britons will be obese by 2025, with the country being mainly obese by 2050.

- Half of Britons will be obese by 2050

- Target for halting childhood obesity slips back 10 years

- Obesity epidemic in Britain?

- Obesity could cost £45.5 billion a year by 2050.

QUESTION

1. How might they influence your understanding of the findings of the report?

2. Why do you think that the writers might have chosen the style and content of each headline?

EVIDENCE ACTIVITY

P2

For **P2**, you have to describe the key elements of research methodologies.

Choose two pieces of research that have been published in a professional journal or magazine. Identify the methods of research that have been used and use your findings to illustrate the key elements of research methodologies.

22.3 Be able to identify a suitable topic and produce a plan for a research proposal

We will now look more specifically as how a piece of research is conducted.

TOPIC AND HYPOTHESIS

A hypothesis is a tentative proposal that is made to explain certain facts requiring further investigation to prove the truth of the statement. For example, 'health and social care students smoke less than other students of the same age' is a hypothesis which could be tested to see if was true or not. This will be done by looking for evidence to see if the statement can be proved or disproved. A working hypothesis may be used when trying to explain how certain things happen. It may be used for a while and then changed if other facts come to light. The establishment of a sound hypothesis is an important first step to conducting research. A research question is an exploratory statement or question which opens up a line of enquiry.

Whether it is a small-scale research project, like the one that you will be undertaking, or a large-scale piece of government research, the first step is to identify an appropriate topic. Earlier we explored the purpose and role of research and these principles need to be kept in mind. For example, will the purpose of the research be to identify a need, provide further knowledge, highlight gaps in provision or used to plan provision? The outcome may be to inform policy or practice, extend knowledge and understanding, improve practice, aid reflection, monitor progress or used to enable the examination of topics of contemporary importance.

Identifying a topic

Choosing an appropriate topic needs careful thought. There are so many aspects to health and social care that the choice is very wide. All research begins with the researcher identifying an area of particular interest. It may start with a rather general statement about a particular field of health or social care – for example, the lifestyles of individuals or the care of elderly people. From this rather vague area of interest the research question can be gradually narrowed down. One

CASE STUDY: SEJAL'S RESEARCH

Sejal is studying health and social care and has to choose a topic to research. During one class they discussed the effect of diet on an individual's health. Sejal was interested to find how varied the different diets of her class were. She is thinking of becoming a nutritionist in the future and studying dietetics at university. With this in mind she thought it would be interesting to research some aspect of diet.

Sejal started to consider what aspect of diet she could research. Her brother and one of her close friends are both vegetarian. Sejal thinks that they might both miss out on some essential requirements in their diets. However, they both seem to be very healthy – unlike several of her non-vegetarian friends. She was interested in how people choose to become vegetarian. This led to the idea of investigating why people became vegetarian and the difference between the diets of vegetarians and non-vegetarians and how they link to their health. She realised that she needed to narrow down her research topic. She did some initial reading around the subject which helped to clarify what was possible to undertake. Sejal came up with the hypothesis 'Vegetarians have healthier lifestyles than non-vegetarians'.

QUESTION

Suggest reasons why Sejal came up with her topic and how she developed her hypothesis.

very important starting point for you is to be sure that you are choosing an area that you are interested in – you are going to spend a lot of time and thought on this work!

Literature search

This involves conducting a systematic and thorough search for published material on a specific topic, looking at a range of secondary sources such as books, journals and the internet. From these sources it is possible to summarise what is already known. However it is important to ensure that any information found as part of a literature search is accurate, up to date, reliable and unbiased.

Ethical issues

There are certain ethical considerations that apply to all research. Researchers must respect the rights of those who are part of a research project in the same way that their rights must be respected in other circumstances. Those taking part in research should not have their physical, social and psychological well-being harmed. There should not be any unwanted intrusion into their privacy and their rights to anonymity and confidentiality must be upheld. Informed consent should be freely obtained from participants.

Key words

ethical – relating to moral principles

Research tip

The guidance published by the Department of Health for research in health and social care is called the Research Governance Framework (published in April 2005). It can be found on the website www.dh.gov.uk .

CASE STUDY: SEJAL'S LITERATURE SEARCH

Once Sejal had identified the topic of her research project she started her literature search. She was unsure how to research the healthy lifestyle of vegetarians as this could include diet, exercise and other lifestyle choices, but decided to start with diet. She wanted to get information about food and what constituted a healthy diet. She visited the Learning Resource Centre and found some books which included basic information about diet. She also found some recent journals covering aspects of diet particularly linked to the diets of teenagers. There was also a programme on TV about the schools meals programme and the options for children. This was based on government recommendations for healthy diets. Sejal realised that she needed to know more about vegetarian diets. When she first put 'vegetarian' in the computer search engine she was overwhelmed by the number of responses and uncertain which source to use. She then realised that she could get much of the information she required from the official websites of the vegetarian and vegan societies. She felt much more confident that she was getting accurate information although she realised that they were promoting a vegetarian lifestyle.

Once she realised how much information there was, she refined her hypothesis and research to: 'Vegetarians eat a more healthy diet than non-vegetarians'.

QUESTIONS

1. What sources did Sejal use in her literature search?

2. What might influence her choice as to whether or not to use the information she found?

3. Why did she change her hypothesis?

Much research, particularly in health and social care, is likely to encounter ethical issues which need to be addressed. Researchers need to be aware of their own views, values and outlooks and must try to ensure that their attitudes do not influence either the research or the reporting of their findings.

Different methods of research may raise their own ethical issues. For example, when using observational methods, there are obvious problems in using covert methods, such as hidden recorders or two-way mirrors. A participant's consent should be obtained before including them in a research project. If consent has not been obtained before the research is undertaken retrospective consent should be obtained.

Interviewers may put pressure on people to participate. This may be verbal persuasion but at other times inducements such as sweets, drinks or financial reward may be offered. However, people have a right to decide for themselves whether or not they wish to be part of a research project.

> **Think** Why do you think the volunteers took part in the new drug trial mentioned on page 149? If an organisation offers free tickets, money or even a free holiday would you feel more pressurised to take part in their research? How easy is it to say no?

The right of an individual to confidentiality must at all times be respected and it should not be possible to identify people in research reports. This may be difficult if an individual with distinctive characteristics is included in the study; for example, if there is only one male in a group of female subjects. The Data Protection Act 1998 safeguards the rights of individuals when data about them is being collected and processed. You need to make sure you know and understand how the Act might apply to your work and abide by it.

From time to time some research involves an element of risk. There may also be occasions when some participants may benefit more than others.

CASE STUDY: SEJAL AND ETHICAL ISSUES

Before going any further with her research project Sejal decided to assess whether there were any ethical issues that she needed to consider. She wanted to get a wide range of opinion so needed to ask a number of people to participate in her research. She identified the need for ensuring that her subjects were fully informed before giving their consent. She also identified the need for confidentiality. This meant that she had to consider how she would survey the participants and, if she wanted to interview them, where she could do so in privacy. She also thought carefully about her questions, realising that they might be quite invasive and personal. Another area she thought about was the possibility of bias. Sejal is not a vegetarian and has had frequent arguments with her brother about his beliefs. She realised that she would need to make sure that her attitudes did not affect her conclusions.

QUESTION

1. What ethical issues might arise as a result of Sejal's research project?

For example, in clinical trials some individuals might receive a new drug which has both benefits and risks associated with it while others provide a 'control' group and receive neither the benefits nor run the risks that may be part of the trial.

Another ethical issue which is more difficult to identify is the problem of bias caused by the attitudes and norms of the researcher. It can distort the findings of the research and the conclusions can lack objectivity. For instance, a difference in culture may lead to misinterpretations of certain actions.

Formulating a realistic hypothesis

With such a choice of areas to research the biggest challenge is probably choosing the right topic! Research must be relevant to the person who is undertaking it. It needs to be in an area that they understand, or it might be an integral part of their job. You could apply the same criteria to your research: jot down a list of topics that you are interested in researching. Now review them – are they relevant to what you are doing? For example, is it relevant to what you are studying as part of your course? Does it link with your work experience? Are you motivated to study the subject in more depth?

Secondly, any piece of research needs to be realistic. This means that it is within the scope of the person doing the research or that the resources are available. You need to be realistic as to what you can cover in a small-scale project. It has to be practical in terms of scope, time and opportunity. The people who are going to be interviewed or surveyed need to be available and willing to participate.

CASE STUDY: SEJAL'S AIM

Having identified her hypothesis as 'Vegetarians eat a more healthy diet than non-vegetarians', Sejal then wrote out her aim which she believes is achievable within the constraints of her small-scale research. Her aim was stated as: 'The aim of this research is to find out whether there is a difference in the diet between vegetarians and non-vegetarians and specifically if the vegetarian diet is generally healthier.'

QUESTIONS

1. Do you think this aim is achievable?

2. How might Sejal meet her aim?

Having considered any problems that you can identify and having chosen your topic, the next step is to come up with the hypothesis or research question that you are going to follow through as part of your research. All research has an aim to which the research is directed. It may be to prove or disprove the hypothesis that has been identified. Once the aim is identified then the objectives – or how the aim will be met – can be set.

OUTLINE OF THE PLANNED RESEARCH

The careful planning of the research is crucial for the success of the project. This applies to all types of research whether it is large or small. It may be necessary to present the plan to other people, for example an ethics committee, in order to get approval for the research to go ahead. The outline plan should include information on the reasons for undertaking the research, the target group, the proposed methods, time scales, the action plan and how the project will be monitored and if necessary changed.

You need to start making your plan now for your own research project, following the steps outlined in the next section.

Methodology

By now you have identified your topic and decided your hypothesis or research question. The next step is to think about which method or methods are most appropriate to use. Look back at the various methodologies described earlier to remind yourself what is involved in each method. You will probably decide between the following *primary sources* of evidence:

- questionnaires – with further thought as to how these should be worded

- interviews

- observation

For your *secondary sources* you can use the range of evidence found in books, journals or on the internet.

You may wish to start by reading around the topic. It will be important to keep a careful record of where you have found your information so that you can acknowledge your sources through referencing correctly, and also so you can find the information again if necessary. Make sure to put some time into your plan which allows you to do this.

When planning to use questionnaires, you need enough time to develop the questions and print out the questionnaires. Depending on whether they are to be posted, self-completed or handed out, the plan must allow a realistic timescale for the production, completion and analysis of the questionnaire. If possible, it is useful to pilot the questions first.

Interviews need to be planned not only for what questions you are going to ask but who you intend to question. If you are hoping to speak to busy professional people you will need to think ahead and book a time with them.

Observation schedules also need to be considered, particularly if you need to obtain consent before starting to observe your subjects.

Target group

A well-designed hypothesis or research question will clearly indicate the target group of your research. Researchers must decide who they need to collect information from. **Population** is the term used to describe the total number of people to which the research applies. For example, if you are researching the effects of a vegetarian diet on vegetarians, then the population will include all vegetarians. It is rarely possible to interview everybody to whom the research might apply, unless the population is very small, or unless it is a government survey like the national census.

Key words

population – the total number of people in a research group sample.

Therefore a sample needs to be identified which is as representative as possible of the population of the research topic. This is very important if

CASE STUDY: SEJAL'S TARGET GROUP

Sejal decided that in order to investigate whether vegetarians had a more healthy diet than non-vegetarians, she needed to use a questionnaire and possibly some interviews. She identified her target group as vegetarians and non-vegetarians. She chose a sample of 20 people – 10 vegetarians and 10 non-vegetarians. She gave them questionnaires to complete. She also interviewed four people to gain more information – two vegetarians and two non-vegetarians.

QUESTION

How did Sejal plan to get a representative sample?

the researcher wants to be able to apply the findings to the whole population. You will have to decide on how big a sample you need in order to ensure that you reflect the characteristics of the population you want to study. For example you need to think whether you need to have representation that covers age, gender, ethnic group or class if these are variables that might influence the findings of the research. Random sampling methods are used to try to eliminate any personal bias by the researcher in choosing who should participate. In a random sample all individuals in a given population have an equal chance of being asked to participate.

Rationale

A research project needs to have a purpose and reason why it is to be carried out. A rationale is the explanation of why the research has been undertaken. For the individual there will be the reasons why the research is important or interesting to them personally. For example, you might explain the relevance of the research to your own work or future career. The rationale should also indicate who the target audience might be and who might be interested in the results. Any links with other previous research will be mentioned. Finally, there should be some indication as to how the results of the research could be used. For example, could any findings be generalised and applied to other settings?

CASE STUDY: SEJAL'S RATIONALE

Sejal wrote the following rationale for her project.

'I want to demonstrate through my research whether or not the vegetarian diet is healthier than a non-vegetarian one. I have decided to carry out this research project because a healthy diet is very important. In recent years there has been a rise in the number of diet-related diseases such as heart disease and diabetes. If a person can lead a healthier lifestyle by having a vegetarian diet this is very important. There have been a number of studies of vegetarians which have shown that they generally eat healthier diets than non-vegetarians. I will be able to compare my findings with research that has already been published.

I am particularly interested in researching this topic as several of my friends are vegetarian and I would like to explore the reasons why they have chosen this diet. The topic fits in well with the study of health and health promotion that we have covered as part of the course in health and social care. I have a particular interest as I intend to do further study into dietetics in the future.'

QUESTION

List the main reasons that Sejal gives for her choice of topic.

Time scales

Effective time management is essential when undertaking any project and is a very useful skill to develop. The time scale for the research must be established at the beginning of the project. In order to set time scales, you need to consider when the work must be completed and how long it will take. Times can then be incorporated into the action plan. It is always useful to build in some extra time to allow for something to run late.

Figure 22.6 Plan your time effectively

Action plan

The action plan indicates the details of exactly what will be done, when, and with what resources. It will form the 'blueprint' of the research, giving guidance which can be followed throughout the project. It will be necessary to build in points when the action plan can be reviewed. Time spent at this stage may save time later.

Monitoring and modification

All projects need to be monitored to ensure that they are staying on track. Opportunities for such monitoring should be built into any action plan when it is drawn up. It will be important to return to the original statement of purpose to check that it is still being met and that the research has not diverged from the original intentions. Sometimes unforeseen problems occur. In this case it may be necessary to make modifications. Any such modifications should be carefully noted and may form part of the final discussion, with an explanation of why they happened.

RESOURCES

The available resources have already been discussed. As part of the planning for the research proposal you should identify the resources that are actually going to be used. A range of resources is necessary to demonstrate the depth of any research.

Before submitting the plan and research proposal it is likely that some secondary sources will have already been consulted. This should give some idea as to the lines of enquiry that will be followed. It may be that certain information is still required. An outline of the broad areas of secondary research still to be done is an important part of the research proposal.

It is important that any research includes reference to any 'standard' information on the topic being researched. For example, if researching what constitutes a 'healthy diet' it would be important to refer to the official government guidelines on healthy eating. Any very similar research should also be acknowledged. Good research projects demonstrate that the researchers have taken their information from a range of appropriate sources and not relied entirely on a narrow view of the topic.

CASE STUDY: SEJAL'S SOURCES

Sejal planned to use a range of secondary and primary sources. She had information from the Vegetarian Society but decided that on its own this might give her a narrow range of information. She planned to access government guidelines on diet as well as information from books, journals and the internet.

QUESTION

How did Sejal plan to ensure that she had a range of sources for her research project?

EVIDENCE ACTIVITY

P3 – M1

For **P3**, you need to have identified the topic that you intend to research and undertaken a literature review. You should have done this by now.

For **M1**, you should also justify why you have chosen this topic and your hypothesis.

22.4 Be able to conduct the research and present the findings

To recap: you have identified your topic, proposed a hypothesis and produced an outline of the planned research, including an indication of what resources you are planning to use. Now you are going to undertake the research. This section takes you through the steps in order to produce a successful piece of work and present your findings.

The outline of the process should follow these stages:

Planning

- choosing a research topic
- proposing a hypothesis or research question
- reviewing prior research into the topic
- identifying type of data needed
- choosing appropriate research methods
- writing out aplan for managing your time

Undertaking research

- choose population sample
- design appropriate research instruments to collect data
- make arrangements to contact sample
- gather data from sample
- undertake further secondary research if necessary
- regularly monitor and review progress

Analysis

- analyse data collected from primary research linking to research aims
- analyse any secondary research findings and link with own findings
- evaluate research including research methods
- draw conclusions from analysis
- make recommendations

UNDERTAKING THE RESEARCH

You will need to be particularly well organised as you start doing the research part of your project. You may be carrying out both primary and secondary research, and the information needs to be carefully recorded both for its content and also its source.

Primary and secondary research

For your primary research you should have identified the type of data that you need and who you will question, decided on which methods are most appropriate and designed your research instruments. You should look back at your plan to see how and when you had planned to undertake your research. Remember that if you are using a questionnaire you may want to pilot it first.

Before selecting your topic and proposing your hypothesis you will have started your secondary research. You should now review what else you need to cover.

Statistics

Once you have completed your own primary research and undertaken appropriate secondary research you may have collected a lot of data. It may be in the form of qualitative or quantitative data depending on your research methods. There will also be statistics in the secondary research that you have studied. Whatever form it is in, this data will need to be processed appropriately so you can analyse your findings.

Qualitative data may have been collected through interviews or observations. It may have been recorded by hand or through tape recordings or videos. Some of the information given may have strayed off the point and will need to be discarded. Extracts from the interviews may be used in order to illustrate certain points. However, most of the information will need to be categorised in order to identify the trends or themes.

Monitor and review

You should have built in a system of monitoring and reviewing the progress of your research project. For example, you might monitor the returns from a postal questionnaire to see whether a further reminder needs to be sent. It is also essential to review how the research is progressing and whether your choices of methods are producing the information you require. If reviews are carried out at appropriate intervals there will be an opportunity to adapt if necessary. Not all research goes to plan, so be prepared!

> **Think** Have you checked all the stages and prepared everything ready to start?

Figure 22.7 Front cover of Sejal's research project

The research report

The report that you make on your research is the tangible result of all your hard work. You will need plenty of time and the appropriate resources not only to analyse your data and draw conclusions from your findings but also to present it all. The presentation of the findings will affect the final outcome of the work.

A research report usually follows a standard format:

Title

Contents

Abstract

Introduction

Literature review

Aims and objectives

Method

Results

Discussion

Conclusions

Recommendations

Bibliography

Appendices

The title and contents are obvious. An *abstract* is a summary of the contents of the report. It introduces the topic of the research, summarises the process and presents some of the findings. It needs to be done in about 150 words and it is often easier to leave it until the end. You may have found an abstract useful during your literature search to help you decide whether or not a report is relevant.

INTRODUCTION

In your introduction you will state your hypothesis or research question and explain why you are undertaking the research – your rationale. The introduction will also present the findings of your secondary research and literature review. This should summarise the current research that has taken place in relation to your chosen topic.

METHOD

The next section will cover the hypothesis of your research, your aims and objectives and your choice of methods. You should explain how you developed your hypothesis and how your aims and objectives influenced your choice of research method. The primary research methods should be described briefly and any factors that helped or hindered your research commented upon. Any research tools that you devised, such as questionnaires, should be identified and a blank copy attached in the appendix.

Secondary research will also be described and any sources clearly acknowledged. Data from all sources must be recorded. Triangulation is the term given to describe how the validity of data can be verified by using more than one method of research. Whenever this has been possible it should be highlighted.

RESULTS

Compiling the data

The presentation of the results can be undertaken in different ways and will depend on the methods that have been chosen. Qualitative data is likely to have come from interviews and to be descriptive. It may have been collected through written note taking or by using a tape recorder. It is important that any report accurately represents what was said. It may be possible to identify certain themes that run through a number of interviews. For example, research into the proposed closure of a local health facility might gather very similar views expressed in different ways which were all against the closure. Compiling this data may involve summarising the opinions and also including direct quotes from some participants.

Quantitative data is usually presented in the form of graphs and charts. Whenever *triangulation* of results has been possible it is usual to highlight this by grouping the findings together. For example, qualitative research such as interviews can produce information which can then be checked using a quantitative method. Conversely, patterns and trends illustrated in quantitative research can be explained or illustrated using qualitative methods.

> ### CASE STUDY: SEJAL'S QUALITATIVE RESEARCH
>
> Sejal asked some qualitative questions such as 'Do you think being a vegetarian contributes to a healthy lifestyle? If yes, how?'
>
> She reported the qualitative response by quoting one participant:
>
> 'My energy levels are higher. This means I do more exercise. This means I keep my weight down.'

The use of *graphical representation* can help illustrate the findings and may be easier to understand than reading a lot of figures within a text. There is a huge choice of different ways in which graphs and charts can be produced including pie charts, bar charts, histograms and so on (see below). Computer software is available to support the presentation of your data. As there are so many different software packages you will need to discuss with your teacher/tutor what is available to you.

STATISTICAL INFORMATION

Statistical information is collected together and then must be examined more closely. From your primary research you can total the responses and start to make a more detailed analysis of your findings. The types of questions that you have asked will lead to different numbers of responses for different questions. For example, if you have asked a question which requires a 'yes' or 'no' answer you will be able to have a simple comparison of those who give a positive response with those who have a negative one.

Another type of question gives the respondents a range of answers from which to choose; for example, there might be a statement which then offers a scale of agreement or disagreement such as 'Vegetarians live healthier lives than non-vegetarians' which could have a response scale from '1 Agree strongly' to '9 Disagree strongly' with steps in between, so that 5 is a neutral point of neither agree or disagree. Findings based on questions such as this need to be analysed by first compiling a frequency distribution table. This collates all the responses and shows where on the range they lie.

CASE STUDY: SEJAL'S FINDINGS

Sejal asked how many days a week her participants drank alcohol: never; 1 day a week; 2 days a week; 3 days a week; more than 4 days a week. Sejal collated her findings in the table below.

Response	Number of answers	
	Vegetarian	Non-vegetarian
Never	4	3
1 day a week	2	2
2 days a week	2	2
3 days a week	1	1
More than 4 days a week	1	2

Mean, median and mode

Statistics can be viewed in a number of ways. A common method of analysis is to establish the *mean* value. The mean is the average value. It is calculated by adding together all the numbers and dividing the total by the number of items, each of which has a numerical value. For example in a data set consisting of 2, 3, the mean value is 2.5. This is arrived at by adding 2 + 3 and dividing by 2 (the number of 'items' in the set).

CASE STUDY: SEJAL'S STATISTICS

Sejal found the mean number of times that alcohol is drunk by the vegetarians she surveyed as follows.

Never drinking alcohol was given a value of 0. She made these calculations:

Total number of vegetarians = 10

0 x 4 = 0
1 x 2 = 2
2 x 2 = 4
3 x 1 = 3
4 x 1 = 4
Total 13

Mean: 13 divided by 10 = 1.3 times a week.

The average or mean number of times that alcohol is drunk by the vegetarians surveyed is 1.3 times a week.

QUESTION

Now you should do the calculation for the non-vegetarians, using the table above.

The mean value does not always represent the findings accurately enough as it may include extremes at either end. This may skew the figures. For example, if a survey of house prices included one very expensive house in a neighbourhood of otherwise more average houses it would have too big an influence on the average house price for an area.

It is therefore useful to be able to look at data in other ways. The *median* value is the middle value in a set of values. There is an equal number above and below.

The *mode* is the score or value that occurs most frequently. For example, if a data set contains the following responses:

Answer   A 1

   B 1

   C 2

   D 4

   E 1

The most frequently occurring response would be Answer D, so the modal value is Answer D. It is useful to calculate the mode as it provides a good summary statistic which is not affected by any extreme values at either end of the distribution.

In Sejal's research she identified that the modal value for vegetarians was that they never drank alcohol. Is it the same for non-vegetarians?

METHODS OF PRESENTATION

Having done all the calculations, you need to decide the best way to present the information. Your report must be clear in presenting your findings. It will make it more interesting (and demonstrate your skills) if you use a number of different presentation methods. For example, a report that only had a series of pie charts may not convey all the findings in an interesting way. You may have the opportunity to present your findings to the class in an oral and visual presentation. This could include the use of posters or a powerpoint presentation. However, neatly drawn information is still just as acceptable.

The most common methods of presenting data include:

- bar charts

- histograms

- graphs

- pie charts

- tables.

Research tip

Look at 'Saving Lives: Our Healthier Nation' on http://www.archive. official-documents.co.uk/document/ cm43/4386/4386.htm for lots of examples of different methods of presentation

Bar charts

A bar chart is a chart which has rectangular bars which reflect the values which they represent. They can be drawn vertically or horizontally. There can be many variations in the way bar charts are presented.

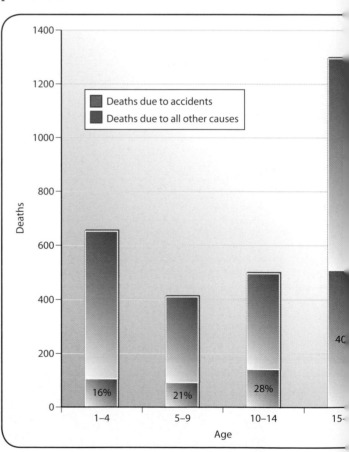

Figure 22.8 A bar chart showing child deaths due to accidents from Saving Lives: Our Healthier Nation

Histograms and graphs

A histogram chart is a form of bar chart where bars are drawn above each score with the width reflecting the limits of the score and the height representing the frequency. It is used to represent continuous data. There are no gaps between the bars of a histogram.

A graph can also be used to give a visual representation of information.

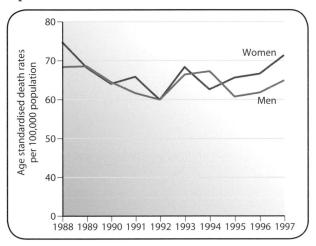

Figure 22.9 A graph showing accidental falls in the elderly, from Saving Lives: Our Healthier Nation

Pie charts

As suggested by the name, pie charts are a way of representing the information in the form of a circle with segments – hence a 'pie'.

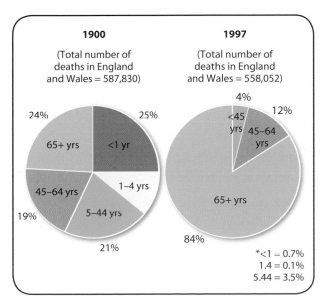

Figure 22.10 A pie chart showing age at death, from Saving Lives: Our Healthier Nation

Tables

Tables list the findings of research in columns so that the information can be read clearly, although they do not have such an immediate visual impact as other methods. Sometimes the information can be presented in a novel or interesting manner by using graphics or illustrations to represent the data. For example, Birmingham Health Authority used the illustration below to highlight the impact of the introduction of traffic calming.

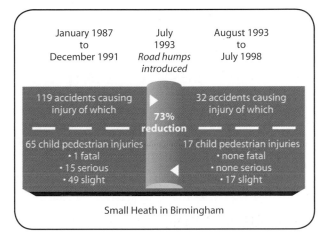

Figure 22.11 A table about traffic calming, from Saving Lives: Our Healthier Nation

METHODS OF ANALYSIS

There is a lot of IT software available to help with the presentation of your results. In addition, you may wish to use IT to help analyse your findings. Remember, however, that you must put in accurate information! You should see your teacher/tutor about the type of software that will help to process your statistical information.

Conclusions

Drawing conclusions from your findings is the next very important step. An analysis of the data will give you the information on which to base your conclusions. You will be able to demonstrate differences in opinions between different groups and compare your primary data with the secondary sources you have reviewed. Does the research that you have undertaken agree or disagree with the findings of others?

Bias and error

You may have heard the phrase, 'Lies, damned lies and statistics' (attributed to the politician Disraeli in the nineteenth century) which is popularly used as a reminder of the danger in placing too heavy a reliance on statistics! It recognises that statistics can be used to support inaccurate arguments. The likelihood of error should also be identified in any reporting of the research.

There are different ways in which errors can be made. For example, the calculations may have been done incorrectly so it is worth checking your work carefully. Another problem is caused by making the wrong correlations between two variables and therefore assuming that one is the cause of the other. For example, in 1998 Dr Andrew Wakefield made a correlation between the giving of the MMR vaccine to children and the development of autism. However, autism is often diagnosed at about the same age as children have the vaccine. Numerous studies since have failed to show any cause and effect. It is likely that he made the wrong correlation.

Another type of error that can be made when using statistics is extrapolation. This means applying results beyond the range of the research. It is very important to be aware of the limitations of small-scale primary research and not make claims beyond the scope of the work undertaken.

Errors can also occur in the way evidence is collected. If there is a very low response rate or a particularly small number of respondents it can be a major cause of error. Questions can be poorly worded and misunderstood, so that the answers cannot be used as planned. When using a postal questionnaire the reason for non-returns will not be known and any guessing at the cause for the low rate will produce error. Small samples are very often not representative.

CASE STUDY: SEJAL'S SMALL SAMPLE

Sejal interviewed 10 vegetarians and 10 non-vegetarians, all aged between 17 and 25 years old. Any conclusion she draws cannot necessarily be applied to all vegetarians as her sample is small and not representative of the population.

Bias can creep into research, particularly if the researcher has a particular interest in the subject. Care needs to be taken to ensure that questions are worded in an unbiased manner. The tone and attitude of the questioner needs to be neutral so that the respondent answers truthfully. It can be particularly hard to ask children questions as they may be inclined to give the answer that they think the questioner wants.

Key words

bias – distortion of result; prejudice; influence

ETHICAL ISSUES

Ethical issues may also arise if the statistical results are inappropriately used or misused.

EVIDENCE ACTIVITY

P4 – P5 – M2 – D1

To meet the requirements of P4 you need to carry out the primary research and collect and record appropriate data.

For **P5**, you must present and report your findings in a relevant format, identifying sources of bias or error.

For **M2**, you should review the methods of research that you chose in relation to the results obtained, any sources of bias or error and ethical considerations.

For **D1**, you must discuss how the methodology of the research project could be altered to reduce bias and error.

22.5 *Be able to evaluate the research project*

EVALUATION AND CONCLUSION

The final part of your research project is the evaluation and conclusion, and certain points must be included to ensure that you cover all aspects. You will compare your findings to the research question or hypothesis that you first posed. At this point you may find that all your results appear to support the theory. This will allow you to confirm your findings by producing arguments that support your original hypothesis. However, on the other hand, you may find that not all your results lead to definite conclusions and the answer to your research question is not clear. It is important that you do not try to draw conclusions which are not supported by the evidence. If necessary you may conclude that your hypothesis has not been proved or that further research is necessary.

The report should explain what the data indicates and describe the conclusions you have made based on the data. This leads to a discussion of the findings, showing how you have come to your conclusions. This will be a summary of the findings and charts and graphs can be used to illustrate your points.

The relationship to current research needs to be covered in the report. This will probably link back to the secondary research that you undertook.

Comparisons and contrasts can be made with other research.

Any conclusions cannot be based on one piece of evidence. For example, Sejal's findings that vegetarians eat the recommended amount of fruit and vegetables each day would not be enough to conclude that they therefore had a healthy diet. The vegetables could all be fried or prepared in an 'unhealthy' way, or they might be missing some other vital food category like a mineral, such as iron. Other results would be required to build up the evidence base.

The evaluation should also identify any limitations of the research project. This could include the number and representation of the sample.

CASE STUDY: SEJAL'S EVALUATION

Sejal identified that her research had been limited as it was a small sample with a very small number of male participants. She considered that a potential area of further research was to increase both the number of males and the size of her sample to see whether the same results were found. She also suggested that some objective ways of measuring health could be used.

CASE STUDY: SEJAL'S CONCLUSIONS

Once Sejal had identified the topic of her research, she compared vegetarians and non-vegetarians and their consumption of five portions of fruit and vegetables a day. She undertook secondary research about the role of fruit and vegetables in the diet. This is how she reported her findings:

'There has been a national campaign called '5 a day' to promote healthy eating. Eating fruit and vegetables is important because they provide essential antioxidants which reduce the risk of heart disease, arthritis, cancer and other diseases. As you can see from the graph, 90 per cent of vegetarians eat five portions of fruit and vegetables each day compared with only 50 per cent of non-vegetarians. This could be due to the food choices of vegetarians whose meals consist mainly of vegetables while non-vegetarians eat meat as part of their diet.'

Limitations may be posed by such requirements of confidentiality or health and safety considerations.

The findings may lead to consideration of potential areas for further development of research. For example, the age range might be extended or the research might be repeated in five years time to see if there have been any changes.

The evaluation should include a discussion of any controversial issues, such as any implications of the research which might infringe an individual's human rights, or other ethical issues, such as confidentiality or data protection. You should also make sure that you have explained any problems that you have identified through error or bias in your research.

RECOMMENDATIONS

Having undertaken the research and drawn conclusions from your findings you are now in the position to make recommendations. It is important that any recommendations are very clearly linked to the facts that you have discovered through your research. These recommendations may involve practical actions or take the form of suggesting further research. It is important that the recommendations are soundly based within the remit of the research undertaken. Remember that research is the basis of evidence-based practice. Recommendations from research therefore can have important implications on the work of health care practitioners and influence the introduction of new policies.

At the end of your report you should include a list of references of the sources that you have consulted. Throughout the text you should show acknowledge the source of any information you have used. The most usual system is the Harvard referencing system for literary sources. In this system the author's name and the date of publication appears in brackets in the text. At the end of the report the references are listed in alphabetical order (by author's surname) and should include the author's surname and initials, date of publication, title of book and name of publisher. Articles published in journals should also be referenced in the same way, giving the

name of the journal and its date of publication – including its volume number if appropriate. Information found on the internet must also be referenced in such a way that the author is acknowledged and all websites should be clearly identified. The principle is that a reader should be able to find all sources if necessary. So putting in a search engine such as Google or Yahoo is not sufficient!

Example

Any quote or reference from this book would appear in your bibliography (reference list) as:

Crittenden, M., Garnham, P., Harvell, J. and Higgins, H. (2008) *BTEC National Health and Social Care Book 3*, Harlow: Pearson Education

Any other information, such as a blank copy of the questionnaire, should be included in the appendix. It is not necessary to include all the completed questionnaires. You may also have some letters that you have sent out to gain permission for your research. These too can be included in the appendix along with any other documents that provide useful information. However, you should not include large quantities of print-outs from the internet.

EVIDENCE ACTIVITY

P6 – M3 – D2

For **P6**, you must look back at your original hypothesis and discuss how your findings relate to it.

M3 involves analysing the findings of the research in relation to the original hypothesis.

For **D2**, you should analyse the purpose and role of research, drawing on the piece of research undertaken.

22.6 *Understand the implications of and ethical issues related to using research in health and social care*

There are implications and ethical issues related to any research, but these issues become greater when the research has greater application to individuals or the public as a whole.

IMPLICATIONS

When considering the implications of any research, certain questions should be asked in order to understand why the research is taking place. It is obvious that research is usually undertaken because the organisation which commissions the research has an interest in its outcome. For example, the government will commission research from many different bodies in order to shape public policies. Sometimes research is commissioned by companies with a financial interest in the outcome of the research. For example, a pharmaceutical company will want to research the benefits of certain drugs in treating a disease.

Figure 22.12 Pharmaceutical companies undertake drug research and testing

Human rights

The human rights of participants must always be a prime consideration. The principle that the well-being of the participants should always be ensured is generally accepted in research. Sometimes there are risks in research and these risks need to be weighed against the potential benefits that may come from the findings. The human rights of the individuals involved can be safeguarded by ensuring that the participants are fully aware of the implications. Clear information should be given and informed consent obtained. However, for those who cannot give consent, safeguards are required to make sure that their rights are maintained. Research is sometimes undertaken in countries where human rights legislation and protection is not so sophisticated. For example, clinical trials have taken place amongst poor people in the developing world where it is cheaper to do the research. Individuals may be persuaded to join the trials for small sums of money or in return for medication.

Validity and reliability

The validity of any research means that the evidence collected accurately reflects the reality of what has been studied, i.e. the methods used to collect the data have ensured that results are consistent with what has been said or observed. The reliability of the research is based on whether or not the research could be repeated exactly and the same results obtained.

Consequences

The consequences of research obviously depend on the findings but also on the experiences of the participants. Some research may cause anxiety and stress and efforts should be made to minimise such problems. The outcomes may prove beneficial in the long run but can also cause change and upset. For example, in 2006 new research showed that showed that the guidance for the treatment of hypertension (high blood pressure) should be changed. The National Institute for Health and Clinical Excellence (NICE) issued new guidelines which meant that many thousands of patients had to visit their GP to change their medication.

Publication

The publication of research findings can have implications. It is important that individuals cannot be identified through references to places or events with which they could be associated. Publicity can also spread the information very swiftly. The nature of the media that is read by the general public may mean that the full story behind any findings is not explained. Sometimes 'scare' stories will circulate and cause people unnecessary anxiety. On the other hand, sometimes the publication of research can allow a more open investigation and debate about issues.

Access to information

Some information is confidential to individuals but much is now accessible. The Freedom of Information Act 2000 gives access to information that is held by public authorities.

Client group vulnerability

Some groups of people are particularly vulnerable when research is undertaken. These include children, those with learning difficulties or mental health problems and the elderly. When research that involves any of these client groups is proposed, great care needs to be taken to ensure that appropriate consent is obtained and they are safeguarded throughout the research process. The publication of information on any of these groups could be detrimental to their well-being.

ETHICAL ISSUES

Confidentiality and data protection

The issue of confidentiality is at the centre of much research that is undertaken in health and social care. Research reports should never identify the participants in any way, whether by name or by association. The identity of participants should be protected and anonymised.

The Data Protection Act 1998 protects the rights of individuals when data is being collected about them. The purpose of the Act is to protect the rights of the individual about whom data is obtained, stored, processed or supplied. The Act applies to both computerised and paper records.

In research it means that participants must be informed about how any data that is collected from them will be used and for what purpose. They also have the right to see the results of the research. However, if the basic principles of confidentiality are maintained then there should be no problems arising from properly conducted research.

Policy procedures

Researchers are always obliged to follow any procedures that are laid down, either by the organisation in which they are researching or the professional bodies that govern health and social care. These may take the form of codes of practice or policy procedures. For example, the British Psychological Society publishes a code of conduct and the ethical principles that should be followed, as do universities, the NHS and social care organisations.

Authenticity

The authenticity of any research must be established. From time to time it emerges that some research is not genuine and that results have been manipulated or invented.

The media reports on many research findings. Often in the newspapers or television the report has to be shortened and only the headlines used. This means that the full extent of the research is not always reported.

Use and misuse of data

As we have seen, data can be used in many ways to support research. The appropriate and accurate use of well-researched data will ensure that any findings can be relied on and applied successfully. However, data can also be misused, producing incorrect or inaccurate information. This can have far-reaching implications.

Research tip

You can find out more about SCIE and look at some of the key reports by going to www.scie.org.uk

CASE STUDY: SALLY CLARK

In 1999, Sally Clark, a qualified solicitor, was wrongly convicted of murdering her two young sons. At her trial an expert witness, Professor Sir Roy Meadow, testified that the chance of two children in the same family dying from Sudden Infant Death Syndrome (cot death) was 1 in 73 million. In fact he had miscalculated data and the true figure is closer to 1 in 200, if not lower. He had failed to recognise that the risk of cot death within the same family increases rather than decreases.

Sally Clark eventually had her conviction quashed and was released from jail in 2003. Sadly, she never recovered from the effects of her loss, conviction and imprisonment and died, aged just 42, in March 2007.

EFFECTS ON POLICY AND PRACTICE

The role and purpose of research can be to make changes in policy and practice. Although there can be some disadvantages and ethical implications to consider, the benefits of good research can have far-reaching results in improving the health and social care of many individuals. For example, the aim of the Social Care Institute for Excellence (SCIE) is stated as:

'SCIE's aim is to improve the experience of people who use social care by developing and promoting knowledge about good practice in the sector. Using knowledge gathered from diverse sources and a broad range of people and organisations, we develop resources which we share freely, supporting those working in social care and empowering services.'

SCIE also maintains a research register for social care which includes ongoing and completed research that has been subject to independent ethical and scientific review.

EVIDENCE ACTIVITY

P7 – M4

For **P7**, you must outline any possible improvements to the research, referring to any relevant implications and ethical issues.

For **M4**, you should discuss whether your research could have any implications on current practice.

Vocational Experience for Health and Social Care

unit 44

If you are doing this unit it means that you are undertaking work experience of at least 200 hours, in a minimum of three different health and social care settings. The aim of this unit is that you should gain further understanding and knowledge of the organisation, practices and policies of the work placements that you visit. It also enables you to review your own personal effectiveness by completing reflective accounts of your experiences. This should lead on to a discussion about your personal development needs and help with your planning for the future.

In addition, by undertaking a number of work experience placements you will have opportunities to gain evidence to support many of the units that you are studying.

As part of the assessment for this unit you are expected to keep a portfolio of evidence and a reflective practice journal, which will record the evidence from your work experience placement that demonstrates how your knowledge, understanding and skills have developed.

Learning outcomes

By the end of this unit, you will:

So you want to be a...

NHS Trust Work Experience Manager

My name Fiona Walters

Age 23

Income £21,000

This job requires organisation, tact and empathy to ensure placement is a satisfying experience, both for the individual and for the work area.

What do you do?

I organise the work experience placements for young people in the NHS Trust. These include students from local schools and further education colleges, as well as those who are studying vocational courses in higher education at college or university.

What are your responsibilities?

I liaise with work areas in the trust to identify where placements are possible. I support staff in preparing for the students so that they know what is involved. I sometimes have to 'sell' the idea to them by persuading them how important it is for the future of the NHS. I also visit the schools and colleges to talk to the students about what to expect. All applicants must fill in an application form and then I interview them. I am responsible for ensuring that all the correct paperwork is completed, such as insurance and health and safety requirements.

How did you get your job?

I had been working as a 'temp' following university, where I studied for a degree in social administration. When I was at school I had undertaken work experience in my local NHS trust so while I was deciding what I wanted to do in the future, I had been doing some voluntary work at the weekends.

> ## " I enjoy seeing how enthusiastic the students are. "

This brought me into contact with the voluntary services department and when a vacancy for a manager came up I was asked to apply.

What training did you get?

It was rather in at the deep end as it was a new project! I went through the induction for all new employees in the Trust which included health and safety and equal opportunities training. There are lots of opportunities through the staff development programme to do many different types of training. I got lots of support from my managers.

What are the hours like?

I work mostly nine to five. Occasionally I do some promotional events, such as school careers conventions, which can be in the evenings.

What skills do you need?

You need to be very well organised. It is also important to have good interpersonal skills as I meet a wide range of people every day, from hard-pressed professionals on the wards to a group of students in a college who all want the same work experience placement! You need a thorough understanding of the work of health and social care professionals and some good powers of persuasion.

Grading criteria

The table below shows what you need to do to gain a pass, merit or distinction in this part of the qualification. Make sure you refer back to it when you are completing work so you can judge whether you are meeting the criteria and what you need to do to fill in gaps in your knowledge or experience.

In this unit there are four evidence activities that give you an opportunity to demonstrate your achievement of the grading criteria:

page 177   P1

page 184   P2

page 188   P 3, P4, M1

page 190   P5, M2, D1

To achieve a pass grade the evidence must show that the learner is able to...	To achieve a merit grade the evidence must show that, in addition to the pass criteria, the learner is able to...	To achieve a distinction grade the evidence must show that, in addition to the pass and merit criteria, the learner is able to...
P1 Describe the structure and function of one health or social care organisation	**M1** Explain how development of knowledge and understanding can be linked to improved practice	**D1** Evaluate own development as a result of workplace experiences.
P2 Present and review a portfolio of evidence demonstrating knowledge and understanding of workplace practice	**M2** Explain how improving own personal effectiveness can enhance the experience of the patient/service user.	
P3 Maintain a reflective practice journal to monitor development of own knowledge, understanding and skills		
P4 Identify links between knowledge and understanding and effective practice		
P5 Describe own effectiveness in work in health and social care.		

44.1 *Understand the structure and function of a placement organisation*

PLACEMENT STRUCTURE

All organisations, whether large or small, need to have a structure so that they can function effectively. The way an organisation is structured will depend on such things as its size and what its main aims are. Health and social care organisations range from very large NHS trusts employing thousands of people to small privately-run businesses, such as care homes or playgroups. You may gain experience of a number of different organisations as you undertake your work experience placements and will have the opportunity to see different structures and the effect on the functioning of the workplace.

Aims and role

The aim of an organisation is often stated in its 'mission statement', which explains the main purpose of the organisation and why it exists. These are often expanded to show how the aim will be met. Each organisation is likely to have its own specific organisational culture. The organisation's culture influences how people are treated and the way in which the work of the organisation is carried out. It may also have implications for its structure and its attitude to risk-taking, or the ways in which its employees are organised and rewarded. Charles Handy suggested four different organisational cultures (C. Handy, *Understanding Organisations* Penguin, London, 1985).

Key words

organisational culture – the attitudes, experiences, beliefs and values of an organisation

These four cultures were:

- The Person Culture – the individual is the focus of a person culture. The individuals tend to believe that they are more important than the organisation itself. Some professional health care partnerships have a person culture.

- The Power Culture – concentrates power among a few. It is like a spider's web with control spreading out from the centre. Power is in the hands of those in the centre who make all the decisions.

- The Role Culture – where there are clearly delegated authorities within a highly defined structure. Typically, these organisations form hierarchical bureaucracies. A person's position defines how much power they have.

- A Task Culture – teams are formed to solve particular problems and power derives from expertise. The emphasis is on achieving results, and individuals can be given a lot of control over how they undertake certain tasks.

Here are two examples of mission statements.

Examples

Mission Statement

We aim to provide high quality, locally-based health and social care services that are responsive to the needs of users, carers and local communities, taking account of ethnicity, culture and gender.

Our School Aims

Our school aims to provide a broad, balanced, relevant education, based on the National Curriculum. All of our children, whatever age, sex, race, ability, cultural background or religion, are guided to achieve full potential in the areas of knowledge, skills and personal development.

The school might go on to suggest the following ways in which the aims will be met. For example:

- The school will be a safe and happy school in which learning is valued as an enjoyable experience.

- The environment will be stimulating and well resourced so that high standards can be reached.

- A sense of community will be encouraged both within the school and with the outside community.

- The children will be encouraged to develop sensitivity and tolerance towards others, respecting and appreciating each other's feelings, views and capabilities.

- The children will be helped to develop moral values, and the confidence to make and hold moral judgements, developing habits of self-discipline and acceptable behaviour.

- The bonds between school and home will be promoted and strengthened by close co-operation between staff, parents and children.

- Children will be encouraged to work co-operatively together and to develop social skills.

- All children will have access to equal learning opportunities and taught to avoid prejudice and stereotyping.

> **Think** Consider the mission statement for one of your work experience placements. How do they plan to meet their aim?

The stated aim of an organisation may give some indication of the organisation's role in providing health and social care. Health care may be commissioned from a number of different organisations, some of which will be part of the public sector while others are privately owned and run. However, they may all have a role in meeting the needs of a local population. For example, mental health services for a local population may be provided from the statutory, private or voluntary sector. Health and social care services are organised differently in England, Wales, Scotland and Northern Ireland. They are provided at national, regional and local levels.

> **Think** Can you identify the role played by your work experience placements in providing health and social care in your area?

Policies and procedures

In order to meet the aim of the organisation a number of policies, procedures or codes of practice will be developed. A *policy* is a statement of the way in which an organisation intends to tackle a particular issue. For example, every organisation is expected to have an equal opportunities policy which states its approach to ensuring that both its staff and its clients have equality of opportunity. Such a policy is likely to cover how recruitment and promotion of staff are undertaken to ensure equality, and how any issues of harassment or racial discrimination will be dealt with.

A *procedure* is a written instruction of how staff should act in certain situations. It identifies a certain way of getting something done. Procedures are the steps that are used to achieve a principle or objective or to carry out a policy. These cover a very wide range of different topics.

A *code of practice* is a set of written rules which are intended as a guide to acceptable behaviour in certain circumstances.

Care organisations are required by law to have in place certain policies and procedures – for example on equal opportunities, health and safety and the reporting of accidents in the workplace. If you look back at Unit 3: Health Safety and Security in Health and Social Care you will see some of the legislation that enforces the implementation of certain policies and procedures.

Policies and procedures are put in place to make sure that the organisation meets its legal requirements and also to maintain high quality care. The policies should ensure that 'best practice' is followed by the staff. The organisation should review and monitor the effectiveness of all policies and procedures on a regular basis to make sure that they are effective and are being followed. Large organisations have departments whose responsibility is to carry out regular audits of the standard of care and implementation of any procedures.

You will have experienced some of the policies and procedures when you first attended your workplace. You should have had an induction which covered such matters as health and safety, including what you should do in the case of a fire.

The following is a list of the policies at a nursery school. As you can see, there are quite a lot!

Admissions policy	Medication policy
Emergency policy	Illness policy
Fire drill procedure	Health and safety policy
Outing policy	Accident policy
Equal opportunities policy	Special needs policy
Access to information policy	Complaints procedure policy
Child protection policy	Behaviour and disciplinary policy
Anti-social behaviour policy.	Biting policy
Bullying policy	Curriculum development policy
Failure to collect a child	Lost children policy

Think How do the policies and procedures in your work experience placement link to the aims of the organisation?

ROLES AND RESPONSIBILITIES

The culture of the organisation and its role and aim will influence how it is structured. Staff at every level will have certain roles and responsibilities. Many organisations will have a board of directors who set the direction for the organisation and oversee its workings. For example, NHS trusts are run by a board of directors, some of whom are non-executive – they are not involved in the day-to-day running of the trust.

The main responsibilities of a NHS board are to:

- ensure high quality patient care

- monitor performance and ensure objectives are achieved

- determine the strategic direction of the trust

- maintain a high standard of corporate governance and professional conduct

- maintain the trust's financial viability.

Staff organisation

The chief executive officer (CEO) is accountable to the board for all aspects of the trust's work. Large organisations such as these have complex structures with different directorates headed by senior executives. These tend to have hierarchical management structures. This means that decision making is usually concentrated at the top of the organisation and there is a line management system. Each person is responsible to a supervisor or manager to whom they report.

Think If you are working or have worked in a large organisation with a hierarchical management system, what are the lines of responsibility and accountability? Go up as far as the chief executive.

Smaller organisations may have much 'flatter' management structures with far fewer layers of decision making. Sometimes the responsibilities are shared equally, with everybody contributing and no one person having the final responsibility. Examples of this may be found in small voluntary groups or self-help groups.

The management structure of an organisation should be planned so that people can work together effectively to meet the aims of the organisation. The responsibility for making decisions must be clear and communications should be good. Staff need to be supported to do their work effectively. This can be achieved through good supervision or line management, providing education and training, and having staff support groups. Good communication can be key in ensuring that all staff feel involved in the organisation. Regular meetings and information sharing help staff feel valued. Sometimes this can also be achieved through a company newsletter or similar type of communication.

CASE STUDY: LAKESIDE RESIDENTIAL CARE HOME

Lakeside is a home for 30 residents. Each person has their own room with en-suite facilities. All the meals are provided from a central kitchen. In the dining room the residents are able to choose the table where they want to sit and there is a choice of menu every day. There is a communal lounge and a friendship club which encourages the residents to socialise. Carers ensure that all the needs of the residents are met. They help them with their personal care, their dietary needs and support them socially and emotionally.

Lakeside was established as a charity 25 years ago by a trust set up under the will of a local benefactor, to provide care for those in need in the area. A group of local people act as trustees of the organisation on a voluntary basis. They meet every three months to discuss a range of issues. They have a responsibility to ensure that the residential home is run efficiently, that it meets the needs of the residents and complies with all legal requirements. They also visit the home and speak to the staff and residents on an informal basis and join some of the social activities, such as the garden fete. The trustees are responsible for the appointment of a manager and for setting the salaries of the staff.

According to the job description, the manager:

- is expected to provide the residents of Lakeside with services appropriate to their needs and in accordance with the policies of the trust

- is responsible for ensuring that all activities are conducted within existing frameworks of legislation for the care of the elderly

- will have responsibility for the leadership and management of designated staff.

As well as a manager there is an administrator who is responsible for the financial aspects of the home and the support staff. A deputy manager deputises for the manager in her absence and takes particular responsibility for arranging the duty rotas of the staff. The rest of the staff consists of four senior carers and a number of full and part-time carers. The senior carers also have some special responsibilities such as training co-ordinator and medication supervisor. They oversee the other staff and report to the manager. There are two office staff, three kitchen staff, a caretaker and two gardeners who report to the administrator.

QUESTIONS

1. Using the information above, draw a management structure that might apply to Lakeside.

2. How could the trustees ensure that the residents receive high quality care?

3. Suggest ways for communicating with and between the staff. Why might this be important?

The **role** that a member of staff has within an organisation should be identified in their job description. When an individual applies for a position in an organisation the job role is clearly explained. However, sometimes the job may change over time and new roles are undertaken. In these cases it is important that the job description is updated.

Key words

role – what an individual is appointed or expected to do

With every role there are certain **responsibilities** that the individual has and for which they can be held **accountable**. There are some areas for which everybody has a responsibility at some level, such as safety and security. For example, in order to maintain a safe environment, all staff must report any obvious hazards such as wet or slippery floors.

Key words

responsibilities – what an individual will be answerable for
accountability – being responsible to someone or for something

At the beginning of your placement you should take time to clearly understand what is expected of you – your role and what responsibilities you therefore have. It is important that you do not step outside your role while on work experience. This might cause problems for you, the staff and the clients.

If you look at the 'job exposed' case studies in this series of books you will see descriptions of a number of roles in health and social care. Each person also gives a short account of their responsibilities.

Figure 44.1 You may do work experience in a nursery

PATIENTS/SERVICE USERS

Health and social care provision covers a very wide range of services. For example, there is care of children in hospitals, nurseries and schools, services for individuals with special needs, including learning disabilities, the care of the elderly in hospital, residential care, support for people with mental health problems, health promotion, nursing, maternity services and scientific jobs. It may be that you specifically requested to work with a certain group of clients or perhaps you have found yourself going to a placement where you have very little knowledge of the type of provision. All organisations aim to provide services and meet the needs of an identified client group.

The people who use the services may be known as patients, clients or service users or might be identified by their age, such as children, teenagers or adults. The way in which the needs of individuals are to be met forms part of the 'mission statement' or aim of the organisation.

Example

A local authority in London, such as Brent, is responsible for – among other things – the learning disability services. The mission statement for the organisation states:

We aim to ensure that health and social services are provided for people with learning disabilities and their carers, living or originating in Brent, to enable them to live in the community with dignity.

This identifies the groups for which they are making provision as people with learning disabilities and their carers. The statement goes on to indicate in broad terms how their needs will be met.

We shall achieve this by delivering person-centred services that are tailored to meet individual needs to improve the lives of people with a learning disability in Brent. This will be realised by offering opportunities that provide choice and independence. We will seek to involve and empower users, parents, carers and employees through increased communication and choice, for a brighter future together.

Research tip

Find out more by going to
www.brent.gov.uk/socserv2.nsf

Organisations are structured so they can meet the needs of the identified client group through the ways in which they provide resources and staff.

Example

The London Borough of Brent provides Community Teams for Learning Disabilities (CTLD). The CTLD is an integrated team of social services and health professionals. The team is made up of care managers, review officers, transitional workers, psychologists, occupational therapists, a bereavement officer, outreach workers, crisis intervention officers and community nurses. The CTLD provides a seamless service by managing all the community assessment, care management and treatment services operated by health and social services.

In addition, Brent has day centres, residential placements and respite care. The planning to meet the needs of each client will be undertaken at an individual level within the scope of the service.

Think What are the main characteristics of the service user group for your work placement? How is the organisation structured to meet the needs of the group?

SERVICES AND RESOURCES PROVIDED BY ASSOCIATED ORGANISATIONS

Sometimes the organisation itself will not provide all the services that a service user requires. In these circumstances partnerships may have been formed with other organisations so that together they can ensure that the client receives all the care they need. This may require a number of agencies to work together. It is known as inter-agency working and there are an increasing number of examples of this. The reforms that were introduced under the 'care in the community' initiative required social services and health authorities to work together.

Many issues in health are also influenced by the social circumstances of the clients. This is particularly true for elderly people or those with mental health problems. The care of children is shared between education, health and social services. It is important that all these different agencies work together in order to maximise the help and support that can be given to any individual, their family or community.

Example

For example, Brent Learning Disability Partnership: *'works closely with other departments in the Council such as Children's Services, Mental Health Services, Older People Services, Education etc. and other agencies such as Kingsbury Community Hospital, Parents and Carers and the Voluntary and Independent Sectors. The help we offer may be provided directly by the Partnership or by another commissioned organisation.'*

Think What are the services that are provided to the clients of your placement by other organisations or agencies? In what ways do they work in partnership and how do they communicate with each other?

ROLE AND PERFORMANCE IN PLACEMENT

Work placements provide many opportunities for individuals. These include:

- the development of workplace skills

- gaining self-confidence and self-awareness

- gaining understanding of the health and social care industry, its organisations, staffing and clients

- application of academic study and linking of theory and practice

- opportunities to take responsibility for your own learning

- career opportunities.

It is important that the role and responsibilities of the learner in the placement is very clear to the individual, the employer and the responsible teacher/tutor or workplace co-ordinator.

Before starting the placement you should do some research into the place where you are to work so that you know the type of organisation and the clients. If possible, you should have a preliminary meeting with the employer. This will help you to plan your aims and objectives in discussion with the workplace supervisor and your teacher/tutor. It will also give the employer an opportunity to understand what you are hoping to get from the experience.

Whether or not you meet your supervisor or manager before attending for the first time, you need to be clear about your aims and objectives. However, these must then be discussed in order to ensure that they will fit in with the organisation and the care that is being provided to the clients.

Here are some tips to help you get the best from your placement:

- Prepare carefully for your placement by researching the organisation.

- Arrive punctually and always telephone if unable to attend.

- Be enthusiastic and show a positive attitude.

- Wear appropriate clothing – check with your teacher/tutor if you are unsure.

- Be aware of your responsibilities regarding health and safety.

- Accept instruction and direction from your supervisor and undertake appropriate tasks and projects as requested.

- Communicate with your teacher/tutor or workplace supervisor if you have any concerns.

- Keep regular and careful records of your work.

- Review your work to ensure that you are meeting your aims and objectives.

The employer will, in discussion with your teacher/tutor, have identified what role you will undertake while on work experience. They will also ensure that any learner will have a comprehensive induction and provide a supervisor or mentor in the workplace. The tasks that are within the scope of the learner are identified and any restrictions or boundaries explained.

Work experience placements should be enjoyable for both the learner and employer. An enthusiastic and willing learner who is keen to learn will receive a good response from an employer. Most employers are dedicated to their work and always wanting to encourage students to enter the caring professions.

EVIDENCE ACTIVITY

P1

For **P1**, you need to describe the structure and function of one health and social care organisation.

While you are at your work experience placement, you should collect information about the structure and function of the organisation. You will need to do this for at least three different organisations. You should then write a report which describes the function of the organisation, including the setting, the clientele, how it meets the needs of the service users and how it fits in to the local or regional provision of health or social care.

44.2 Be able to demonstrate knowledge of workplace practice

PRACTICE SITUATION

The ways in which care practice is undertaken will vary depending on the setting, the user group and the role of the individual delivering the care or education. For example, the practices of a health care assistant are different from those of a specialist nurse or physiotherapist. During your work placement you will have the opportunity to participate in some workplace practices and to observe others.

Setting

The workplace setting could include: care settings, such as hospitals, residential or nursing homes; education settings, such as playgroups, nurseries or primary schools; or social services settings, such as youth clubs and resource centres, facilities for those with learning disabilities or voluntary organisations. For each type of setting there will be certain practices or ways of doing things, some of which will be the same and others that will vary according to the setting.

Patient/service user group

The client group will also dictate the workplace practices. Some clients or service users will be particularly dependent, while others will be more autonomous and independent. Young children and vulnerable adults require higher levels of supervision and care.

> **Think** What is your work experience placement like? Can you describe to a friend the setting, the client group and the roles undertaken by yourself and the other individuals you observe or work with?
>
> *You can include your responses in your portfolio of evidence (see Evidence activity P2 on page 184).*

KNOWLEDGE AND UNDERSTANDING

As you work with different clients or service users, you will start to understand some of the different practices that apply to the specific group. Some practices will be used across a number of different groups while others will be very specific to that group.

Needs

The needs of different groups or individuals are likely to be very specific to their own particular circumstances. These needs will have been assessed in order to provide appropriate care. It is useful to consider different needs under the PIES classification.

- Physical – the physical needs of an individual – including their physical health.

- Intellectual – the intellectual development or stimulation.

- Emotional – emotional needs and emotional health, including ability to express emotions.

- Social – the opportunity and ability to have social needs met.

Another way of assessing needs is through the 'hierarchy of needs' as outlined by Abraham Maslow in his 1943 paper 'A Theory of Human Motivation' (see page 20).

Practical care skills

Remember the Care Values? You will have studied them when undertaking some of your other units. They are a set of values and principles which are common to all health and social care practitioners and which underpin practice. The five main areas are:

- promoting anti-discriminatory practice

- maintaining confidentiality

- promoting and supporting individuals' rights

- acknowledging individuals' personal beliefs and identities

- promoting effective communication.

You should see these principles being put into practice while you are in your workplace. You will also observe a number of practical care skills. These will include helping individuals to meet their hygiene, dietary, mobility and communication needs, as well as providing activities to meet social, emotional and intellectual needs. You will be able to participate in some activities and develop your own skills, while other more specialist skills you will be able to observe. For reasons of confidentiality and personal privacy some activities are not appropriate to be undertaken by a learner. However, whenever possible you should try to gain knowledge of how and why certain procedures are done.

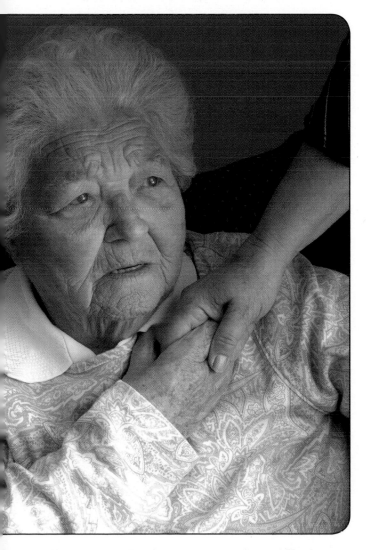

Figure 44.2 Going into care can be a difficult time

CASE STUDY: GOING INTO A HOME

Joan has recently been admitted to Lakeside residential home. Before this, she was living independently on her own in a bungalow a few miles away. She was very active in the community, visiting local friends and attending a lunch club twice a week. Here she took part in a number of activities she enjoyed such as quizzes, talks and outings. However, six months ago Joan started having some 'funny turns' and fell and broke her hip. While she was in hospital it was decided that she would not be able to return to her home immediately as she did not regain her mobility; she also suffered a minor stroke which has left her right arm rather weak. Joan is now worried that her friends will not be able to visit her as it will be too far for them to travel.

QUESTIONS

1. Using either PIES or Maslow's hierarchy of needs, suggest what needs Joan had when she was admitted to Lakeside.

2. What practices might ensure that these needs are met?

Think What are the practical care skills that you have taken part in or observed? How is each type of need met?

You can include your responses in your portfolio of evidence (see Evidence activity P2 on page 184).

Knowledge of roles

The roles of the staff in any organisation are reflected in their care practices. Although some jobs cover many different practices, others are very specific. By looking at the job description the role of an individual should be very clear. However, sometimes it may be more difficult to identify what someone's role is from observing their practice. The role of the cook is likely to be very obvious, but the different levels of care workers or nurses may not be when first observed!

CASE STUDY: CLASSROOM ROLES

Josh is undertaking work experience in a local primary school. On the first morning he met with the headteacher and the school receptionist. The headteacher welcomed him and discussed the plans for his placement. She then asked the receptionist to give Josh a short tour of the school and to explain the main health and safety issues before taking him to the classroom. When Josh first entered the classroom he noticed that there were four adults in the group of 30 children. They were all working with the children – some in groups and the others with individuals. He was told that in addition to the classroom teacher there was a classroom assistant, a special needs helper for a boy with hearing difficulties and a parent who came in to help with the children's reading. As he watched, Josh could see that the four adults were all undertaking slightly different roles. He made a note to ask each one what they did each day.

QUESTIONS

1. What differences and similarities might Josh find when he compared the roles of the four adults?

2. Describe the care practices that are associated with the different roles of the individuals in your work placement.

You can include your responses in your portfolio of evidence (see Evidence activity P2 on page 30).

Communication

Good communication is essential to all care practice. In Unit 1 you studied how effective communication is developed in health and social care. While in your placement, you will constantly see examples of communication and personal interactions and have many opportunities to explore and develop the skills necessary for effective communication. Remind yourself of the main points by looking back at Unit 1. You may also want to use your placement to carry out one of the evidence activities required for that unit.

Think What are the different types of communication and interpersonal interaction that can be seen in the workplace? What factors inhibit or support good communication?

You can include your responses in your portfolio of evidence (see Evidence activity P2 on page 184).

In some placements there are well-established partnerships with other organisations and opportunities for inter-agency working. There may be occasions when you are able to see evidence of such practices.

INFORMATION

The way in which information is handled in a care setting is very important. There will be important information that affects how an individual is cared for contained in reports and records. Other information may come from relatives and friends. The information may be in verbal, written or electronic form. Most organisations will have established procedures as to how information is received, handled and stored. It is important to know and understand what those procedures are and to ensure you know what your role and responsibilities are. For example, you may be told something by a service user or asked to take a telephone message. You need to be certain that you follow the guidelines given to you and pass on any messages accurately.

Recording and reporting

Any information has to be recorded. The content must be recorded accurately and must also be recorded in the right place. Too often, information, such as test results, can be scribbled down on scraps of paper which may then be lost or forgotten. Phone calls from relatives, although seemingly unimportant to a busy staff member, may mean a lot to a service user who is feeling very isolated from their family. Any record needs to be readable, with careful attention to spelling to ensure accuracy. Information must be passed on and reported to the appropriate person. It may be circulated to other care staff, carers or outside agencies, depending on the relevance of the information.

Sharing information

Each organisation will have different methods of sharing information and you should make yourself familiar with the practices of your workplace. The most common ways of sharing information are by telephone or face to face, or by written methods such as letters or reports, fax and email. Phone contact can be verbal or by text message. It is important when making or receiving telephone messages that the identity of the individual at the other end of the line is clear. This may mean asking someone to spell out their name and the name of the person to whom the message is addressed. Many workplaces will have a book or pad on which all telephone messages should be recorded.

Post and faxed material need to be delivered to the correct person. Although post can remain unopened and therefore confidential, faxed material is not so secure as it can be seen by anyone passing by the fax machine. It is important to make sure that all the intended number of pages have been received when collecting a document that has been faxed.

Confidentiality

Security and confidentiality of information are extremely important. Organisations have policies for dealing with electronic information. They need

to abide by the regulations in the Data Protection Act with regard to information held about their clients. Most computers in the workplace are password protected and are only available to certain individuals.

Confidentiality requires that information is kept safe and only passed on when there is a clear need to do so. Service users have a right to confidentiality, but only when that right does not affect the rights of others or if they may be in danger of harm to themselves. For example, if an elderly person is found in a very dirty home which is cold and infested with rats and mice, they would be in danger of harm to themselves and also causing a public health risk – putting others in danger. In these circumstances, the individual's right to confidentiality regarding information about them being passed on is superseded.

It may be appropriate to ask an individual if certain things which might be regarded as confidential can be passed on. In all other circumstances, personal information, should be kept confidential. In some circumstances it may be important to make it clear to an individual that if they continue to share certain information, it will be passed on. This may occur when someone is told information which is outside their competence to deal with. An example of this would be if a resident confided in a work experience student something that might affect their health or well-being. In such circumstances the student would need to explain that they were in the organisation on work experience and they must pass on any such information to their supervisor.

Other professionals need to know information about clients and service users. However, when information is passed on professionally it is on the understanding that they should keep it confidential.

Relatives do not have an automatic right to be told information unless the client is under-age. Even in the case of young people under the age of 18, it has been established that they may have a right to confidentiality under the Gillick principle. This was the outcome of a case which went to the House of Lords and states that parental powers to control their children dwindle as the child matures. The rights of parents should give way to the child's right to make decisions when 'he or she is of sufficient understanding and intelligence' to be able to make up his or her own mind. This means that parents will not automatically be informed if, for example, their daughter is given contraceptives by her GP or requests a termination of pregnancy. It will be up to the doctor to decide whether or not confidentiality should be maintained in such circumstances.

The basic rule should be that all information given by an individual or on their behalf is confidential and should not be disclosed to anyone else without their consent.

Think What is the policy of your placement regarding confidentiality and the disclosure of information? How is information is handled?

You can include your responses in your portfolio of evidence (see Evidence activity P2 on page 184).

Storage of information

Records of information, particularly confidential information, need to be kept securely. This includes any files, charts, reports notes or any other written record whether in written or electronic form. This means that arrangements should be made to store records in places that are safe and can be locked. Only designated people should be able to access such records. Care must be taken to ensure files are not left lying about – especially if documents are being transferred from one location to another. Unfortunately there are often stories about files being stolen from cars or left on trains!

Electronic records must also be kept safe with access restricted by passwords.

Good record keeping relies on effective filing systems that allow information to be stored safely but easily accessed when required. In large organisations such as the NHS, the filing and retrieval of records takes up a large amount of time and there are individuals who are specifically employed to undertake these tasks. In smaller organisations, everybody may be required to file and retrieve information – so the policies regarding this are very important.

Manual systems include filing records by name or number, very often in lockable cupboards or trolleys. Computerised systems will be set up to ensure that information cannot be accidentally deleted. Each setting is likely to have special arrangements depending on their own special circumstances.

Think How are records kept secure in your placement setting?

SKILLS FOR EFFECTIVE TEAMWORK

As well as gaining knowledge about workplace practices, your work experience will provide you with the opportunity to work as part of a team and observe how the members work together. It will enable you to gain a greater understanding of the skills required for effective teamwork.

There are many different professionals working in health and social care. Very often a service user will receive care from a number of different people all working together as a team to make sure that the individual receives the best care possible. Effective teamwork relies on individuals working well together in a professional relationship. A good member of a team will be reliable and punctual. A willing and positive attitude contributes to the smooth running of the work. Good communication between team members is also important.

You are likely to see different people taking on different roles within a team. You may identify a leader of the team or others who play supporting roles. Most teams have a cheerful and supportive relationship between members who enjoy working together. You may need to fit into the team and make your own contribution. It may take a little time to feel really part of the team but usually it will be a very rewarding experience.

Think What skills are used by the individual team members which contribute to successful teamwork in your placement? How have you fitted in and been part of the team?

You can include your responses in your portfolio of evidence (see Evidence activity P2 on page 184).

44.3 *Be apply to apply knowledge and understanding*

LINKS BETWEEN THEORY AND PRACTICE

An exciting part of work experience is the opportunity to see theory applied to practice. Decisions about health and social care policy are expected to be based on evidence and all health care practices are developed from evidence-based research. This means that workplace practice should be in line with what is regarded as the best approach to care. Research is always being undertaken to ensure that practice is regularly reviewed and updated so that care is of the highest standard.

Health and social care workers are encouraged to question and reflect on the care they give. The idea is that workers should not be drawn into old habits and always doing things in the same way because 'that is the way we have always done it'. As part of your work experience you will have plenty of opportunities to see evidence-based care and reflect on health care practices.

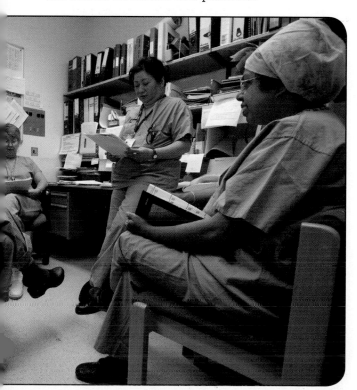

Figure 44.3 Planning nursing care

Before you start your work experience placement, you should look back at the units you have already covered. Consider some of the optional units that you plan to study and look at their content. Identify some of the theory that you might expect to see in practice. In particular, identify any work that requires you to give practical examples.

The following section will suggest some of the areas where you should expect to link theory and practice in order to demonstrate your knowledge and understanding. There may also be times when you observe some practice and you want to understand the theory behind it. You will have the chance to ask questions and to do your own research – it will all increase your knowledge and understanding!

Organisation of service provision

Each work placement will be a health or social care provider. All providers fit within a local and national framework. If you have undertaken Unit 6 you will have studied the way in which health and social care is structured and should know about the different levels of provision – primary, secondary or tertiary. You will also have an understanding of how health and social care is organised and regulated. You may have looked in depth at certain types of provision, and explored the funding mechanisms and how they fit into the national framework. You will have identified a range of health and social care professionals, such as nursing staff, social workers, and professions allied to medicine, as well as managers, technical staff and other support workers. As part of your studies you will have also considered the different needs of clients or service users and any barriers they may find when accessing health and social care services.

> **Think** Using your work experience placement, can you give examples of how health and social care service provision is organised?
>
> *You can include your responses in your portfolio of evidence (see Evidence activity P2 on page 184).*

Policies and procedures

Now consider some of the policies and procedures at your workplace. Can you link them with examples of theories that you have studied? One might be the promotion of equality and individual rights through workplace policies and procedures. The principles you will have learnt include the Care Value Base promoting individuals' rights, choices and well-being, maintaining confidentiality, promoting anti-discriminatory practice, acknowledging individuals' personal beliefs and identities and promoting effective communication. This can be applied to both the service users and the staff. The Care Value Base is derived from care principles which respect the worth and dignity of every individual and ensure social justice, promoting the health and social welfare of all. The organisational policies and procedures set out the ways in which members of staff should act when dealing with specific circumstances and put into practice the principles of good care practice.

Care practices

The care practices that you undertake or observe will differ depending on the setting and client group. Based on the principles and values of good care, and supported by the organisational policies, codes of practice and procedures, practitioners provide appropriate care services. Effective care practice depends on high quality professional skills, including good communication and teamwork. During your work experience you will see the needs of individual clients being met through the skills of those caring for them. You should be able to make appropriate links with some of the theories that you have studied. For example, in Unit 1 you have looked in depth at effective communication in health and social care.

> **Think** What examples of care practices that you have observed or undertaken can be linked with a theory that you have studied?
>
> *You can include your responses in your portfolio of evidence (see Evidence activity P2 on this page).*

Health and safety

The importance of health and safety in the workplace will have been emphasised during your induction to your work experience and you should have remembered a number of issues that you have already studied and discussed. Look back at Unit 3 where you have considered, in detail, health, safety and security in health and social care. There will be many examples of the principles of health, safety and security that you have studied. Remember that you also have responsibilities for both your own safety and the safety of others while on your work experience.

EVIDENCE ACTIVITY

P2

For **P2**, you need to demonstrate your knowledge and understanding of workplace practice.

You should have built up a portfolio of evidence from your different work experience placements. There must be evidence from at least three different workplaces, not including the one used for Unit 6. Go through your evidence to make sure that you have covered all the criteria. It is important to have referenced and organised your portfolio.

You will now have a range of evidence from your coursework and your portfolio which will demonstrate how theory and practice is linked. You may need to ensure that you have all the facts you need by asking additional questions.

You should review all your evidence and present your findings, using your portfolio to demonstrate your knowledge and understanding of workplace practice. You can do this by identifying some of the theories that you have studied, and then use examples of practices that you have seen in your workplace to show that you understand and can apply the theory.

44.4 *Be able to review personal effectiveness*

'There is only one corner of the universe you can be certain of improving and that's your own self'

(Aldous Huxley, 1944)

REVIEW

It is essential for all health and social care practitioners to review their practice regularly in order to ensure that it is of the highest quality. There is a duty of care owed to all service users and this can only be fulfilled if working practices are kept up to date and improvements made as necessary. New research, policies and guidelines are frequently introduced in health and social care and it is the responsibility of staff, and the organisations in which they work, to ensure that they are working to the most up-to-date information. As an individual it is important to know how to evaluate your own work and make improvements in your practice.

This section will support you in developing your skills of reflective practice and will help you monitor your own development through maintaining a personal reflective practice journal.

Reflection

The first step in reflecting on your own practice is to know yourself! All of us are individuals with different personalities and our own personal values and beliefs. These have been built up through the influences of our family, friends, school, work, the local community, religious beliefs, culture etc. People usually choose friends who share their own views and attitudes. However, at work there may be colleagues who have different views but with whom it is necessary to work very closely when providing care. Service users may also hold different ideas and sometimes express views or attitudes with which you may not agree. It is important to be aware of your own reactions and be sure that recognise your own preferences or prejudices.

Figure 44.4 *What is happening?*

> ***Think*** Look at the illustration. Can you describe what is happening in different ways? How are the descriptions influenced by your own views and attitudes?

If you can recognise your own beliefs and attitudes, this will help you to understand your reactions to certain situations and, if necessary, take steps to ensure that the care you give is not compromised in any way. Remember the care principle that the views and wishes of individuals should be promoted and respected.

> ***Think*** Which of your own views and attitudes might have a bearing on your work in health and social care? What are your expectations of someone who is more than 80 years old, or someone with a learning disability?

When you have considered and come to understand your own personal views, it will be important to keep these views in mind to ensure that you do not slip into making unfounded assumptions about people or situations. Identifying the factors that have influenced you will make it possible to reflect on how they affect the way that you work with and relate to other health care practitioners and service users.

Knowledge and understanding

Another area of reflection is to consider your level of understanding and knowledge at a certain point in time. You may look back at what you have learnt since starting your health and social care course compared with what you knew about healthcare previously. It is particularly relevant to review the progress that you have made since starting your work experience placements. For this you will need to have a baseline with which you can make comparisons. It may be that you have already had some work experience and it is already showing you how much you did not know before!

Start by identifying the amount of experience that you have had with the client group or setting before starting your work experience. You can include the theory lessons that you have had as examples of the knowledge and understanding that you had at the beginning. Do you have any technical or creative skills that might be of use in health and social care? What about your communication skills? Are you good at listening or able to talk to people easily?

There are a number of personal skills that are useful in any type of workplace. These are known as transferable skills (abilities that can be of equal use in more than one job setting). If you have already done some other types of job, such as working in a restaurant or supermarket, you will have developed some of these skills which can now be applied to your work experience. These skills might include communication skills, the ability to work well in a team, showing initiative, self-organisation and being flexible to different circumstances.

In Unit 6 (Book 1 page 215) there is an example of a profile of a student on a health and social

care course. Look at it now. Could you produce the same sort of analysis for yourself?

The purpose of reflective practice is to improve your practice by regularly reviewing what you do and how you are doing it. It means thinking things over carefully to see if improvements could be made. The theory known as Kolb's learning cycle can be useful here. Kolb identified four different stages:

- Stage 1 – An event or situation occurs. It can be a regular occurrence or an unusual one. This is known as a concrete experience.

- Stage 2 – You think about it – reflective observation.

- Stage 3 – Some general rules are worked out about the experience through analysis and understanding of the situation – abstract conceptualisation.

- Stage 4 – Next time the experience occurs you can make changes by applying the rules or theories that you have worked out – active experimentation.

As this is a cycle the stages can be repeated again and the pattern continues, as can be seen in the diagram below.

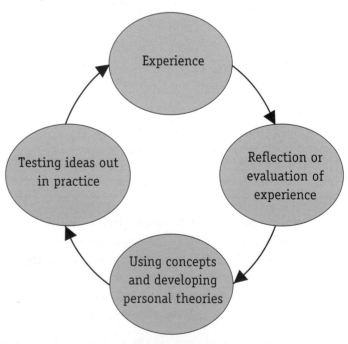

Figure 44.5 The Kolb learning cycle
Source: adapted from Kolb (Pearson Education)

Other theorists have suggested that individuals have different learning styles or ways of learning. Honey and Mumford (1982) suggested that there are four main types of learning style which complement the learning cycle. Some people are better at some of the styles than others. These learning styles are characterised as:

- The activist – people who enjoy having new experiences and spend less time on reflecting and analysing.

- The reflector – people who like to sit down and think things through.

- The theorist – someone who likes to analyse situations against established theories.

- The pragmatist – someone who likes to try to put new things in practice.

> ***Think*** What sort of learning style do you think describes you best?

Placement experience

After all of this you perhaps know yourself a bit better! Now is the time to start thinking about how you will make progress while on your course and undertaking your work experience. You will need to do this by monitoring your progress while you are on your work experience. You can do this by keeping a reflective practice journal to review anything you have learnt and any changes that you have made because of this.

CASE STUDY: MEENA'S REFLECTIVE DIARY

Meena is doing work experience in a nursery school. She is used to being with young children as she has a large close-knit family with several nieces and nephews. She has done quite a lot of babysitting for them and enjoyed helping them with their games and reading books. Meena likes art and is quite creative. As she is going to be at her placement near to Christmas she hopes that her skills can be used in making decorations with the children.

After settling in to the nursery Meena decides to keep a reflective diary of her experience. She chooses two key issues to focus on. One is the beginning of the day when the children arrive and the practices that are in place when the parents leave the children. The second is the way in which the children are given their mid-morning snack. She had observed the way in which the staff had persuaded a little boy to say goodbye to his mother, although he had been rather reluctant to come into the nursery. At mid-morning the staff had taken great care to ensure that the children all had suitable food, including those with special dietary needs. Principles of health, safety and hygiene had also been upheld. Several of these practices were new to Meena. She spent some time thinking about what she had observed. She linked back some of her findings to theories she had studied. She felt that she now had a greater understanding of how she should act in similar circumstances. The next day she asked if she could help by welcoming some of the children at the beginning of the day and also to become involved with giving out the mid-morning snacks.

QUESTIONS

1. What skills and experience did Meena bring to her work experience?

2. How did she set about improving her practice in the nursery?

3. What stages did she go through?

As part of monitoring your progress you may need to set certain dates when you will review and comment on your progress. There may be formal or informal training sessions which you can attend while on work experience. Your workplace supervisor or teacher/tutor may make regular appointments with you to discuss your progress. You should keep a record of all these in your journal.

Keeping a reflective journal is more than just keeping a diary of the things that you did. It requires you to think or 'reflect' on why or how they were done. You need to be able to record the experiences and feelings and try to include the effects that you observed on the clients or other staff members.

Personal and professional development

As well as gaining increased knowledge, understanding and skills in health care practice, work experience will give you the opportunity to consider your own personal and professional development. This may involve your personal goals in gaining your qualification or the opportunity to further develop skills in your chosen area. It will certainly give you the chance to review your career aspirations. The experience of working in a sector in which you hope to make a career in the future will be a great benefit in confirming (or otherwise!) your choice of career pathway. When you are applying to enter professional training, or to get a job in health and social care, the value of having had relevant experience cannot be rated too highly.

> **Think** What personal and professional goals have you set for yourself? Has the experience of being on work placement helped you to achieve any of the goals?

EVIDENCE ACTIVITY

P3 - P4 - M1

For **P3**, you need to maintain a reflective practice journal to monitor the development of your own knowledge, understanding and skills.

You should keep a journal or diary of your work experience and record your experiences and feelings. Choose some examples of how you were able to link your theoretical learning with your practical experiences. Plan in some set dates when you will monitor your progress in terms of your knowledge, understanding and skills.

For **P4**, you need to identify links between knowledge and understanding and effective practice.

For **M1**, you need to explain how the development of knowledge and understanding can be linked to improved practice.

From each of your work experience placements, choose some examples of effective health or social care practice. For each example, explain how the practices are underpinned by knowledge and understanding of an appropriate theory or reflection. You could use examples of good communication or of meeting client's physical, mental, intellectual, social or emotional needs. You should be able to look back in your own reflective practice journal to give you ideas. For a merit, for each example explain how, by developing knowledge and understanding, practice can be improved.

EFFECTIVENESS

How self aware are you?

Figure 44.6 How good are you at judging your own performance?

Can you judge how effective you have been while on your work experience? It can be difficult to be able to do that completely or accurately, so it is often very useful to get feedback from others. Your teacher/tutor or workplace mentor will be happy to talk to you about your progress and how you have developed while on work experience.

At other times there may be feedback from some of your work colleagues or your manager. This can be in the form of feedback sheets, witness testimonies and end of placement reports. From time to time a client may wish to give you feedback, for example by giving you a thank you card. You may wish to use these in your personal reflective journal as an opportunity to further develop your skills and practice.

You should also add any feedback from others to your personal portfolio.

RECOMMENDATIONS

The outcome of being on work experience placements for an extended time, in order to achieve this unit, is that you will have many opportunities to add to your own personal development plan. As part of Unit 6 you may have already developed your plan. However you should now revisit this plan and make any amendments that may be necessary because of your extended work experience.

In Unit 6 you set yourself targets in the following areas:

- knowledge – obtaining the qualifications you need

- skills – by improving or gaining relevant skills

- practice – learning about codes of practice and ethics in careers that interest you

- values and beliefs – by determining where your values and beliefs lie and where they could be best put to use

- career aspirations – by understanding where you hope to be working in the short and long term.

Remember that your targets should be **smart**:

- Specific

- Measurable

- Achievable

- Realistic

- Timebound.

You should reflect on the ways in which work experience has helped you reach some or all of your targets and set yourself new ones.

By updating your plan you will be able to outline a pathway for your achievement in each area. This will again mean setting yourself targets and making plans. These plans can be:

- Short term – outcomes that you expect to achieve within six months. It may include very short-term plans with weekly or monthly goals.

- Long-term plans – these are plans you expect to take longer than six months to achieve. It could be even a 5 or 10 year plan.

One area that will certainly have been influenced is that of your career choice. Being on work experience should have enabled you to get a realistic insight into careers in health and social care. Even if you have not been able to experience the exact career that you want to follow, you will have had plenty of opportunities to see at close hand health and social care professionals and their day-to-day work. Perhaps you have been surprised by what you have seen!

After you have been on work experience it might be helpful to revisit the career options that you identified when you first joined the course. For each career, list the qualifications, skills and attributes that are essential or desirable for someone who wants to work in that field. Now, in light of your work experiences, map your own skills, qualifications and attributes. How do they match up? Use the evidence from your reflective practice journal to help you evaluate your own development and progress towards meeting the requirements of your possible career pathway.

EVIDENCE ACTIVITY

P5 – M2 – D1

For **P5**, you need to describe own effectiveness in work in health and social care.

For **M2**, you need to explain how improving your own personal effectiveness can enhance the experience of the patient/service user.

For **D1**, you need to evaluate your own development as a result of workplace experiences.

For **P1**, you should evaluate your own contribution to your work experience placements. You should illustrate your answers by giving examples of feedback that you have received.

For **M2**, describe how you made improvements to your effectiveness during your work experience and how this affected the care you were able to give the patients or service users with which you worked. Give examples of how the care you gave them was enhanced.

For **D1**, you should look back at your journal to see how you have changed and developed since the start of your work experience. You might want to give examples under these headings: knowledge, skills, practice, values and beliefs and career aspirations. Link each one with some aspect of your work experience.

ADDITIONAL RESOURCES AND REFERENCES

UNIT 10

Further reading

Barker, J & Hodes, D (2002) *The Child in Mind – A child protection handbook*, London: Routledge

Corby, B. (2000) *Child abuse: towards a knowledge base*, Milton Keynes: Open University Press

Pledge, D.S (2003) *When Something Feels Wrong*, Minneapolis: Free Spirit Publishing

Useful websites

British Association of Play Therapists
www.bapt.info/

Children's Rights Alliance for England
www.crae.org.uk

Implementation of the Convention on the Rights of the Child

Community Care www.communitycare.co.uk

'Paralysed around culture' by Anabel Unity sale, 16 March 2006, discusses child protection issues in faith communities.

Curriculum online www.curriculumonline.gov.uk

Department for Children, Schools and Families
www.dfes.gov.uk

Care Matters, time for change (White Paper)

The Children Act and Reports (1989)

Children looked after in England (including adoption and care leavers), 2005–06

Department of Health www.dh.gov.uk

General information, a useful glossary, policy documents and circulars

What to do if you're worried a child is being abused (2003)

Working together to safeguard children (1999)

Framework for the Assessment of Children in Need and Their Families (2000)

Every Child Matters www.everychildmatters.gov.uk

Adoption

Foster care

Office of Public Sector Information (OPSI)
www.opsi.gov.uk

Children Act 1989

Human Rights Act 1998

Data Protection Act 1998

Involving parents

www.standards.dfes.gov.uk/locate/pupilsupport/parents/home-school/involvingparents/

www.teachernet.gov.uk/wholeschool/familyandcommunity/workingwithparents/

NSPCC (National Society for the Prevention of Cruelty to Children) www.nspcc.org.uk Keeping children safe: a Toolkit

Sure Start www.surestart.gov.uk

Sure Start programme

Teachernet www.teachernet.gov.uk

Early Years Foundation Stage, for advice on child protection

Unicef www.unicef.org

Convention on the Rights of the Child

UNIT 14

Further Reading

Clancy, J. McVicar J. (1995) *Physiology & Anatomy A Homeostatic Approach* London: Edward Arnold

Kingston, B. (1998) *Understanding Muscles A practical guide to muscle function* Cheltenham: Stanley Thornes

Minnett, P. Wayner, D. and Rubenstein, D. (1989) *Human Form and Function* London: Collins Educational

Moonie, N. et al (2000) *Advanced Health and Social Care* Oxford: Heinemann

Ogden, J. (1996) *Health Psychology A Textbook* Buckingham: Open University Press

Stretch, B. et al (2002) *BTEC National Health Studies* Oxford: Heinemann

Stretch, B. & Whitehouse, M. et al (2007) *Health and Social Care Book 1* Oxford: Heinemann

Stretch, B. & Whitehouse, M. et al, (2007) *Health and Social Care Book 2* Oxford: Heinemann

Journals/Magazines

Community Care

Health Visitor Today

The Lancet

The Nursing Times

Useful websites

General

BBC www.bbc.co.uk

Click on Health: Doctor's advice for 'Ask the doctor'.

Community Care www.communitycare.co.uk

Social care journal.

The Medical Journal of Australia www.mja.com.au/

NetDoctor www.netdoctor.co.uk

For general information about health issues, as well as about specific conditions.

NHS Direct www.nhsdirect.nhs.uk

Information about diagnosis and treatment of common conditions.

Specific

British Heart Foundation www.bhf.co.uk

British Lung Foundation www.lunguk.org

Motor Neurone Disease Association www.mndassociation.org.uk

> **Professor Stephen Hawking** www.hawking.org.uk
>
> Click on 'Disability' for information on his experience of the motor neurone disease amyotrophic lateral sclerosis.
>
> **Patient UK** www.patient.co.uk
>
> Search for motor neurone disease.

The National M.E. Centre www.nmec.org.uk

For information about chronic fatigue syndromes.

UNIT 19

Useful websites

The Association of Public Health Observatories www.apho.org.uk

For information, data and intelligence about people's health and health care.

Cabinet Office www.cabinetoffice.gov.uk

Improving the life chances of disabled people (2005)

Child poverty action www.cpag.org.uk

Community Health Profiles www.communityhealthprofiles.info/

Health Profiles designed to help local councils and the NHS decide where to target resources to tackle health inequalities in their local area. Health Profiles are quality assured by APHO.

Every Child Matters www.everychildmatters.gov.uk

Click on Children's and Young People's Health; Teenage Pregnancy.

Joseph Rowntree Foundation www.jrf.org.uk

One of the largest social policy research and development charities in the UK

National Statistics www.statistics.gov.uk

For information about a wide range of demographic data.

New Policy Institute, The Poverty Site www.poverty.org.uk

UK statistics on poverty and social exclusion.

Official Documents www.official-documents.co.uk

Reference facility for Command Papers, House of Commons Papers and key Departmental Papers.

World Health Organization www.who.int/

Publications, media resources, health statistics, health articles and current health news.

UNIT 21

Useful websites

Department of Health

> www.bdaweightwise.com Search for Body Mass Indicator
>
> www.dh.gov.uk Click on 'Policy and guidance' then Health Topics, followed by 5 A Day for the school fruit and vegetable scheme.
>
> www.dh.gov.uk For up-to-date information regarding health and social care policy, health and nutrition related publications and nutrition and illness.

National Health Service

NHS Direct www.nhsdirect.nhs.uk/

5 A Day www.5aday.nhs.uk/

British Nutrition Foundation
www.nutrition.org.uk/

Provides nutrition information for teachers, health professionals, scientists, and general public as well as publications, conferences and educational resources.

Food Standards Agency

www.food.gov.uk

For information about legislation related to food handling, safety and hygiene.

Also search for genetically modified and novel foods.

www.eatwell.gov.uk/

For information about 'ages and stages', keeping food safe and food labels.

British Dietetic Association www.bda.uk.com

Impartial advice about nutrition and health. It will also provide advice about careers in Dietetics.

Community Nutrition Group

www.cnguk.org/

A British Dietetic Association specialist interest group made up of Dietitians working in the field of community nutrition and public health.

European Union

http://ec.europa.eu/food/food/biotechnology/novelfood/index_en.htm

Information about public health, food safety, consumer affairs and legislation.

The Institute of Food Research www.ifr.ac.uk/

Focus on science, food and nutrition-related disciplines. Downloadable information sheets.

Cancer Research UK
http://info.cancerresearchuk.org/

Click on 'Healthy Living' then 'Diet and Healthy Eating' for information and activities linked to food and health.

UNIT 22

Useful websites

Department of Health www.dh.gov.uk

Search for Research Governance Framework for Health and Social Care.

Official Documents www.archive.official-documents.co.uk

Search for 'Saving Lives Our Healthier Nation' for examples of different methods of presentation.

Social Care Institute for Excellence (SCIE)
www.scie.org.uk

Check some of the key SCIE reports on knowledge-based good practice guidance; involving service users, carers, practitioners, providers and policy makers in advancing and promoting good practice in social care and enhancing the skills and professionalism of social care workers.

UNIT 44

Honey, P. and Mumford, A. (1982) *The manual of learning styles*, Maidenhead: Peter Honey

Kolb, D.A. (1984) *Experiential Learning: Experience as the Source of Learning and Development*, London: Financial Times/Prentice Hall

INDEX

Pearson Education
Edinburgh Gate
Harlow
Essex
CM20 2JE

© Pearson Education 2008

ISBN: 978-1-40586-812-9

Printed and bound in China SWTC/01
Illustrations by Oxford Designers and Illustrators
Indexed by Richard Howard

Acknowledgments
The Publisher is grateful to the following for their permission to reproduce copyright material:

Department for Environment Food and Rural Affairs for the tables "Summary of factors which may reduce the nutrients in food" and "Basal metabolic rate" from Manual of Nutrition. MAFF. 10th edition 1995, Crown Copyright 2007; Department of Health for material from the leaflet What To Do If You're Worried A Child Is Being Abused, 2003 by the Department of Health, and the table "Adults in the poorest fifth are around twice as likely to be at risk of developing a mental illness as those on average incomes. The differences are greater for men than for women" by Health Survey for England, Crown Copyright 2007; Food Standards Agency for material from The Balance of Good Health plate, 2001, Food Standards Agency, Crown Copyright 2007; The Government Actuaries Department (GAD) for material from "Population projections by the Government Actuary"; "National population projections 2004-based" and "Projected populations at midyears by age last birthday 2004-based" by The Government Actuaries Department © Crown Copyright 2005; National Statistics for material from "Improving the life chances of disabled people 2005"; "health profile statistics for Hampshire and Hackney"; "Death Registrations, 502,599 in England & Wales in 2006; "Age-standardised mortality rate for all causes by sex, England and Wales"; "Education - Exam results differ by social status"; and "Attainment of five or more GCSE grades A* to C: by parental NS-SEC 2002, England & Wales" by National Statistics, Crown Copyright 2007; NSPCC for the table "Signs and symptoms of abuse" adapted from the NSPCC and NCMA publication Safeguarding children: A guide

for childminders and nannies copyright © NSPCC, reproduced with permission; Pearson Education, Inc. for a figure from Organizational Psychology: An Experiential Approach 3rd edition by J McIntyre, I M Rubin and D A Kolb copyright © 1979, pg 38, reprinted by permission of Pearson Education, Inc, Upper Saddle River, NJ; The Stationery Office for material from "Framework for the assessment of children in need and their families" 2000 by the Department of Health; Childhood Matters Report of the National Commission of Inquiry into the Prevention of Child Abuse Vol. 2, 1996 by the Department of Health; UK unemployment: by ethnic group and sex, 2004 by the Department of Health; material and the graphs "Child pedestrian deaths: England one for the worst records in Europe" by the Department of the Environment, Transport and the Regions, "Traffic calming can cut pedestrian road accidents" by Birmingham Health Authority from city of Birmingham data and "Age at death at start and end of the 20th century" by Registrar General & Office for National Statistics from Saving Lives: Our Healthier Nation; and the graphs "Accidents kill proportionately more children as they grow up" and "Deaths from accidental falls in older people are not reducing" by Office for National Statistics Crown Copyright 2007; and World Health Organization for the table "Number of healthy years' life expectancy by country" © World Health Organization 2007. All rights reserved.

In some instances we have been unable to trace the owners of copyright material and we would appreciate any information that would enable us to do so.

The publisher would like to thank the following for their kind permission to reproduce their photographs:

(Key: b-bottom; c-centre; l-left; r-right; t-top)

Alamy Images: 175; Christopher Baines 16; Gabe Palmer 37; Paul Panayiotou 86; PCL 68-69, 70; Photo Network 134-135, 136; Photofusion Picture Library 83, 183; Ian Shaw 179; Homer Sykes 123l; Peter Widman 168-169, 170; Janine Wiedel 144; Woodystock 98-99, 100; **Mary Crittenden:** 88; **DK Images:** 10-11, 12, 154, 157; **Sally and Richard Greenhill:** 48, 56, 58l, 64, 82; **Alexandra Milgrim:** 146; **No Trace:** 189; **PA Photos**: 94, 167; **Pearson Education Ltd:** 11t, 41t, 69t, 99t, 135t, 169t; **Photofusion Picture Library:** 58r, 139, 185; **Rex Features:** 23, 73, 76, 97, 123r; **Science Photo Library Ltd:** 40-41, 42, 51, 52, 53l, 53r, 57, 104, 138, 145, 165; **Roger Scruton:** 101, 103

Cover photo © Pearson Education

All other images © Pearson Education

Picture Research by: Thelma Gilbert

Every effort has been made to trace the copyright holders and we apologise in advance for any unintentional omissions. We would be pleased to insert the appropriate acknowledgement in any subsequent edition of this publication.